This volume is dedicated to

Ian A. G. Shepherd
(1951–2009)
Archaeologist for Grampian and Aberdeenshire
1975–2009

A TALE OF THE UNKNOWN UNKNOWNS

A Mesolithic Pit Alignment
and a
Neolithic Timber Hall
at Warren Field, Crathes, Aberdeenshire

Hilary K. Murray, J. Charles Murray and Shannon M. Fraser

*with contributions by Anne Crone, Althea Davies, Claire Deacon,
Brian Dolan, Richard Evershed, Mhairi Hastie, Gail Higginbottom,
Stephen Lancaster, Peter Marshall, Robert McCulloch, Andrew Meharg,
Alison Sheridan, Andrew Smith, Catherine Smith, Lucija Šoberl,
Scott Timpany, Richard Tipping, Graeme Warren
and Sandy Winterbottom*

Oxbow Books
Oxford and Oakville

Published by
Oxbow Books, Oxford, UK

ISBN 978-1-84217-347-3

A CIP record for this book is available from the British Library

This book is available direct from

Oxbow Books, Oxford, UK
(Phone: 01865-241249; Fax: 01865-794449)

and

The David Brown Book Company
PO Box 511, Oakville, CT 06779, USA
(Phone: 860-945-9329; Fax: 860-945-9468)

or from our website

www.oxbowbooks.com

Library of Congress Cataloging-in-Publication Data

Murray, Hilary.
 A tale of the unknown unknowns : a Mesolithic pit alignment and a Neolithic timber hall at Warren Field, Crathes, Aberdeenshire / Hilary K. Murray ... [et al.] ; with contributions by Anne Crone ... [et al.].
     p. cm.
 Includes bibliographical references.
 ISBN 978-1-84217-347-3
 1. Warren Field Site (Scotland) 2. Mesolithic period--Scotland--Aberdeenshire. 3. Neolithic period--Scotland--Aberdeenshire. 4. Dwellings, Prehistoric--Scotland--Aberdeenshire. 5. Plant remains (Archaeology)--Scotland--Aberdeenshire. 6. Palynology--Scotland--Aberdeenshire. 7. Excavations (Archaeology)--Scotland--Aberdeenshire. 8. Aberdeenshire (Scotland)--Antiquities. I. Crone, Anne. II. Title.
 GN774.22.G7M87 2009
 941.2′4--dc22
                                2009030023

Front cover: The Warren Field excavations in the wider landscape with Crathes Castle in the background. (Photograph by Moira Greig. © Aberdeenshire Archaeology Service. AAS-05–02–CT34)

Back cover: The timber hall during excavation in 2005, looking south. (© Charles Murray)

This publication was made possible by a generous grant from Historic Scotland

Printed in Great Britain by
Short Run Press, Exeter

Contents

Contributors

Anne Crone
AOC Archaeology Group
Edgefield Road Industrial Estate
Loanhead, Midlothian, EH12 9SY
United Kingdom

Althea Davies
School of Biological and Environmental Sciences
University of Stirling
Stirling, FK9 4LA
United Kingdom

Claire Deacon
Department of Plant and Soil Science
University of Aberdeen
King's College, Old Aberdeen, AB24 3UU
United Kingdom

Brian Dolan
Department of Archaeology
University College Dublin
John Henry Newman Building
Belfield, Dublin 4
Ireland

Richard Evershed
Organic Chemistry Unit
School of Chemistry
Cantock's Close
University of Bristol
Bristol, BS8 1TS
United Kingdom

Shannon Fraser
The National Trust for Scotland
The Stables, Castle Fraser
Inverurie, Aberdeenshire, AB51 7LD
United Kingdom

Mhairi Hastie
Headland Archaeology Ltd
13 Jane Street
Edinburgh, EH6 5HE
United Kingdom

Gail Higginbottom
School of Archaeology and Anthropology
Australian National University
Canberra
Australia

Stephen Lancaster
Headland Archaeology Ltd
13 Jane Street
Edinburgh, EH6 5HE
United Kingdom

Peter Marshall
Chronologies
25 Onslow Road
Sheffield, S11 7AF
United Kingdom

Robert McCulloch
School of Biological and Environmental Sciences
University of Stirling
Stirling, FK9 4LA
United Kingdom

Andrew Meharg
Department of Plant and Soil Science
University of Aberdeen
King's College, Old Aberdeen, AB24 3UU
United Kingdom

Charles Murray
Murray Archaeological Services Ltd
Hill of Belnagoak, Methlick
Ellon, Aberdeenshire, AB41 7JN
United Kingdom

Hilary Murray
Murray Archaeological Services Ltd
Hill of Belnagoak, Methlick
Ellon, Aberdeenshire, AB41 7JN
United Kingdom

Alison Sheridan
Archaeology Department
National Museums of Scotland
Chambers Street, Edinburgh, EH1 1JF
United Kingdom

Andrew Smith
Department of Physics
University of Adelaide
Adelaide, 5005
Australia

Catherine Smith
SUAT Ltd
55 South Methven Street
Perth, PH1 5NX
United Kingdom

Lucija Šoberl
Organic Chemistry Unit
School of Chemistry
Cantock's Close
University of Bristol
Bristol, BS8 1TS
United Kingdom

Scott Timpany
Headland Archaeology Ltd
13 Jane Street
Edinburgh, EH6 5HE
United Kingdom

Richard Tipping
School of Biological and Environmental Sciences
University of Stirling
Stirling, FK9 4LA
United Kingdom

Graeme Warren
Department of Archaeology
University College Dublin
John Henry Newman Building
Belfield, Dublin 4
Ireland

Sandy Winterbottom
School of Biological and Environmental Sciences
University of Stirling
Stirling, FK9 4LA
United Kingdom

List of Illustrations

List of tables

Acknowledgements

The authors would like to thank all the funding bodies: The National Trust for Scotland, Historic Scotland, the Russell Trust, the Society of Antiquaries of London, Aberdeenshire Council, the Mackay and Brewer Charitable Trust, the P. F. Charitable Trust, the Prehistoric Society, the Robert B. Jeffrey Trust Fund, Mrs J. Y. Nelson's Charitable Trust, Miss Ross's Charitable Trust, and the National Trust for Scotland Aberdeen and District Members' Centre. Many thanks are due to Tamara Templer and Buz Whibley of the National Trust for Scotland Development Department.

We are indebted to all those who worked on site as staff and volunteers, especially to Dave Harding for his contribution and to Derek Alexander, Jill Harden and Robin Turner of the National Trust for Scotland Archaeology Team for their help throughout. Our thanks are also due to the tenant farmer Neil Barclay and his manager Bill Johnston, and the staff of the National Trust for Scotland at Crathes Castle, in particular Charlie Sutherland, Callum Pirnie and Dave Wood. Thanks are due to the Inspectorate of Historic Scotland for their advice and help, particularly Patrick Ashmore, Gordon Barclay, Sarah Govan, Ann MacSween and Rod McCullagh, and to Ian Shepherd of the Archaeology Service, Aberdeenshire Council for his considerable support throughout. Our thanks to the many people who have discussed the site and for the generosity of those who have given access to unpublished comparative material or drawn our attention to other parallels, in particular John Barnatt, John Cruse, Julie Gardiner, Petri Halinen, Karen Hardy, Chris Hayden, Gill Hey, Magnus Kirby, Jane Kenney, Bruce Mann, Nigel Trewin and Alasdair Whittle. We are very grateful to those who have read and commented on drafts of the text, especially Gordon Barclay, John Barrett, Strat Halliday, Ian Ralston and Caroline Wickham-Jones. We would like to thank the Royal Commission on the Ancient and Historical Monuments of Scotland and Moira Greig of the Archaeology Service, Aberdeenshire Council for permission to use aerial photographs of the site, and Gordon Barclay, Ian Ralston and CFA Archaeology for permission to use comparative plans in Fig. 21. Thanks are also due to Jan Dunbar for the lithic illustrations and the reconstruction drawings. Thanks go to Jane Bunting for analyses of the scale and extent of woodland disturbance. Heartfelt thanks are due to all the specialists who have contributed so much to our understanding of this site. Finally thanks to Clancy for his patience throughout.

Alison Sheridan would like to thank Trevor Cowie, Moira Greig and Ian Ralston for permission to cite the unpublished report on the Balbridie pottery assemblage and Marion O'Neil, Duncan Anderson and Craig Angus for their work on the pottery illustrations. Graeme Warren is very grateful to Patrick Shannon and Brian Jackson for assistance with the geological identifications and to Alison Sheridan for help in seeking advice on this material.

This book is published with the aid of grants from Historic Scotland and the National Trust for Scotland.

Chapter 1

The Warren Field Project: place and context

1.1 Background to the excavation

The site

Warren Field, Crathes, Aberdeenshire lies within the estate of Crathes Castle, now in the ownership of the National Trust for Scotland (NTS) (Fig. 1). It is *c*.600m north of the River Dee and less than a kilometre from an early Neolithic timber hall excavated at Balbridie, on the south bank of the river (Ralston 1982; Fairweather and Ralston 1993). A complex of cropmarks was first identified on aerial photographs taken in the very dry summer of 1976 by the Royal Commission on the Ancient and Historical Monuments of Scotland (Fig. 2). These revealed two main features: an alignment of pits (NGR: NO 737 966; NMRS NO79NW18), and a large, rectangular feature interpreted as a timber building (NGR: NO 739 967; NMRS NO79NW17). A large number of far smaller, dispersed features were also visible in the area between the building and the alignment.

The building was protected as a Scheduled Ancient Monument in 1978 and the whole field, which had been in arable cultivation prior to 1976, reverted to grazing. In 1982 the Scheduled area was enclosed by a wire fence with buried rabbit wire. The fence not only proved ineffective, but the lack of grazing within the enclosed area actually encouraged rabbit activity. All fencing was therefore removed from the vicinity of the building in the late 1980s. Outwith the Scheduled area, the field was used for various recreational events, which involved activities such as the erection of marquees stabilised by pegs penetrating the ground 0.5m or more, or the display of heavy agricultural machinery.

In 1991 Warren Field was shallow-ploughed to reseed the grass and a programme of fieldwalking was undertaken; no prehistoric material was recovered (Begg and Hewitt 1991). A geophysical survey undertaken in 2000 by students of Glasgow University Archaeology Department appeared to show the outline of the building (Jones 2000). However, there was no clear understanding of the level of preservation of the known archaeological features and given the vicissitudes suffered by the building since its discovery, and the fact that the field was known to have been in cyclical cultivation since at least the late eighteenth century, damage might have been considerable. The NTS therefore established a project to assess the condition of the pit alignment and the building, and to evaluate the nature of the other cropmark features within the field.

The project also sought to address various research objectives. Pit alignments are rare in northeast Scotland; additionally, the class itself is not well understood, as it includes monuments varying widely in scale, nature, function and date (from the Neolithic to the early modern period), of which too few have been excavated to refine the picture. Rectangular timber structures are also rare in the cropmark record in northeast Scotland and more generally in northern Britain and although the Warren Field structure superficially resembled two other excavated sites interpreted as roofed Neolithic buildings – Balbridie (Fairweather and Ralston 1993) and Claish Farm, Stirlingshire (Barclay, Brophy and MacGregor 2002) – there were suggestions that it might equally represent the lowland element of medieval rural settlement, another elusive feature within Scottish archaeology. At the same time, understanding

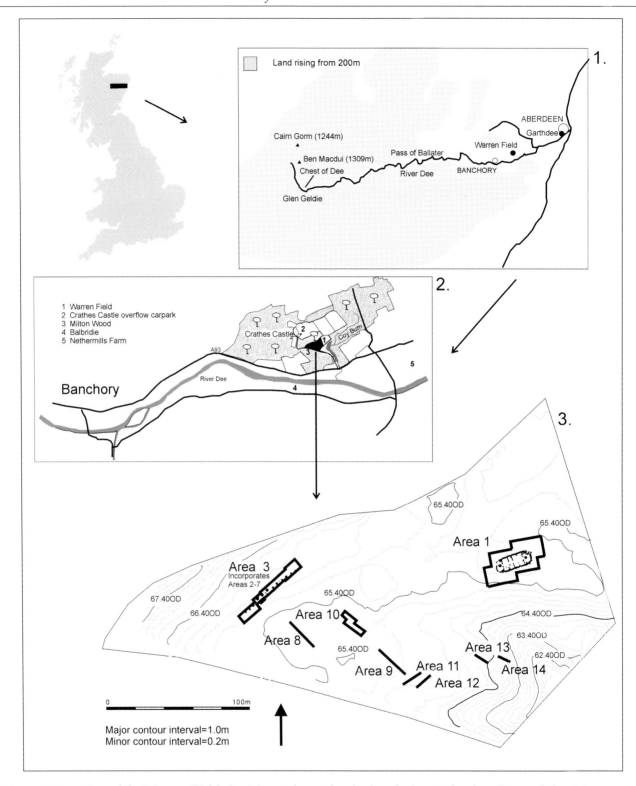

Figure 1. Location of the Warren Field site. Map 1 shows the site in relation to the river Dee and the rising ground to the west. The Mesolithic and Neolithic site at Garthdee and the Mesolithic sites at Chest of Dee and Glen Geldie are also marked. Map 2 shows Warren Field in relation to the Neolithic hall at Balbridie, the Mesolithic site at Nethermills and the small Neolithic sites at Crathes Castle Overflow Car Park and Milton Wood (this report). Map 3 shows the excavated areas (Based on the Ordnance Survey map © Crown Copyright NTS licence No. 100023880)

of the relationship of rectangular timber halls to other, more ephemeral, early Neolithic settlement evidence in Scotland, including potential turf and/or timber-built structures, is very limited. The occurrence of two such enigmatic monuments as the pit alignment and the hall in close proximity, alongside a series of other cropmark features, provided an opportunity to explore such issues at a landscape scale.

A small evaluation excavation was undertaken in 2004 (Murray and Murray 2004). Ploughing had truncated the site so that only negative features survived, cut into the underlying sands and gravels. Topsoil was removed by hand to evaluate finds distribution in the cultivated ground. A second resistivity survey was carried out over the site of the building, directly before excavation (Kidd 2004). Comparison of the excavated plan with the results of the 2000 and 2004 surveys was disappointing and emphasizes the difficulties encountered in the interpretation of geophysical data in a glacial geological context. As a result of this evaluation, the full plan of the timber structure was exposed – by now confirmed as an early Neolithic building – and more of the pit alignment was excavated (Murray and Murray 2005a). Samples from the pit alignment taken in 2005 indicated that it had been in use from the Mesolithic. To confirm this dating, two further pits in the alignment were sectioned and sampled in 2006 (Murray and Murray 2006). Extensive evaluation of the wider cropmark complex was undertaken in 2005 and 2006. In both of these seasons, the topsoil was machine-stripped with a flat-edged ditching bucket. The excavation was undertaken by Murray Archaeological Services Ltd on behalf of the National Trust for Scotland.

Archive

All archive material will be deposited with the National Monuments Record of Scotland, Edinburgh at the date of publication. The finds have been deposited in Marischal Museum, University of Aberdeen.

1.2 Geomorphic setting

Richard Tipping

Warren Field is a flat surface at *c*.55m OD. To the west and north the ground rises in a gentle slope

in bedrock. To the east the deeply incised narrow gorge of the Coy Burn, 10–15m below the terrace surface, receives water draining the Loch of Park, 4 kilometres to the northeast of Warren Field. The terrace forms the surface of an unknown thickness of sands and gravels (Fig. 1); around 2m of gravel are poorly exposed in the sides of the Coy Burn. The terrace fill is very probably of glacifluvial origin, though the terrace is higher and thus older than those mapped along Deeside by Brown (1992).

The aerial photograph (Fig. 2) shows two sets of geomorphic features marked by dark, slightly damper channels on the otherwise very well-drained terrace surface. These features are not all identifiable morphologically. The first set of channels (marked A to C on Fig. 2) are generally longer, east-west trending channels. The two parallel channels at extreme left seem to split to leave a very low ridge of pale sand, and the ridge is possibly a mid-channel bar. This ridge, not distinguishable topographically today, was the locus for the pit alignment. The channels marked D TO G in Fig. 2 are parallel, more deeply entrenched in the terrace surface, and flow from north to south, widening slightly downslope. Channel C in the middle of the field seems to lead to channel F, suggesting that water flowed for a time contemporaneously in both sets of channels but it is thought that channel C is intercepted by channel F, making channel F later, and channels A–C are thought to predate channels D–F.

There is no direct dating of the channels: no channel examined contained organic matter that could be radiocarbon dated. Archaeological features tend to be formed, or are more easily seen, on what are now drier patches of sand or gravel, but at Warren Field it is not thought that these features were situated to avoid flowing water, as none of the channels is thought to have been active when the archaeological features were made. Channels A–C are aligned with the general trend of glacial meltwater channels along Deeside (Brown 1992), and do not accord with the current southerly slope to the River Dee (Fig. 1). Channels A–C are likely to be of Late Devensian age, formed during deglaciation (Brown 1993). Channels D–F cut into the terrace surface and flow to the incised Coy Burn (Fig. 1). They are likely to have been active when the Coy Burn was downcutting. This period is not known with precision, but since the

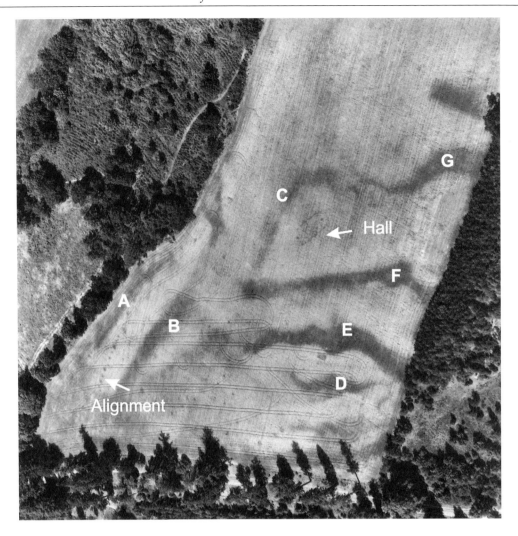

Figure 2. Aerial photograph of the Warren Field taken in 1976. The hall and pit alignment are marked. Letters A–G refer to the report on the geomorphic setting of the site (© Crown Copyright: Royal Commission on the Ancient and Historical Monuments of Scotland. Image KC 632)

Coy Burn has an alluvial fan at its outlet leading to one of three glacifluvial terraces of the Dee at Milton (Brown 1992), it is likely that these channels are also of Late Devensian age.

It is probable that the terrace surface was more topographically differentiated in the early Holocene period because much soil redistribution and surface smoothing has occurred in recent centuries. The early Mesolithic pit alignment follows closely the line of the probable gravel bar between channels A and B, and it may be that in the early Mesolithic period this ridge was still topographically distinctive between two shallow but dry channels. The Coy Burn had probably by this time become a major entrenched gorge to the east.

By the early Neolithic period when the timber hall was constructed, channel C (Fig. 2) may still have been visible as a shallow dry channel. This seems to curl round the site of the hall, and may have been used to demarcate the site.

Chapter 2

A line in the landscape: the pit alignment *circa* 8210–3650 cal BC

2.1 The excavated evidence

Hilary Murray and Charles Murray

The aerial photographs (Fig. 2) taken in 1976 reveal a line of pits extending northeast/southwest along the top of a very low ridge. Between 2004 and 2006 a total of 12 pits were revealed in plan (Fig. 3: Features 20, 19, 18, 16, 22, 5, 6, 7, 9, 10, 11 and 12), extending for a distance of c.50m. There were also a number of smaller features interpreted as post-pits (Fig. 3: Features 21, 17, 2, 3, 4, 8 and 13) which were not visible on the aerial photographs. Detailed examination of the aerial photographs suggests that the line may extend to the southwest with two additional pits and to the northeast with two, possibly three, features of similar size to the excavated pits, but at slightly greater spacing. If these features belonged to the alignment it would have been c.90m long. Any further extension to the northeast, if it existed, would have been removed or obscured by boundaries within the eighteenth-century designed landscape. However, it must be stressed that the field has been in intensive use over the centuries and other anomalies visible on the aerial photographs have ranged in date from prehistoric to modern (see chapter 4.1). It should also be noted that if these other features were part of the alignment, the line would not appear to run so clearly along the low ridge, but to veer off at the northern end.

The line of the excavated pits was not completely straight as there is a distinct curve towards the east at the southern end (features 18–21) and, although a straight line can be drawn between pits 16 and 12, pit 6 lies to the east of this line.

The pits

In 2004, topsoil was removed partly by hand, to reveal the pits between pit 5 and post pit 13. The pits had been cut into very hard, compact silty gravels, below which there were bands of finer, sandier gravels. Pit 5 was partially sectioned in 2004 but, due to very dry conditions, even with spraying, the primary fills of redeposited gravel were indistinguishable from the undisturbed natural gravel and only the secondary fills were excavated. When pits 5 and 6 were fully excavated and the surface of pit 7 re-exposed in wetter conditions in 2006 they were shown to be far larger than first thought. It is probable that pits 9, 10, 11 and 12, which were planned in the dry conditions of 2004, are actually larger.

Seven of the pits and five of the smaller features were fully sectioned and are described in detail below. They ranged in size from c.1m in diameter and 0.55m deep to 2.6m in diameter and 1.3m deep. All of the sectioned pits proved to have had an initial cut partially filled by eroded material and slumping of upcast material. Subsequently each of the pits had been recut All of the pits had been truncated by ploughing. Samples were taken of primary and secondary fills and datable material identified where possible. The sample locations are marked on the pit sections (Fig. 3). In total, 17 radiocarbon samples from the pits have been dated. For a full discussion of the radiocarbon dates see Marshall (chapter 5). The samples from three pits (16, 18, 19) were from charcoal deposited in the base of the pits and can confidently be used to say that these three pits were dug in the Mesolithic in the first half of the eighth millennium cal BC. Pits 18

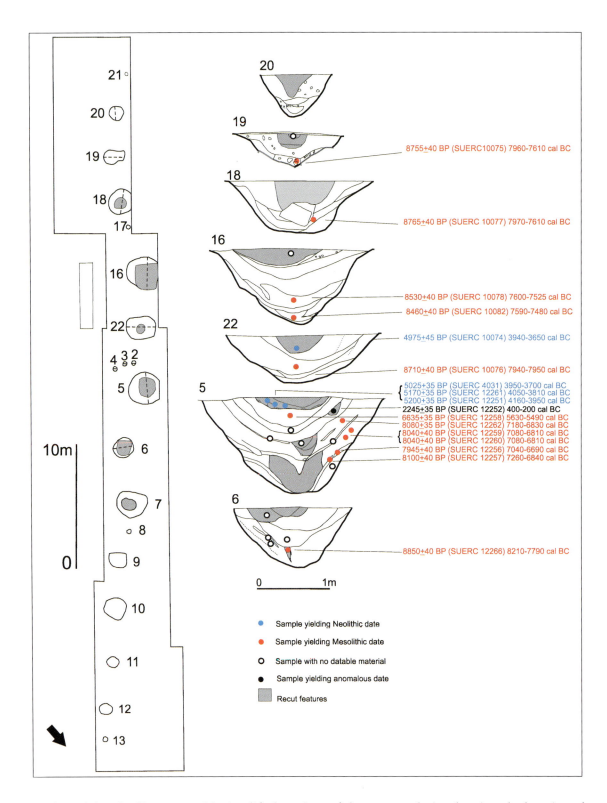

Figure 3. Plan of the pit alignment with simplified sections of the excavated pits showing the location of samples taken for radiocarbon dating

and 19 were dug first and pit 16 some 200 to 400 years later. The dates from primary fills in pits 5, 6 and 22 are from contexts that do not allow the same degree of certainty as they contained material that had eroded into the pits. However, as there is a correlation between the soil chemistry of the primary fills in pits 16 and 5 (this section below), and between the macrofossils in the primary fills of the sampled pits (Lancaster, chapter 2.2), it can be strongly argued that the whole alignment was dug over a period of several hundred years and was revisited on a number of occasions.

With the apparent exception of pit 16, the sectioned pits had been recut at a time when they were almost fully silted up. Unfortunately datable samples could not be identified in most of these contexts but four samples from the final recut of two pits (5, 22) have yielded early Neolithic dates. Marshall is cautious about interpreting these dates as evidence of re-use by people using the timber hall. However, as the pit alignment and the hall are at some distance apart there is little likelihood of totally accidental incorporation of Neolithic material into the recut pits and the evidence may be taken to show that the final recuts appear to have been roughly contemporary with the hall. Artefacts were only found in one pit (5).

The pits are described in the order they occurred in the alignment from southwest to northeast (Fig. 3). All depths are from the top of the undisturbed subsoil.

Pit 20

Pit 20 (Fig. 4) was slightly ovoid, 0.95m × 1.06m, with a maximum depth of 0.55m. The initial fill (20/4) was of clean yellow gravel, probably eroded from upcast material. This was interleaved with a small black deposit including charcoal (20/5). A more pebbly gravel (20/6) sealed this and merged into 20/4, before a second charcoally deposit (20/3) was placed in the pit; this was very similar to 20/5 and the two layers seemed to join, mixed through part of 20/6. It is possible that all this was a single deposition with some slippage of the surrounding loose upcast material at the time of deposition. These layers were sealed by an accumulation of redeposited gravels (20/2) with some stones and silt throughout; this also appeared to have been erosion of upcast material. This upper fill was cut by a small feature 0.50m in diameter and *c*.0.30m deep, filled by fine grey silt (20/1).

Dating
No samples were taken from this pit and there were no finds.

Pit 19

Pit 19 (Fig. 4) was ovoid, 0.8m-1.1m × 1.6m with a maximum depth of 0.45m. It had been cut down to the tops of two large glacially-deposited boulders which formed an angle at the base of the pit into which a black, charcoal-rich deposit with some blackened pebbles had been put (19/5). This appeared to have been a deliberate deposit directly after the pit had been dug, before any erosion of the upcast material had occurred. Samples yielded charcoal of birch and hazel with a seed of fat hen and a small number of tiny fragments of unidentifiable burnt bone. A compact grey sandy deposit (19/4) on either side appeared to merge into 19/5 and seems to have been the result of silting into the hollow between the stones. These were all sealed by a compact fine sandy gravel (19/3) eroded in and filling the pit. The centre of the pit had then been cut by a smaller pit 0.41m in diameter and 0.19m deep, filled by brown sandy silts (19/6, 19/7), the top of which was slightly pink, possibly heat-affected by the overlying deposit (19/2) which was carbon rich but with only very small discrete pieces of charcoal. This was sampled but no wood identifications were made.

Dating
19/5 Sample No: SUERC-10075 (alder/hazel charcoal): 7960–7610 cal BC.
(Fig. 3 and Marshall, chapter 5).

Pit 18

Pit 18 (Fig. 4) was much larger, some 1.8m-2m in diameter and 0.64m-0.70m deep with a flat base. Soon after it was cut there appears to have been some erosion of the sides or slippage of clean sand (18/6) and sandy gravel (18/7) from the upcast material. A black charcoal-rich layer (18/3) up to 100mm thick had then either been deposited or slipped in from the northern edge of the pit. Charcoal samples were identified as hazel. This deposit was sealed by a series of sands and sandy gravels (18/5, 18/2, 18/8, 18/4) which appeared to have slipped in as part of natural erosion of upcast material and accumulated around a large stone in the centre of the pit which lay on and partly pressed into the underlying charcoal-rich

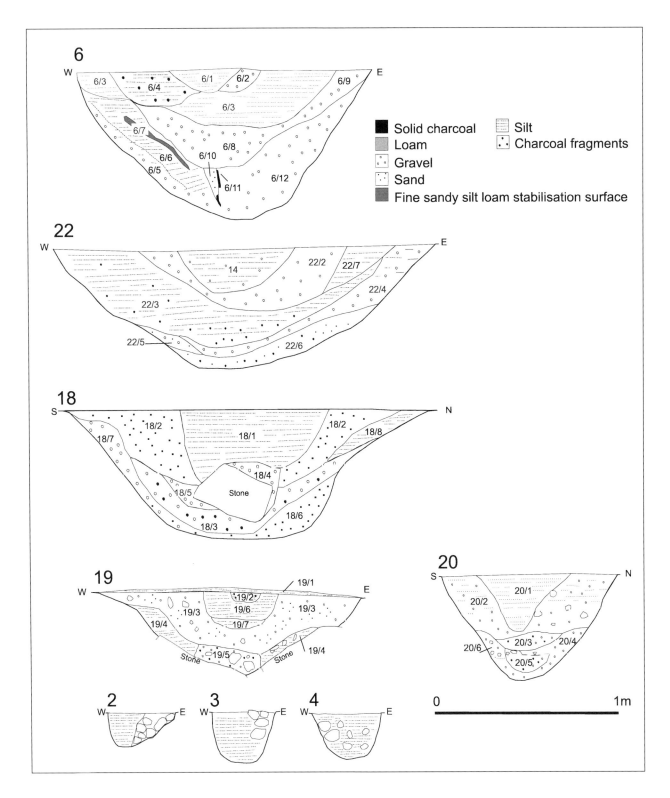

Figure 4. Pit alignment: sections of pits 6, 22, 18, 19, 20 and smaller features 2, 3 and 4

layer. The filled pit had subsequently been cut by a secondary pit 0.80m in diameter at the top and possibly as much as 0.40m deep. This was filled with a very fine grey/black soil (18/1) which incorporated minute charcoal fragments but no discrete pieces for identification or dating.

Dating

18/3 Sample No: SUERC-10077 (hazel charcoal): 7970–7610 cal BC.
(Fig. 3 and Marshall, chapter 5).

Pit 16

Pit 16 (Fig. 5) was 2.1m–2.4m in diameter and 1m deep. The lowest fill (16/9) was gravel eroded from the sides or upcast material. 16/5 was similar pebbly gravel which had slipped in from the northern side of the pit and was interleaved with a black charcoal-rich deposit (16/6) which included hazel charcoal up to 20mm in diameter. Further slippage of gravels from the south (16/4) sealed 16/6 and separated it from another charcoal-rich deposit (16/3) which appeared to have slipped or been deposited from the northern side where it was thickest. Alder and hazel charcoals were identified. This sequence of fills appeared to have been quite rapid as the profile of the pit was steep and would have eroded more if left open for long. There seems to have been further active erosion of the south side while 16/3 was being deposited, as it was interleaved with part of a thick layer of fine sand (16/8). This layer, which was up to 0.30m thick, half filled the pit, leaving a relatively shallow dipping surface which was then covered with very fine silt (16/2) – yellow at the base and grey/brown towards the top. On the northern side this was overlaid by a pebblier layer (16/7) which appeared to have slipped in from the north. A very fine grey soil (16/10) developed over these fills. Interpretation of thin sections (Lancaster, chapter 2.2 and 2007a) indicated that both 16/7 and 16/10 had been land surfaces for sufficiently long for soils to have developed. The remaining saucer-shaped hollow filled, or possibly was filled, with very fine grey silt which contained abundant tiny fragments of charcoal but nothing large enough to be identified for dating. Nine tiny fragments of burnt bone were mammalian but indeterminate as to species (Smith 2007).

Dating

16/3 Sample No: SUERC-10078 (alder/hazel): 7600–7525 cal BC.

16/6 Sample No: SUERC- 10082 (hazel): 7590–7480 cal BC.
(Fig. 3 and Marshall, chapter 5).

Pit 22

Pit 22 (Fig. 4) was another of the larger pits, 1.9m × 2.2m and 0.67m deep. The lowest fill (22/6) was a dark grey/black silt with much microscopic charcoal; it appeared to be an accumulation which had slipped in and possibly been consolidated with some vegetation. It was sealed by redeposited, cleaner, sandy gravels (22/4, 22/5) which were probably derived from erosion of upcast material on the east side of the pit. Another silty layer (22/3) had filled the full width of the partially filled pit. At the top this was grey but blacker towards the base where it contained much charcoal (not identifiable to species) and a hazelnut shell; the charcoal was not in a distinct layer but seems to have been more common at the beginning of this deposition episode. The centre of the pit was finally filled with yellow gravel and some silty sand (22/2, 22/7) which were loose but otherwise identical to the surrounding natural sediment and which probably also represent slippage of upcast material. The filled pit was cut by a smaller pit (14) 0.60m × 0.80m in diameter and 0.23m deep containing dark grey silt with some charcoal. A sample included large pieces of charcoal and two grains of bread/club wheat.

Dating

14 (secondary fill) Sample No: SUERC-10074 (carbonised wheat grain): 3940–3650 cal BC.
22/3 (primary fill) Sample No: SUERC-10076 (hazelnut): 7940–7950 cal BC.
(Fig. 3 and Marshall, chapter 5).

Pit 5

Pit 5 (Figs 5, 6) was the largest and most complex of the pits; it was also the only one in which any artefacts were found. It was 2.6m in diameter and 1.3m deep with fairly steep sides giving a V-shaped profile. A number of depositional events can be distinguished (Lancaster, chapter 2.2 and 2007b). A fine sand (5/15) had slipped into the pit soon after it had been cut, piling steeply against the sides. This appears to have stabilised with soil formed on the top of it (5/14) before further slippage of sandy gravel from the upcast around

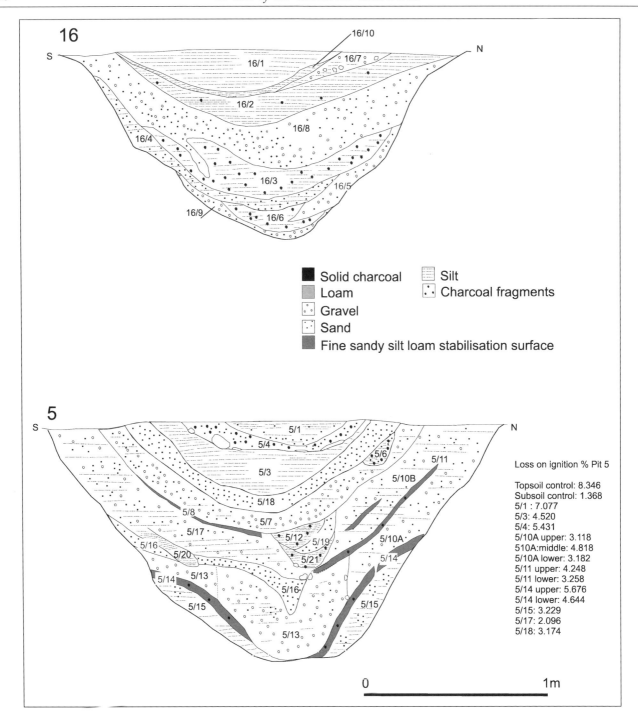

Figure 5. Pit alignment: sections of pits 5 and 16. Loss on ignition results for samples in pit 5 are given alongside the section

the pit (5/10A). The centre of the pit, by then filled to *c.*0.40m from the base, was recut by a pit *c.*0.70m in diameter and 0.40m deep which was filled with a very loose jumble of pebbly gravel (5/13). In the top of this there was a tapering vertical hole *c.*0.20m in maximum diameter and 0.20m deep

filled with very fine sand (5/16) which appears to have slipped in from the south side of the main pit. It is possible that a small post or stake may have been held in position in pit 5 by the pebbles 5/13 and that it was withdrawn, allowing the void to fill with the sand. This episode was followed by

Figure 6. Section of pit 5 during excavation (© Charles Murray)

more periods of slippage of upcast gravels (5/10B, 5/17), interspersed with periods of stabilization and soil formation (5/11, 5/8). Three flint flakes from layers 5/10 and 5/11 are described by Warren (chapter 6.3) as non-diagnostic. The occurrence of flints in both the stabilization surface and the material eroded from the upcast gravel around the pit suggests that they derived from activity adjacent to the pit. The half-filled pit 5, which was then only *c*.1.8m in diameter, was cut by a very small pit *c*.0.30m-0.35m in diameter and *c*.0.25m deep which was filled with dark sandy silt, rich in pulverised charcoal (5/12, 5/19, 5/21). An unburnt flint blade fragment (Warren, chapter 6.3) was found in the upper fill (5/12). This small pit was sealed by another accumulation of gravel (5/7, 5/5 (not on section)) *c*.0.10m-0.15m thick, on the top of which there was a very hard layer of iron pan. In section this gravel appeared to have been cut by another small pit (5/6) filled with gritty sand containing abundant charcoal fragments. However, oak charcoal from this feature was dated to 400–200 cal BC and it is suggested that this may

be an intrusive feature such as a burrow from behind the section. This was sealed by another layer of silty sand which may have eroded from upcast material beside the pit (5/18) and by a silt layer (5/3) which may also have been soil washed in from around the pit. By this time the pit was reduced to a shallow hollow *c*.1m in diameter and at least 0.15m deep (this does not allow for plough truncation). It was not totally clear if pit 5 had been recut at this point although the angularity of the base indicates this is probable. The hollow was filled with very dark, charcoal-rich silty sand (5/4). The upper fill (5/1) was similar but with more evidence of earthworm activity from the overlying ploughsoil. A burnt chunk of flint was found at the base of 5/4 and a cluster of fragments of burnt stone was found within 5/1(Warren, chapter 6.3).

Dating
5/4 Sample Nos: SUERC-4031 (oak charcoal): 3950–3700 cal BC, SUERC-12261 (oak charcoal): 4050–3810 cal BC, SUERC-12251 (oak charcoal): 4160–3950 cal BC.

5/6 Sample No: SUERC-12252 (oak charcoal): 400–200 cal BC. (Anomalous)

5/3 Sample No: SUERC-12258 (oak charcoal): 5630–5490 cal BC.

5/10B Sample No: SUERC-12262 (birch and hazel charcoal): 7180–6830 cal BC.

5/10A Sample Nos: SUERC-12259 (birch charcoal): 7080–6810 cal BC, SUERC-12260 (willow/poplar charcoal): 7080–6810 cal BC.

5/14 Sample Nos: SUERC-12256 (alder charcoal): 7040–6690 cal BC, SUERC-12257 (alder charcoal): 7260–6840 cal BC.

(Fig. 3 and Marshall, chapter 5).

Pit 6

Pit 6 (Fig. 4) was slightly to the east of the main line of pits. It was bowl-shaped with quite steep sides *c*.1.7m in diameter and 0.78m deep. The initial fills were a series of slightly silty gravels (6/5, 6/6, 6/12) which were quite loose and probably represent the slippage of upcast material back into the pit; as this stabilised a consolidation layer (6/7) seems to have formed within the western side of the pit. Very small amounts of charcoal were found in 6/6, probably deriving from activity in the area around the top of the pit. The centre of the reduced pit was cut by a small tapering feature, 0.70m in top diameter and *c*.0.25m deep, which was filled with fine yellow sand (6/10) and an apparently vertical piece of charcoal. Initially this was thought to have been the charred base of a stake which had been in the pit but, as identification of charcoal fragments included both willow/poplar and hazel, this is unlikely. It is possible that there were two stakes or that a stake was withdrawn from the pit and that sand and charcoal fell into the void. A further series of yellow pebbly gravels (6/8, 6/9) may represent another phase of slippage of destabilised upcast material from beside the pit. However, these gravels were rather loose with all sizes of pebbles very mixed, so it is also possible that, as with layer 5/13 in pit 5, this gravel may have been deliberately backfilled to support a stake. The gravel was so loose that it would have settled when the stake was removed; this explanation would explain the rather truncated appearance of the western side. The partially filled pit was then almost completely filled by soft light brown silt (6/3) which included occasional small fragments of charcoal, probably from activity in the area around the pit. The pit was then cut by

a small feature (6/4) which appears to have been *c*.0.45m across and 0.20m surviving depth; the soft dark fill contained a small amount of tiny charcoal fragments. This was itself cut by another small feature *c*.0.50m across and 0.14m surviving depth, the fill was partly clean gravel (6/2) and partly topsoil (6/1) and this may be a relatively recent disturbance, possibly by animal burrowing.

Dating

6/11 Sample No: SUERC-12266 (willow/poplar and hazel charcoal): 8210–7790 cal BC.

(Fig. 3 and Marshall, chapter 5).

Pits 7–12

None of these pits were sectioned.

Smaller features

Seven smaller features were identified after the removal of topsoil. Two (8, 13) were not sectioned. Feature 17 proved in section to be just a dark staining of the undisturbed natural *c*.0.40m in diameter; it may be due to natural leaching but could indicate the position of a ploughed out feature. Feature 21, which was a shallow patch of charcoal 0.20m in diameter, may also have been the base of a ploughed-out post-pit. In contrast features 2, 3 and 4 (Fig. 4) were post-pits 0.35m-0.44m in diameter and 0.18m–0.26m deep with stone packing. Unfortunately none of them yielded any datable material, so, although probable, the association of these post-pits with the pit alignment is purely based on their proximity and apparent correspondence to the alignment of the pits.

Summary

Mesolithic activity

There is a considerable difference in scale between small pits such as pit 20 at *c*.1m in diameter and 0.55m surviving depth and the much larger pits such as pit 5 at 2.6m in diameter and 1.3m surviving depth. An estimate of the original depths of the pits should allow for up to *c.* 0.20m–0.30m of plough truncation, and diameters at the ground surface would also have been slightly greater. There does not appear to have been a pattern to the differences in size; three of the smaller pits (18, 19, 20) were at the slightly curved southwest end of the alignment but this does not seem to be a consistent sequence as pit 6, another smaller pit, was in the centre of the line, next to the large pit 5. The dates indicate that one of the larger pits (16) was dug some 200–400 years after two of the smaller pits (18, 19). Superficially the dates also suggest that the other large pit (5) may have been dug a little later than the smaller pits, but as the earliest date from pit 5 was from a stabilisation layer (5/14) which may have developed some years after the pit was dug, this is perhaps a risky assumption (see Marshall, chapter 5).

Regardless of the differences in size, considerable effort had been expended in digging the pits through very hard, compact silty gravel, although some of the underlying sands and gravels were softer. Pit 19 was dug to the top of large glaciofluvial boulders but no attempt was made to remove them; avoidance by the builders of the frequent boulders at the south end of the ridge may account for the curve of the line at this end. The pollen evidence shows that the pits were dug within open woodland (Davies, Tipping and McCulloch 2007 and Lancaster, chapter 2.2), so the pits may also have been placed to avoid trees or tree roots. The earth dug out of the pits is likely to have been piled up beside them as much of the fill in all the pits appears to have been redeposited gravel which has slipped back in. These gravels appear to have come in from all sides of the pits, suggesting that the loose earth was piled up around each pit, rather than in a linear bank, which might be expected to produce a bias for erosion from one direction.

The soil micromorphology (Lancaster, chapter 2.2) suggests that erosion of the upcast material was intermittent. There were periods when the surface in the pits stabilised with some sparse vegetation. Pollen was too poorly preserved in this context to indicate what grew on these surfaces (Davies, Tipping and McCulloch 2007). The lack of erosion during these stablilisation periods suggests that there was little activity immediately around the pits at these times. These periods alternated with episodes when there appears to have been considerable activity around the alignment that loosened the remaining heaps of earth, causing further slippage and filling of the pits. In some cases small amounts of charcoal were mixed into this slippage. The charcoal could be natural or anthropogenic, but burning does not appear to have been common in these woods (Davies, Tipping and McCulloch 2007) and the flint artefacts that were also incorporated into the fills that had slipped into pit 5 suggest that the charcoal derived from human activity.

PRIMARY CHARCOAL DEPOSITS

Charcoal-rich deposits were found at or near the base of most of the pits (16, 18, 19, 20 and 22). In pits 19 and 20 these were relatively small, compact deposits but in the other pits the deposit was larger and less well defined and may have been deposited or may even have slipped in from beside the pit, for example as if derived from fires on or beside the upcast earth. In pits 16, 20 and 22 the charcoal-rich material was interleaved with sand and gravel; this possibly defines separate deposition events or may simply represent disturbance of the upcast when the charcoal was deposited. Whatever the source of the charcoal-rich deposits, they do not appear to have been deliberately sealed but gradually covered by the slippage described above. Charcoal fragments identified from these deposits were up to 50mm in diameter and included alder, hazel and birch as well as a single hazelnut shell, seeds of grass and fat hen and a few very tiny bone fragments. The birch and hazel could have derived from the woodland in which the pits were dug but alder is unrepresented in the pollen and may have come from the incised valley of the Coy Burn a few minutes walk away – *c.*300m (Lancaster, chapter 2.2).

STAKES

In two pits however, the primary use was different and more complicated. Both pits 5 and 6 appear initially to have remained open and empty with only a little natural slippage. There were no deliberate depositions of charcoal; some charcoal was present in in-washed layers (*e.g.* 5/15 and 5/10A in pit 5) but this was in tiny eroded fragments which may have derived from fires on the surface near the pits. In both pits there is some evidence that the surface of this in-washed material had stabilised before a smaller pit was cut through it, possibly to hold a stake or post which was supported by loose gravel and which had subsequently been pulled out. The loose nature of the gravel makes it difficult to estimate the post diameters with any accuracy but they appear to have been small diameter posts, rather than large timbers.

Subsequently pit 6 continued to fill up slowly like the other pits, but pit 5 had at least one, and possibly two, small pits cut later into the primary fills; the clearest of these (5/12, 5/19, 5/21) contained a charcoal-rich deposit and a fragment of an unburnt flint blade (SF 507) which may be considered to have been a deliberate deposit.

Figure 7. Preliminary chemical analysis being undertaken in pit 16 (© Charles Murray)

CHEMICAL ANALYSIS

Chemical analysis of samples from pits 5, 6 and 16 (Meharg and Deacon 2007) is tantalising as it shows a significantly elevated percentage of copper, lead and silver (and to a lesser extent strontium in pit 16 and zinc and cadmium in pits 5 and 6) in certain specific fills as compared to control samples of the surrounding natural (Fig. 7). As silver cannot be taken up by trees or other living organisms this cannot be ascribed to a concentration of minerals from burning wood. It suggests that the elements were introduced in the form of crushed rock. Rocks including this range of elements are generally uncommon in the region but can be found in an area around the Pass of Ballater, a dramatic landmark some 40 kilometres from Warren Field. The rocks at the Pass of Ballater include quite vivid purples and greens which might have attracted prehistoric people (*cf.* Cummings 2000, 92). The focal nature of the Pass is emphasised later in prehistory by the deposition there of a hoard of two Early Bronze Age flat axes (Ralston 1984, 77–8).

This high concentration of these elements can be linked to specific events which are observed in the stratigraphy of the pits (Figs 4, 5). In pit 16 it was in the charcoal-rich primary deposit (16/6, 16/3). In Pit 5 it was in the primary fill (5/15, 5/14) washed in from the upcast material around the pit, suggesting an activity which had taken place near the pit soon after it was dug. Also in pit 5 it was found in the charcoal-rich fill of a small recut (5/12) and the surface in the pit from which this was dug (5/8). In pit 6 it was found in the fill of a recut (6/4). With the possible exception of pit 6, these contexts are clearly dated to the Mesolithic. It is worth stressing that these anomalies are in specific contexts and do not occur in all charcoal-rich layers.

Neolithic activity

Most of the pits had a defined secondary recut (18, 19, 20, 22, 6, 5) into the top of the almost filled pit; only in pit 16 was this unclear. When these recuts were made most of the pits would have been visible only as shallow hollows in the ground, possibly surrounded by the remnants of the upcast earth. However, the disturbed soil in them may have produced differences in the vegetation which could have been quite striking. The fills of these final recuts were quite silty and although they contained charcoal this generally comprised tiny fragments; only in pits 5 and 22 were there pieces of sufficient size to identify (oak). Two burnt grains (bread/club wheat) were found in pit 22 and tiny fragments of burnt bone in pits 5 and 16. The impression is that the fills of these final recuts were at least partly of inwashed material (Lancaster 2007a; 2007b and chapter 2.2). The burnt chunk of flint (SF502) and burnt stone (SF501) in pit 5 may have been deliberate deposits.

2.2 Palaeoenvironmental Synthesis

Stephen Lancaster

Introduction

The original consideration of the environmental evidence from Warren Field exists as a number of archive reports concerned with palynology (Davies, Tipping and McCulloch 2007), soil micromorphology supported by loss on ignition analyses (Lancaster 2007a; 2007b), analysis of charred plant macrofossils (Hastie 2004; Timpany 2006a; 2006b), and bone (Smith 2007). Fully integrating different forms of environmental evidence is not without its difficulties. The physical circumstances that allow sampling of environmental material for different techniques vary, as do the conditions that determine the survival of different forms of environmental evidence. Different techniques provide information at different spatial and temporal resolutions, although the analyses at Warren Field are characterised by methods that reduce these difficulties. As such, completely parallel sets of data are not often available, a consideration that affects Warren Field.

The geomorphological setting of the site has already been described (Tipping, chapter 1.2). The glacifluvial terrace forms a well drained parent material, and the soils that develop on this are consequently highly oxidised, well drained, and generally somewhat acidic. These conditions affect the type of environmental material that survives and the preservation condition of that material. Calcareous material does not generally survive, as reflected in the survival of only small fragments of burnt bone. Such conditions are not ideal for the preservation of pollen, and a number of contexts sampled for pollen were found to have either no surviving pollen or pollen in too poor a state of preservation to be interpretable. Plant macrofossils only survive through charring in these conditions. Moreover, sands and gravels do not aid the survival of charred plant material: any degree of transport around a site composed of such materials tends to rapidly crumble and abrade charcoal. The physical character of the soils and sub-soils is also significant: the deposits do not cohere well, making sampling for thin-section analysis difficult. The methods by which data were obtained are presented in each of the archived reports.

Soil micromorphology (Lancaster 2007a; 2007b)

A total of three thin-section samples were taken from the pit alignment, two from pit 5 and one from pit 16. Full descriptions of all thin-sections are given in Appendix 2. In all features the sampled deposits largely comprise two components: an unsorted to poorly sorted coarse mineral component of sand with small stones, consisting of quartz, feldspars and fragments of metamorphic rock; and a fine, moderately sorted, organo-mineral component, composed of fine sand and silt sized particles of quartz and feldspar and humified organic matter, with finely comminuted charcoal intermixed throughout the fine material. The fine material has frequently formed as bacillo-cylindrical excrements, generally interpreted as being the product of enchytraeid worms (Bullock *et al.* 1985). The compositional difference from deposit to deposit was largely explicable in terms of the variation in the proportion of these two main components.

The contexts sampled in pit 5 were from the upper fills of the pit and date from both the later Mesolithic (5/3 and 5/18) and the Neolithic periods (5/1 and 5/4). The contexts sampled in pit 16 (16/7 and 16/10) are assumed to be of Neolithic date by association with upper, radiocarbon-dated fills of pits in the alignment. As many of the deposits in pit 5 were too loose to sample for thin-section micromorphological analysis, samples were taken to analyse the carbon content. This was done through loss on ignition analysis, and the samples from pit 5 were compared with analyses taken from the sub-soil and top-soil (Fig. 5). The coarse mineral fraction in contexts 5/3 and 5/18 was poorly to moderately sorted. In addition to the components described above, the later Mesolithic contexts in pit 5 (5/3 and 5/18) contain coarse (> 50 μm) charcoal fragments. These have eroded and rounded forms. These contexts have undergone much reworking by enchytraeid activity and incorporate much fine organic matter, resembling biologically active topsoils under the microscope.

The Neolithic contexts in pit 5 (5/1 and 5/4) have a moderately sorted mineral component, those in pit 16 (16/7 and 16/10) have a poorly to moderately sorted mineral component. The coarse charcoal fraction has eroded and slightly rounded forms. The Neolithic contexts in pits 5 and 16 have also undergone much reworking by enchytraeid activity. There are also possible traces of earthworm excrements in 5/4 and 16/10. The channels that form part of the void space of all the contexts in pits 5 and 16 indicate biological activity in the form of root growth or earthworm burrowing. Like the Mesolithic contexts in pit 5, these contexts resemble biologically active soils. The loss on ignition results from pit 5 were elevated, that of 5/1 being almost the same as the modern topsoil (Fig. 5).

Pollen analyses (Davies, Tipping and McCulloch 2007)

Two features in the pit alignment were sampled: pits 5 and 16. A total of twelve samples were taken, seven from pit 5 and five from pit 16. Due to the soil conditions at the site, insufficient identifiable pollen survived in some of these samples. Rigorous analysis of the state of preservation (Tipping, Carter and Johnston 1994, Bunting and Tipping 2000, Tipping 2000) allowed the interpretation of five samples from pit 5. Tables 17–18 in Appendix 3 show the pollen preservation and pollen concentration values for polleniferous contexts and tabulate the results of the tests applied to establish the reliability of the pollen assemblage. Percentage pollen results are presented in graphical format in Fig. 8.

The samples from pit 5 came from one context, 5/14, dating to the Mesolithic. These were generally the best preserved of the pollen samples. The pollen assemblages are dominated by birch (*Betula*), cf. hazel (*Corylus avellana*-type), heaths (Ericales) and ferns (Pteropsida).

Plant macrofossils (Hastie 2004; Timpany 2006a; 2006b)

A total of 31 samples were processed to recover plant macrofossils. Finely comminuted charred material was found in all the samples, and identifiable material was recovered from 20 samples. Wood charcoal identifications are given in Table 1, other plant macrofossil identifications and counts are given in Table 2. While wood charcoal was moderately common, other charred plant remains were relatively scarce. As one purpose for the recovery of plant macrofossils, both wood and non-wood, was dating, the contexts in which macrofossils were found are mostly well dated. Where radiocarbon dates do not exist, a hypothetical date for a context has been tentatively suggested on the basis of the pit stratigraphy and through analogy with dated contexts in other pits in the alignment. These dates are prefixed with an asterisk in Tables 1 and 2. The Iron Age dated material recovered from Context 5/6 is thought to represent intrusive material (Murray and Murray chapter 2.1).

The Mesolithic contexts

Wood charcoal fragments were recovered from Mesolithic deposits in pits 5, 6, 16, 18 and 19, and other plant macrofossils from Mesolithic deposits in the same pits and pit 22. Wood charcoal from hazel was the most frequently identified taxon, with hazel/alder (*Corylus/Alnus*), birch and willow/poplar (*Salix/Populus*) being the next most frequent, with two pieces of alder charcoal being identified from one context in pit 5 (5/14). A single piece of oak (*Quercus*) was recovered from pit 5 (5/3), which dates to the later Mesolithic. The other plant macrofossils recovered from Mesolithic layers of the pit alignment consist of hazelnut shell (22/3), a fruit from fat hen (*Chenopodium album* 19/5), a vetch seed (*Vicia* sp. 5/12), a fruit from a violet (*Viola* sp. 5/12) and a spikerush nutlet (*Eleocharis* sp. 5/12).

The Neolithic contexts

Wood charcoal fragments were recovered from Neolithic contexts in pits 5 and 6 and other plant macrofossils from pit 22. All the positively identifiable wood charcoal from these contexts in the pit alignment consists of oak. Two grains of bread/club wheat (*Triticum aestivo-compactum*) were recovered from pit 22. (See Lancaster chapter

3.2 for discussion of the presence of bread/club wheat at Warren Field in the wider context of the Scottish Neolithic.)

Bone (Smith 2007)

As noted above, soil conditions at Warren Field are unfavourable for the preservation of bone. What little bone was recovered from the pit alignment survived as small calcined fragments.

The material could not be identified beyond being of mammalian origin.

Formation processes

The infilling processes identified in the pit alignment consist mainly of the slippage of sub-soils and the inwashing of soils, indicated by the texture and moderate to low level of sorting. The composition of the fills is consistent with a local

Table 1. Wood charcoal identifications from the pit alignment (* denotes date suggested on the basis of pit stratigraphy and through analogy with dated contexts in other pits)

Sample	Pit/Context	Age	Identification
2004–4	5/3	Neolithic	*Quercus* sp.
2004–5	5/4	Neolithic	*Quercus* sp.
2006–01	5/4	Neolithic	*Quercus* sp.
2006–02	5/6	Iron Age	*Quercus* sp.
2006–05	5/14	Mesolithic	*Alnus glutinosa*
2006–07	5/3	Mesolithic	*Quercus* sp.
2006–09	5/10A	Mesolithic	*Betula* sp. and Salicaceae sp.
2006–11	5/4	Neolithic	*Quercus* sp.
2006–12	5/10B	Mesolithic	*Corylus* sp. and *Betula* sp.
2006–18	6/4	*Neolithic	*Quercus* sp. and other
2006–19	6/11	Mesolithic	Salicaceae sp. and *Corylus* sp.
2005–11	16/3	Mesolithic	*Alnus/Corylus*
2005–12	16/6	Mesolithic	*Corylus*
2005–10	18/3	Mesolithic	*Corylus*
2005–05	19/5	Mesolithic	*Alnus/Corylus*

Table 2. Plant macrofossil identifications from the pit alignment (* denotes date suggested on the basis of pit stratigraphy and through analogy with dated contexts in other pits)

Sample	Pit/Context	Age	Identification
2006–02	5/6	Iron Age	*Ranunculus* cf. *R. lingua* fruit (1)
2006–04	5/12	*Mesolithic	*Viola* sp. fruit (1), cf. *Eleocharis* sp. nutlet (1)
2006–13	5/12	*Mesolithic	Fabaceae cf. *Vicia* sp. seed (1)
2005–09	22/3	Mesolithic	*Corylus* nutshell? – 1 small fragment
2005–01	22/14	Neolithic	*Triticum aestivo-compactum* grains (5)
2005–05	19/5	Mesolithic	*Chenopodium album* – fruit (1)

origin. The infilling was interspersed with periods of soil formation, indicated by the higher loss on ignition results of contexts 5/11 and 5/14. These apparent phases of stability suggest that once dug, the pits were left as appreciable features in the landscape for a considerable period from the Mesolithic to the Neolithic. The examination of charcoal, both in thin-sections and during plant macrofossil analyses, revealed the eroded and rounded nature of the charcoal, suggesting that this was derived from activity around the pits rather than produced *in situ* within them. The plant macrofossil evidence therefore is indicative of activity in the wider landscape as well as relating directly to the pits themselves.

Environmental reconstruction

Although the key component in reconstructing the early Mesolithic environment is the pollen analysis,

this is supplemented by evidence from other analyses. The relatively limited pollen source area for pit 5 reduces some of the problems of difference of spatial scale between palynological, stratigraphic and other palaeoenvironmental evidence.

Pit 5 was located in the middle of the pit alignment, but the estimated pollen source area for this pit spans the entire length of the pit alignment. Under normal pollen dispersal and deposition conditions, small catchment hollows like pit 5 primarily reflect local pollen production, up to a radius of *c.*100–400m, perhaps extending up to 1 kilometre (Sugita, Gaillard and Broström 1999; Bunting 2002; Broström, Sugita and Gaillard 2004; 2005). Such small diameter sites record the ground flora more clearly than lakes or peat bogs.

When initially infilled, the floor of the pit may have been moist (and so protective of pollen), but it did not retain water: there were no aquatic

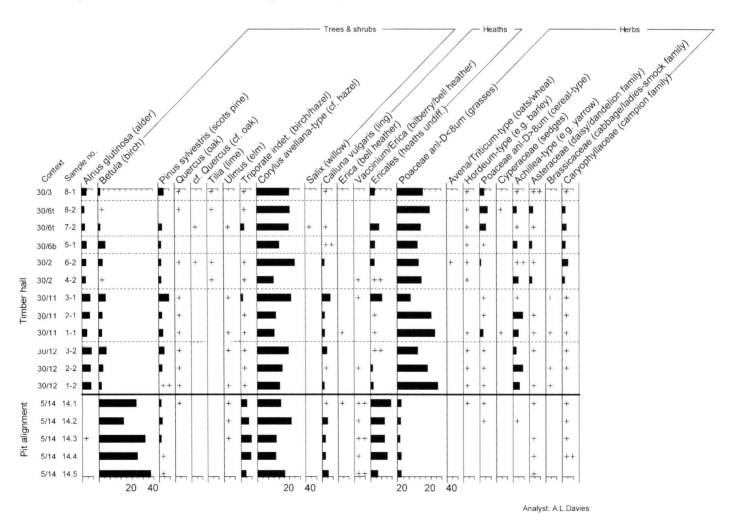

Figure 8. Percentage pollen and spore data from polleniferous contexts from pit alignment pit 5 and timber hall axial pit 30

pollen types in the analyses. The five basal samples from context 5/14 show that the pit alignment was constructed within a birch/hazel wood. The total tree and shrub pollen sum ranges from 61–78% total land pollen (TLP), which suggests a locally extensive but not dense canopy, with good light penetration to the woodland floor (Birks 1973; Caseldine 1981). It is unclear whether the canopy was continuous or whether there were openings, but the pit alignment did not lie at a woodland edge. There was an understorey dominated by heaths with little grass (Poaceae anl-D<8 µm). The woodland predates the expansion of oak in the region at around 5250 cal BC (Birks 1989); this evidence supports the radiocarbon dates from this context. Elm (*Ulmus*) and pine (*Pinus*) were similarly absent from the local woods and probably from the region at this time. A single alder (*Alnus*) pollen grain was recorded, suggesting that the tree

was rare, if not absent from the pollen source area, in accord with models of alder colonisation (Tallantire 1992). Alder is identified as charcoal, however, and the tree may have been present nearby – perhaps growing on the valley floor of the incised Coy Burn, outwith the pollen source area for pit 5. Evidence that alder colonisation was patchy in space and time may account for this early presence of alder at Warren Field (Bennett 1989). There was no pollen evidence for willow or poplar (Salicaceae), which was also present in the charcoal record within the pit. While most of the heath (Ericales) pollen was too poorly preserved to identify more precisely, it suggests a ground cover including ling (*Calluna*) and bilberry (*Vaccinium*) or bell heather (*Erica*). The ground cover taxa also suggest relatively dry soils around the pit alignment. There is no evidence for land-use or vegetation disturbance in the pollen record, although it is likely that the samples span

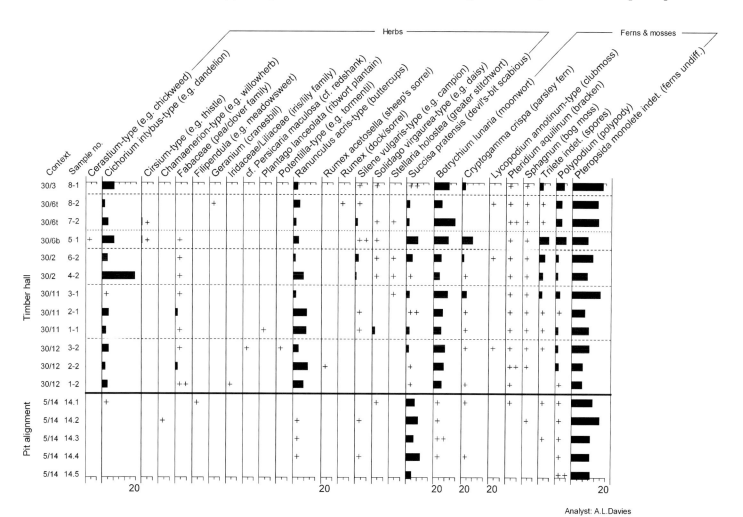

Analyst: A.L.Davies

a short period of time. Fire was also relatively rare in this landscape.

Land use and resources

The environmental evidence adds relatively little to the issue of land use in the Mesolithic: the evidence from the pit alignment does not directly contribute to the consideration of its possible functions. The environmental reconstruction derived from the pollen analysis suggests, however, that if the pit alignment had a monumental function, visibility of it or from it would have been restricted, particularly during the summer. This does not rule out a monumental function, but does raise the issue of who was to know about and see the alignment. The issue of restricted visibility is a greater problem for any possible astronomical function. The possible functions of the pit alignment are discussed in detail below (Murray and Fraser chapter 2.3).

The presence of charcoal from alder implies the gathering and use of wood from different environments to that in which the pit alignment was based. Access to a wet woodland area for fuel gathering is implied by the presence of alder charcoal and perhaps by the willow/poplar charcoal, although the willow/poplar could also represent wood from a solitary tree growing nearby, which would produce insufficient pollen to be noted during the pollen analysis.

Hazelnut shell and seeds of fat hen and possible vetches (Fabaceae *cf. Vicia* sp.) have all been recovered from the Mesolithic contexts. These plants have all been suggested as possible food during the Mesolithic period (Price 1989). The quantities recovered are, however, too small to make a positive interpretation.

Conclusion

The palaeoenvironmental evidence from the Mesolithic contexts of the pit alignment principally indicates the existence of an open hazel and birch woodland. This in itself would be unexceptional for this period and region. The presence of alder charcoal suggests a greater complexity of the landscape beyond the pollen source area, though not irreconcilable with previous models of alder colonisation.

2.3 Discussion of the pit alignment
Hilary Murray and Shannon Fraser

The pollen evidence (Davies, Tipping and McCulloch 2007 and Lancaster, chapter 2.2) indicates that the alignment was dug within a fairly open birch and hazel woodland with low heather and bilberry vegetation. Its location along the top of a low but visible ridge within woodland (Tipping, chapter 1.2) suggests an awareness and enhancement of an existing landscape feature. There is also clear evidence, both from the soil micromorphology (Lancaster, chapter 2.2) and the radiocarbon dates (Marshall, chapter 5), that the alignment was created over an extended period of time and was reworked on a number of occasions. This has important implications for the role and function of the site over time. Both the motivation for digging pits and the way in which existing pits were perceived and used may well have changed over the centuries. Furthermore, we should not assume that the site necessarily ceases to play a role in human lives during periods in which we cannot capture traces of activity archaeologically. This is true not only of the sporadic nature of the growth of and activity at the alignment from perhaps the late ninth through to the mid sixth millennium cal BC, but may also pertain to the 2500–year gap before renewed activity around 4000 cal BC. (It should be noted that the mid-sixth millennium date on oak charcoal from pit 5 might be demonstrating the effect of old oak timber. See Marshall, chapter 5). Interventive activity may have ended here, but the site itself may have continued to play a greater or lesser role in the routine of life for at least some of that time.

The pit alignment in the Mesolithic

Any discussion of the function of the pit alignment tends to be limited by its primary focus on the pits themselves. But beyond the necessity of considering location within the wider landscape, it is also important to remember that when they were dug, the upcast earth would have been very visible around them and it is possible that this may have been as important as the actual pits. A number of possible functions have been explored and the evidence discussed below.

Symbolic use
Two of the earliest pits (18, 19) had primary and apparently deliberate deposits of charcoal. Pit 16,

Fig 9. An impression of the woodland setting: a birch woodland at Mar, Aberdeenshire (© Shannon Fraser)

dug two to four hundred years later, contained a similar deposit as did the undated pit 20. In all of these instances the charcoal deposit had been placed in the pit fairly soon after it was dug, with at most some slippage of sand and gravel from the sides below, or interleaved with, the charcoal. The charcoal deposits did not appear to have been deliberately covered.

The other pits sectioned (5, 6, 22) did not have clear deposits of charcoal, although there was some charcoal in some of the fills that had eroded in from the upcast material around the pits. This is important as it suggests that the fires that created the charcoal were in the wood, near the pits.

Such purposive deposition of discrete, charcoal-rich material, combined with the evidence for intermittent activity and for gradual development of the alignment, in which the place is revisited over a considerable period of time, are features which could conceivably derive from symbolic activity – as is the formal disposition of the pits along a low, natural ridge in the landscape. In such a scenario, a whole range of activities might have been invested with symbolic significance: the excavation of each pit, the removal of soils and gravels and their placement around the edges, the activities connected with the preparation, lighting and use of fires nearby, the gathering together of some of the resulting burnt material and its placement within the pits, the insertion of stakes or small posts in some of the pits. Although undated, there is also the possibility that the posts interspersed among the line of pits formed part of this suggested ceremonial activity.

What such ceremonies might have been, and what they meant, remains elusive – and as we have noted, are unlikely to have remained the same over the life of the monument – but we can perhaps catch the faintest traces of specific activities and seasonal temporalities. The inclusion in the deliberate deposit in the bottom of pit 19 (19/5) of minute fragments of burnt bone and the seed of fat hen, a traditional foodstuff, might suggest the consumption of food as part of activities connected with the monument in mid-summer to mid-autumn, while the burnt fragment of hazelnut shell in pit 22 (22/3) may indicate presence in mid to late autumn.

Much more speculative, but certainly consistent with potential symbolic activities focusing on the pit alignment, is the possible evidence for the use of crushed minerals, possibly deriving from what would then have been spectacularly-coloured outcrops in the area around the Pass of Ballater. The use of pigments deriving from these minerals in the decoration of objects or of the human body (whether as body paint or in the creation of tattoos), might be envisaged as part of ritual behaviour enacted at the monument. In a recent discussion exploring the possible importance of colour in Mesolithic life, Graeme Warren notes that the use of pigments is certainly hinted at by the occurrence of red ochre and of small grinding bowls in Scottish Mesolithic contexts (Warren 2005, 144). Traces of various minerals including zinc and copper were found by Karen Hardy in her analysis of residues on bevel-ended bone tools from west coast Mesolithic sites and interpreted as potentially associated with the use of colour, either as pigments themselves or as mordants for fixing (Hardy 2009). Other evidence for colour in the Mesolithic includes a lump of haematite (red/orange pigment) from the site of Sand (Isbister 2009), as well as the presence of dog whelk (from which a purple dye can be extracted) at the same site (Milner 2009).

Ceremonial places can act as nodes where the rhythms of human life interconnect with other cycles – the succession of seasons, for example, or the movement of celestial bodies over days, months and years. In this context, Andrew Smith and Gail Higginbottom investigated the possibility of astronomical connections at the pit alignment, using dedicated GIS software they have developed to generate horizon profiles for archaeoastronomical purposes (Smith and Higginbottom 2007). It was recognised that as the monument was constructed in woodland, albeit of a fairly open nature, observation of the sky would have been difficult, but that at least the potential for greater visibility existed in the winter and spring, when the trees were without leaves. The study assessed potential correspondence of the alignment with the rising or setting of the sun at solstices and equinoxes, the moon at its most northerly and southerly aspects, the ten brightest stars, and the Pleiades. The orientation of the alignment at 8210 cal BC, at approximately 50°±5° to astronomical north, did not correspond to any significant celestial events. Smith and Higginbottom note, however, that a cyclical phenomenon, in which the full moon appears to roll along the southern horizon around the time of the summer solstice, may have been observable from the site, depending on the level of tree cover. They suggest that while analysis of over 2000 randomly-chosen locations demonstrated that there is a 30% probability of the phenomenon being observed in this area purely by chance, and that it is not therefore a statistically significant occurrence, the possibility of a deliberate connection remains.

Flint quarries
Another hypothesis which was considered was the possibility that the pits in the alignment had been used for quarrying flint. Although it would be unlikely for sources of gravel to be flint-rich in this locality, and although the form and nature of the pits themselves mitigated against their interpretation as flint extraction quarries – a feature not yet attested in Scotland before the later Neolithic – it was considered advisable to test the hypothesis formally, given the unusual nature of the monument. To establish whether the glacifluvial gravels beneath the terrace surface were rich in flint, Richard Tipping examined the composition of the gravel from sieved samples exposed in animal burrows in the valleyside of the incised Coy Burn, around 2m below the terrace surface. The gravel is poorly sorted (50% by weight >16.0mm diam.; 32% <11.2mm diam.), and clasts (rock fragments) are all subrounded to rounded. All clasts are of very durable rocks. Of 150 clasts >11.2mm diam., 60% were of various forms of granite, 20% of quartz or quartzite, 15% of schist and 5% of different volcanic rocks. No flint was recorded. Flint extraction was thus not the purpose of the pits.

Hunting traps
The fact that so many of the pits were originally left open and that pits 5 and 6 had, albeit secondary, stakes set in the base, suggested the possibility that the pit alignment might have been a series of pit traps used in hunting deer or other mammals such

as boar or wild cattle. Originally it was considered that the small size of some pits, the fact that the upcast earth would have been visible in the landscape and the evidence that there would have been burnt material (and therefore, intermittently, the smell of burning) around the pits, all mitigated against such an interpretation. However, there is evidence to suggest that some of these may not have been important considerations.

Re-evaluation of the Mesolithic lakeside site at Star Carr in Yorkshire (Mellars 1999) has shown it to have been revisited repeatedly over 250–300 years from c.8700 cal BC, with burning of reeds possibly used as a hunting technique to attract deer to the fresh new growth of vegetation. This gives a precedent for long term use of a possible hunting site.

Comparison could also be made with the pits used from the late Neolithic (c.2000 cal BC) onwards in hunting reindeer in northern Lapland (Halinen 2005 and pers. comm.). Pits, either individual or up to several hundred in number, were dug in rows that could be a kilometre or more in length. Some of the pits were linked by fences above ground level and were therefore visible in the landscape. They were used by driving the animals along or between the fences and then into the pits. The animals were trapped and crippled by falling into the pits which were usually at least 1.8m deep. The importance of this comparison is that the pit lines were set in very specific locations. They were usually across a natural routeway for the animals, for example between a ridge and a river.

Mye Plantation in Dumfries and Galloway is the only site in Scotland where possible pitfall traps of prehistoric date have been positively identified, although a large Neolithic pit at Newton, Islay may also have been a pitfall trap (McCullagh 1989 and pers. comm.). At Mye Plantation, excavated in 1902 (Mann 1903) and 1951 (Council for British Archaeology 1951, 15) and recently dated to the late Neolithic (Sheridan 2005), there was a row of five pits up to 3m × 2.4m in diameter and up to 2.8m deep, possibly with a fence between them. The pits had numerous stakes in the base, at least one of which, excavated in 1951, had been sharpened on the upper surface. The pit alignment lay roughly parallel to the edge of a low promontory above marshy ground.

These examples show that the smell of burning and the visibility of the Warren Field pits may not

have been a problem and that potentially they could have functioned as a series of hunting pits. However, the small size of some of the pits is impractical even for boar, and their location make this a very unlikely scenario. In particular, the location of the alignment in the landscape is not convincing for hunting traps as it is c.300m from the nearest water at the Coy Burn and does not appear to have utilised any natural land formation in a manner that would have facilitated driving animals towards the line. As Tipping (2007) has suggested, hunting could have taken place in the gorge of the burn, without the need for traps.

Cremation pits
The recent discovery of three Mesolithic cremation pits in Castleconnell, Co Limerick, Ireland (Collins and Coyne 2004; Pitts 2007) of similar date to the Warren Field pits suggests that this is a possible function that should be considered. The three ranged in diameter from c.0.60m to over 2m, each containing cremated bone, one accompanied by a burnt stone axe and two burnt microliths. At Warren Field there was no evidence of cremated human bone. It might be suggested that this was a question of survival but as a few very tiny fragments of burnt animal bone *had* survived on the site this is not a convincing argument. Further arguments against interpreting the Warren Field pits as burials are the absence of grave goods in any primary fill and the evidence that the pits were left open – unlikely in the case of burial.

Parallels
Pits of substantial size are certainly not unknown from Mesolithic contexts in Scotland, but they are generally directly associated with other evidence for settlement activity, as at Kinloch, Rùm (Wickham-Jones 1990) or Newton, Islay (McCullagh 1989). The formal, linear layout and monumental scale that we see at Warren Field has, as yet, no excavated parallels in Scotland. Although no precise parallels have been identified south of the border, thematic similarities do emerge from a handful of sites. Thus, comparison may be made with the four, or possibly five, Mesolithic pits excavated in the car park area at Stonehenge in 1966 and 1988–9 (Allen 1995a, 41–56). Set out in a gentle curve, the pits ranged in diameter from 1.27m to 1.93m and were between 1.27m and 1.55m in surviving depth. Three of the pits had good evidence of having held vertical pine timbers c.0.75m in diameter, a fourth

appears to have held a post which was removed. Three of the pits have yielded radiocarbon dates of between *c*.8820–7730 cal BC and 7480–6590 cal BC, clearly demonstrating development of the monument over a significant period of time (Allen and Gardiner 2002, 143–4). Allen (1995b, 471–3) suggests that they may be interpreted as a series of totem-poles, although he does consider the possibility that they formed part of a herding structure for use in hunting. It is interesting that these pits also appear to have been dug in open woodland, in this case of pine and hazel, which may have been cleared directly around the pits. However, the major significance of this parallel lies in the Mesolithic date of what may be interpreted as a monumental structure and in the possible recognition of this earlier activity as contributory to the positioning of a later ritual monument. Similarly, at Bryn Celli Ddu, Anglesey, two large pits containing pine charcoal have been dated to the seventh millennium cal BC (Pitts 2006). These were part of a row of five pits associated with stone settings and an ox burial, found immediately outside the entrance of a later Neolithic henge and chambered cairn (Hemp 1930).

Another interesting parallel to the Warren Field alignment is at Nosterfield Quarry at Thornborough, Yorkshire (Copp and Toop 2005), another site with later ritual significance, where two pit alignments have been excavated on almost the same northwest-southeast alignment as three later henges. The parallel lines, some 72m long, were 22–28m apart, one with nine pits, the other with eight pits, at intervals of between 10m and 13m. Some of the sections in the interim publication (Copp and Toop 2005, 129, Fig. 58, 59) perhaps indicate that some of the pits had held posts (F204, 209, 215, 68), but in others (F216) the fills appear to have drifted in from around the pit, comparable with the evidence at Warren Field. The dating evidence for the monument is admittedly weak – a single, multiple-entity date on unidentified species – but one of these pits has produced a late Mesolithic date from an upper fill.

These sites, like the Warren Field alignment, show that major structures dating to the Mesolithic are now beginning to be recognised throughout Britain. It may be that other pit alignments were first dug in the Mesolithic but have been dated on later, secondary, activity. A possible example may be the undated phase 1 of the pits of Enclosure 1

at Cowie Road, Bannockburn, Stirling, a site with one late Mesolithic radiocarbon date (Rideout 1997, 36–7, 54–6). Rideout's description of these pits is striking: 'the pits were excavated then left to weather and fill up. The source of the fills is not clear' (1997, 55). Significantly, he suggests that these pits were dug in individual groups, perhaps over a long period of time – thus the monumental aspect of the place may have developed only gradually. The pits were later recut and the upper fills dated to the Neolithic by associated artefacts and radiocarbon dates ranging from the late fifth to mid fourth millennium cal BC.

Clearly, if this were the case, it would have profound implications for the long, pit-defined enclosures and cursus-related monuments in Scotland, which on present evidence are a development of the early fourth millennium. However, we are not intending to suggest here that construction of these monuments necessarily begins in the late Mesolithic. Rather, we wish merely to signal that with the paucity of excavated examples, and with the evidence of the Warren Field alignment demonstrating a tradition of pit-digging to form large monuments which stretches back through the eighth millennium cal BC, it is at least worth considering the possibility that *some* elements of *some* of these monuments may have a deeper antiquity, whether in their materiality or in their ultimate inspiration.

The term 'pit alignment' is a catch-all, descriptive phrase which covers a group of monuments of wide-ranging date and function. Examination of the record for northeast Scotland (the council areas of Moray, Aberdeenshire and Angus), reveals examples as disparate as large-scale, exceedingly regular, pre-Improvement (possibly prehistoric) land divisions at Bellie in Moray, comprising small, close-set pits; undulating lines of massive pits which seem to follow former watercourses or define former topographic features, as at Drumnagair, Aberdeenshire; and early Neolithic pit- or post-defined cursus monuments as at Inchbare, Angus. Although these sites are all of some antiquity, pit alignments in Scotland may extend into the post-medieval period – on the one hand, some may represent the ploughed-out remains of Improvement period hedge-and-tree boundaries or nineteenth-century rifle ranges, while on the other, the practice of 'pitting' to delineate property marches was carried out until the mid nineteenth century – although it is not entirely clear whether the spacing of march pits would be close enough to recognise them as alignments in aerial photographs.

Given this diversity, and the fact that interpretation of cropmark sites from aerial photographic evidence alone is fraught with difficulty, identifying potential comparators for the Warren Field alignment is not an easy task. As Strat Halliday has noted (pers. comm.), some alignments might in fact represent the more robust elements of larger monuments, of which the smaller components are not revealed as cropmarks – as at the Dunragit cursus-type monument, Dumfries and Galloway. However, confining analysis to the northeast of the country in the first instance, a small number of sites which share a series of general characteristics with Warren Field, and with each other, begin to resolve into a loosely-defined group. Some of these appear as isolated cropmarks, while others form part of large complexes likely to represent intermittent inhabitation over several millennia. Some might just prove to be of Mesolithic date.

These pit alignments tend to straggle a little unevenly across the landscape. A general northeast-southwest axis is frequent, though not exclusive, with orientation between north northeast/south southwest and east northeast/west southwest. In addition, the alignments incorporate directional shifts, either in the form of kinks, rather like the southwest terminal end of the Warren Field alignment, or more gentle, curving deviation from the main axis at one end. Generally following the contour of the land, the spacing of the pits is somewhat irregular, as is their size. Unlike some of the examples noted above, they are not monuments of massive scale, lying mostly in the range of 20–60m in length. These alignments tend to lie close to watercourses, on river terraces or on ground rising gently from the valley bottom. As at Warren Field, the features described here would be consistent with the establishment of a monument in woodland, in which a general linear impetus works with and around standing trees, perhaps over a considerable passage of time.

Examples in Moray include a short line of pits at Milltown and two possible alignments at Earnhill, which appear to run along a slightly elevated ridge. At Wester Fintray in Aberdeenshire, a sinuous alignment lies amongst ring-ditch houses and field systems; significantly, a lithic scatter of narrow-blade Mesolithic technology has been identified

here through fieldwalking. Other candidates in Aberdeenshire include Mains of Midstrath, Chapelton, Bent and Pittengardener, the latter lying somewhat apart from an unenclosed settlement complex. Finally, possibilities in cropmark-rich Angus include a gently curving line of thirteen pits at Friockheim and an alignment at Balhungie, overlooking the Firth of Tay.

Neolithic use

The recognition of the 4000 year old pits at Warren Field in the Neolithic is less surprising when one reads the description of the discovery in about 1900 of the pit alignment at Mye Plantation, dated to the late Neolithic (2500–2230 cal BC; Sheridan 2005, 20): 'Mr Beckett's attention was first attracted by a row of depressions on the surface of a wooded area. If there had been one depression only, probably no notice would have been taken of the place' (Mann 1903, 371). Similarly, at Gardom's Edge, Derbyshire, an alignment of pits, which on excavation proved to be of Iron Age date, was clearly visible on moorland with some birch scrub before excavation 2000 years later (Barnatt, Bevan and Edmonds 2002). The pit sections at Warren Field suggest that in the Neolithic they would have been visible only as a line of shallow, saucer shaped hollows, all but one of which was then deliberately recut.

With the exception of pit 5, in which the burnt stone fragments (SF 501) in the top fill gave an impression of a deliberate sealing of the pit, the Neolithic fills appear to have comprised inwashed material. This contained charcoal but often in very tiny fragments, minute pieces of burnt bone and a couple of burnt grains – all material that could have derived from a 'domestic' hearth. The temptation is to derive this material from the Neolithic timber building only 150m distant and perhaps to suggest that it was brought from the building to link it with any supernatural power attributed to the pits. However, it is salutary to note that 300m to the northwest, in the Crathes Castle Overflow Car Park site (Murray and Murray chapter 4.2), truncated post-pits were identified, containing early Neolithic modified carinated bowl pottery (Sheridan, chapter 6.1). Any archaeological remains in the ground between have been destroyed by an early twentieth century tree plantation, but it is possible that this was the remnant of a settlement associated with or slightly later than the timber building, and that this may have been the source of the material in the pits of the alignment. It is also possible, of course, that this material derived from activities taking place around the monument itself, perhaps of a formal, ritual character. In contrast, the source of the burnt, flaked stone placed in the top of pit 5, while probably relatively local (Warren, chapter 6.3), is not the river terrace upon which Warren Field lies. This re-working of the alignment, with the removal of certain materials in the re-excavation of the pits and the deposition of others, from different places, might form part of the symbolic renegotiation, and perhaps appropriation, of the values of a place already laden with meaning.

There is possible evidence from Chapelfield, Cowie, near Stirling (Atkinson 2002) for the Neolithic reworking of earlier features. Three pits (I, II and V) were excavated which were dated to the Mesolithic (ranging between 6240–5970 cal BC and 4540–4330 cal BC) and were described as having been used for 'the deposition of organic based materials ... but for what purpose is not known' (Atkinson 2002, 188). Two of these pits (I, II) had recuts and contained early Neolithic material in their upper fills. Other pits on the site were considered to have been dug in the Neolithic and to contain structured deposits of pottery and lithics.

This re-use of sites originating in the Mesolithic occurs elsewhere in Scotland. For example, at Garthdee, Aberdeen (Murray and Murray 2005b), a Mesolithic pit was sealed below the occupation floor of an oval, early Neolithic building. Significantly, the location of this pit was apparently acknowledged at least at the beginning of the life of the building, the lack of artefactual material directly above the pit contrasting sharply with the rest of the floor surfaces. At Spurryhillock, Aberdeenshire (Alexander 1997) – a site which produced evidence for early Neolithic activity – a pit measuring 2.3m × 1.78m and 1.35m in surviving depth was dated to the fifth millennium cal BC (pit 619: 4720–4370 cal BC and 4910–4540 cal BC). The lowest fill was a deposit of unabraded charcoal which had been slowly covered by alternating inwashed layers of sand and charcoal. At Cowie Road, Bannockburn (Rideout 1997), a hazelnut which gave a Mesolithic date was found in a fire pit which also contained early Neolithic pottery. At Biggar Common, South Lanarkshire (Johnston 1997) a late Mesolithic stake-built structure and burnt spreads with early Neolithic pottery were

sealed below a long mound. It is surely necessary to question if all these occurrences were coincidental or if there was often a deliberate choice of sites that had evidence of earlier use.

Indeed, one of the most interesting features of the few known Mesolithic sites in Britain which display an element of monumentality – Warren Field, Stonehenge Car Park, Bryn Celli Ddu and Nosterfield Quarry (discussed above) – is that they see symbolic activity in the Neolithic. Not only that but, as at Warren Field, the spatial relationship of the earlier to the later activity at Bryn Celli Ddu and Thornborough demonstrates a formality which seems hardly likely to be the product of chance. The pattern which seems to be emerging is one in which places which bear the faintest traces of a previous human presence – which with their deep antiquity may have come to be invested with mythic origins – witness physical elaboration in the fourth and third millennia BC.

Other excavated sites hint that this pattern may turn out to be widespread. Allen and Gardiner (2002) have published a useful reassessment of a number of Neolithic monuments in southern England, including causewayed enclosures, cursus monuments and long barrows, which they suggest drew on the contemporary symbolism of places in which a 'sacred history' several thousand years old was embedded. There are other tantalising possibilities – as in the probable Mesolithic flint burin tightly jammed into a crevice of a natural monolith around which the chambered cairn at Gwernvale, Brecknock was constructed (Britnell 1984, 50, 122), or the parallel lines of posts underlying the probable early fourth millennium ditches of the Stanwell Cursus at Perry Oaks, Middlesex (Lewis and Brown 2006). Closer to home, a series of linear pits with Mesolithic dates may form the spatial framework for early Neolithic monumental developments at the site of Fordhouse Barrow in Angus (Proudfoot 2001). The meanings will have changed, of course, but the power of place, passed down in the stories woven around it, seems to have endured.

Living in the landscape

On balance, and accepting that there may be functions which have simply escaped us, a symbolic role for the Warren Field pits seems to us the most likely. Even as its meaning altered with the passing of time, and as it perhaps drifted in and out of the focus of people's lives over the millennia, the alignment appears to have been a place 'from which people could reference their own identity and history' (Cummings 2000, 88). It can be described as a monument following Mercer's definition (2004, 39): it required effort to create and it was a 'marker' that was used and reused at intervals over a long period – in similar vein, perhaps, to the shell middens of coastal areas. As a monument it can be set in the regional framework of evidence for people moving along and living beside the eastern seaboard and main river systems – the valley terraces of the Ythan, the Don and the Dee – from the early ninth millennium BC.

Mesolithic inhabitation is attested along the entire length of the River Dee, from near the river mouth with flint scatters on a number of sites in Aberdeen (Kenworthy 1982; Murray and Murray 2005b) to the high uplands near its source, at Chest of Dee and in adjacent Glen Geldie (Fraser 2003; 2005; Ballin 2004; Clarke 2007). The presence of flint from east coast sources at these upland sites may be the result of exchange between different regional groups, but is perhaps more likely to represent the scale of people's routine movement between the mountains and the North Sea. Our understanding of the detail of these routines is limited, not least due to the paucity of known upland sites in Scotland, and to ongoing deconstruction of traditional archaeological models which assume long-term winter aggregation in the lowlands and short-term summer dispersal into the uplands (*e.g.* Spikins 2000). As Spikins notes, it seems more likely that seasonal routines of movement will have varied considerably from year to year, in terms of their nature, timing and frequency, and in the composition of groups following particular routes through the landscape. Within this complexity, the bonds of morality, spirituality, genealogy and individual life histories will all have been caught up in the interconnections among places and people.

There are notable concentrations of Mesolithic flint from the river banks nearest to the Warren Field site, stretching from Banchory, 3 kilometres upstream, to Nethermills Farm, Crathes, 2.5 kilometres further east, where a Mesolithic site with a possible oval building has been excavated. This site is not yet fully published and no radiocarbon dates are available as yet (Kenworthy 1981; Boyd and Kenworthy 1992). Warren has suggested that the extensive lithic scatters along notable salmon rivers in eastern Scotland represent repeated visits over centuries and perhaps millennia, and that they may be meeting places for widely-scattered groups of people taking advantage of the seasonal abundance of fish so they may gather together (Warren 2005, 143); for the Dee, this could be at various times between February and September. Transactions of all sorts, from the material to the metaphysical, might take place at such times – moments of negotiation, celebration and dedication.

Such a context would certainly chime well with an interpretation of the Warren Field pit alignment which places it within the realm of symbolic activity. It would have been no more than ten minutes walk from the river, well within the range that would be expected to be used for gathering or hunting. Hints of this sort of movement lie in the fact that neither the alder nor willow represented in the charcoal from primary fills appear to have been growing in the woodland around the pits and are likely to have been gathered elsewhere – possibly near the Coy Burn, which runs down into the Dee. And yet, the monument sits somewhat apart from the intense activity along the lowest river terrace, both topographically and in the absence of lithic artefacts in its immediate environs. The impression is of isolation, of a place visited only occasionally, or by a restricted number of people. It may be that while large gatherings congregated in the area during the salmon and sea trout runs, only particular individuals or small, selective groups spent time at the monument. A whole host of possibilities exists – from the activities of ritual specialists carried out on behalf of the wider community, to the rites of passage of groups of young men or women. It may be, of course, that larger groups did come together at this site, but that whatever took place there simply did not demand – or permit – the use or deposition of lithic artefacts.

Whatever the specifics may have been, the activities carried out at the pit alignment, in its gradual creation and transmutation over immense stretches of time, will have contributed to an understanding of how people, animals, mythic and spiritual forces, and the elements of land, sea and sky, all interact in a world which makes sense. Entwined in a web of named places and pathways through landscapes familiar in differing

*Figure 10. Looking northeast along the pit alignment. Each person is standing in the centre of one of the pits (©
Charles Murray)*

degrees to people of different ages, sex and
affiliation, references to other times, places and
people were captured in the activities at Warren
Field. As Edmonds notes (1999, 117), these human
connections will also have been expressed in acts
such as the consumption of food together as part of
the activities focused upon the monument – traces
of which may be caught in the environmental
evidence from the Warren Field deposits.

Superficially this does not appear to have been
a visually dominant monument in the landscape.
However, it is important to stress that the nature
of the fills suggests that the earth dug from the
pits was piled alongside them. The alignment
when first created may have been far more
obvious for the heaps or banks of earth than for
the pits themselves. This would have made it very
visible, even in the open woodland suggested by
the pollen evidence. We should also be aware of
the potential for the contribution of other, more

ephemeral elements to the constitution of place:
offerings of fruits, nuts and other foodstuffs,
perhaps, or flowers and other vegetation, feathers,
and so on. Carvings might have embellished the
trees amongst which the alignment threaded
– indeed, the trees themselves may have formed
an integral part of the monument. Particular items
of decorative clothing or other organic materials
and objects, all used in ceremonies around the
pits, may have been left behind deliberately. As
with the rags tied to the trees around the 'cloutie
wells' which still survive in some parts of Scotland,
an accumulation of organic material in different
stages of decay can produce a visibly distinctive
effect. Upright posts at different points along the
alignment may also have had a visual impact
at certain points in time, perhaps, like the pits,
separated by hundreds of years or more. In this
regard, we should not forget the possibility that
the undated line of posts revealed *c*.40m to the

southeast (Area 10: Murray and Murray chapter 4.1) might fit in somewhere in the vast expanse of time over which the pits remained visible.

As time passed the piled earth would have become lightly covered in fallen leaves and sparse vegetation. The evidence of the pit fills shows that when the surrounding earth was disturbed by people revisiting the site, there was slippage back into the pits. Gradually the pit outlines would have become more blurred and the surrounding piles or banks less dominant. The later Mesolithic use of pit 5 is quite different in nature, being a deposit into the partly filled pit. Perhaps by this point there was a memory that this was an important place but the nature of that importance was lost or changed into a new, different significance. With the passage of centuries, the origins of the pit alignment might have become drawn beyond the remembered biographies of past generations, into the founding stories of mythical ancestors and other beings.

Thousands of years later, the Neolithic recuts into the pits illustrate an acknowledgement of the earlier monument, the value and meanings of which may have shifted over and over again. Embedded as it is within our imperfect understanding of the nature of the changes in traditional lifeways occurring in the centuries around 4000 cal BC, it is a moot point as to whether this was based on the recognition of an unusual and possibly frightening physical phenomenon in an alien landscape, or on changing perceptions of the knowledge passed down through oral tradition amongst indigenous hunter gatherers, or within the complex context of interaction and knowledge exchange among local groups and incomers. Whatever the case, the relationship between the present community and the traces of past endeavour, whether human or mythical, was being renegotiated; the resonance of their power was being channelled in new ways. The removal of the materiality of the past in the re-excavation of parts of the pits; the insertion, possibly, of posts along the alignment or nearby (the undated post-pits both in the alignment and in Area 10); the deposition of new materials which in effect may finally have removed the remaining depressions in the landscape; will all have carved out new meanings within a landscape undergoing a profound physical and social transformation, as woodland was cleared on the river terrace for cereal cultivation and as areas of grassland developed (Lancaster, chapter 3.2). This opening-up of the landscape may have brought new connections into focus. For example, the axis of the alignment would have encompassed the path of the summer solstice sun, low in the sky, not long after rising (Smith and Higginbottom 2008, fig. 3). While probably not visible in the Mesolithic due to the extent of tree cover, this link might perhaps have become obvious with the lengthening and broadening of the horizon in the early fourth millennium BC.

The precise relationship between the pit alignment and the timber hall at Warren Field – and, indeed, of the Balbridie hall on the opposite bank of the river – remains elusive. It is not impossible, however, to suggest that the awareness of the earlier monument, the pit alignment, may have been instrumental in the choice of site for the building and for the cereal cultivation which took place around it. Perhaps the effort invested in the pit alignment helped to make the place right for new ways of living, and these new traditions right for the place.

Chapter 3

A new kind of place: the timber hall
circa 3820–3690 cal BC

3.1 The excavated evidence

Hilary Murray and Charles Murray

The building was orientated with its long axis approximately east northeast/west southwest (Fig. 1). At its maximum extent it was 24m long and 9m wide externally, with fairly straight side walls and rounded ends. The interior, *c.*22.5m × 8m (between inner wall faces), was divided by partitions into four areas (Figs 11, 12). A large pit was situated at each end of the building on the long axis. The structure of the side walls, the end walls, the internal partitions and the axial pits will be discussed individually. It must be stressed that the site was plough truncated and only negative features remained so there were no surviving floors or occupation deposits and the absence of a hearth may be an accident of survival/non-survival and should not be used in any discussion of function.

Structural details can be discussed with some confidence because most of the timbers in the external walls had been charred, in many cases extending to and including the base of the post. In some instances the charring was up to 50–60mm thick, resulting in the survival of a charred outer casing of the timber around a rotted core (Fig. 24). As a result the size and profile of the timbers was preserved with greater clarity than can be deduced from post-pipe impressions. The excavation strategy, intended to maximise structural detail, was to section *c.*50% of the outer wall posts and 100% of the posts at the east and west ends and the internal features. Particular emphasis was placed on contexts where there appeared to be a sequential relationship. Posts or post-pits which clearly cut other features (Fig. 12 shown in blue) are described in this report as secondary; some may represent a sequence of work within a single construction episode, others were clearly replacements or repairs. Full details of the sectioned posts (Figs 13–15) are given in Appendix 1.

The side walls

The north and south walls were fairly straight for much of their length, but curved very slightly inwards at the ends (Posts 81, 172, 31 and 38). They were built of large vertical timbers set in a series of segmented wall trenches. Both round and split timbers had been used, many of the split timbers appearing to have been roughly halved. Timber identification showed oak as predominant, especially at the eastern end of the building, with ash and willow/poplar also used (Fig. 22). The timbers ranged in size between a post 0.25m in diameter and a split timber of 1m × 0.25m, but the majority were between 0.40m and 0.70m across (longest dimension). Larger timbers stood at the ends of wall segments (31, 38, 60, 77, 146 and 161). Overall the posts in the eastern half of the building were more carefully aligned than those in the western half, with an apparently greater emphasis on the regularity of the inner rather than the outer face. This appears to coincide with the part of the building where oak was the dominant wood identified. Many of the bases of the posts were irregularly tapered, matching the type of cuts produced in experimental felling with stone axes (Coles 1973, plate 3). Many had been placed 0.10–0.20m above the base of the wall trench on a bed of backfilled loose gravel (Fig. 13). This would not only have counteracted the uneven bases but

Fig 11. Aerial view of the timber hall, looking west (Photograph by Moira Greig. © Aberdeenshire Archaeology Service. AAS-05-03-CT80)

might also have facilitated manoeuvring of the timbers to attain a level wall top.

The south wall was defined by six trenches ranging in length between 1.6m and 3.4m and in width averaging 0.60–0.80m, although trench 106 widened to 0.90m to accommodate the large post 108, and trench 133 widened to 1.08m for post 31. The sides ranged between almost vertical and slightly angled, with rounded terminals and flattish bases. Depths, which are likely to have been partially degraded by plough damage, were between 0.22m and 0.50m. There were twenty-eight posts in the wall trenches (fifteen of which have been sectioned) and another post (113), which may be secondary, in an individual post-pit. Nineteen of the timbers could be identified as being in the round but six had clearly been split, the rest were indeterminate.

The north wall consisted of four or five trenches, the junction between trenches 115 and 97 being obscured by the secondary post 167; this clearly cut

trench 115 but its relationship to trench 97 was not established. The trenches ranged in length between 1.7m and 5.6m. The average width was between 0.60m and 0.80m but trench 115 widened to 1m to hold post 38 and trench 64 widened to 0.94m at its west terminal. Depths were between 0.18m and 0.55m, being significantly shallower at the northwest corner of the building which appeared to have suffered greater plough damage. There were twenty-seven primary posts in the wall (nine of which have been sectioned) and three posts (61, 131, 167: all sectioned) which appeared to be secondary. Thirteen of the timbers could be identified as in the round but another sixteen were either clearly or probably split, the rest were indeterminate.

The end walls

The curved ends of the building are treated separately as they appeared to be structurally distinct from the side walls (Fig. 14).

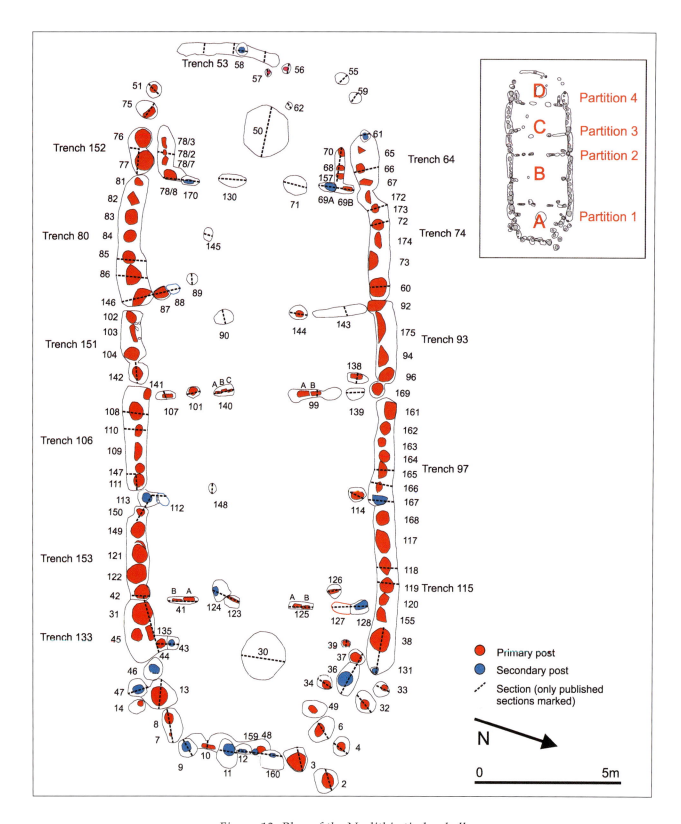

Figure 12. Plan of the Neolithic timber hall

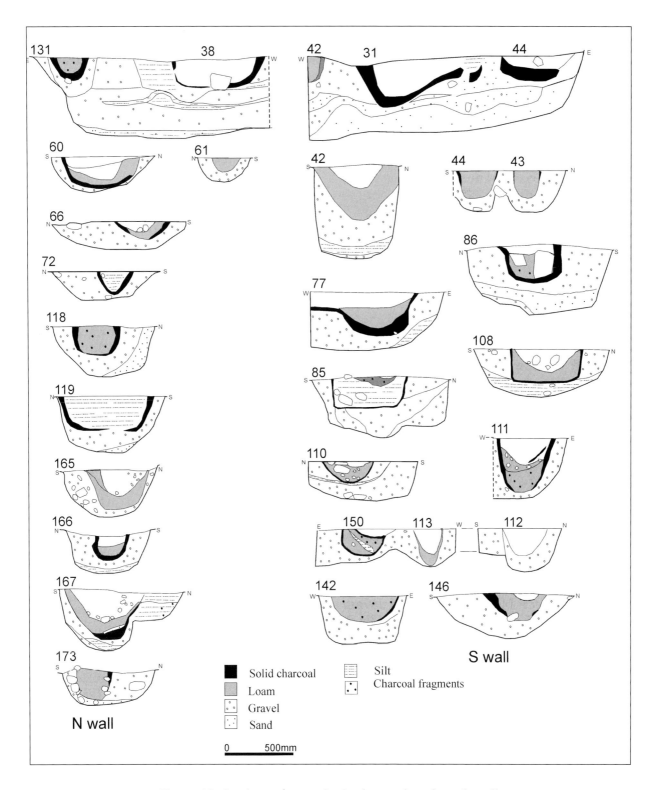

Figure 13. Sections of post-pits in the north and south walls

The east end of the building comprised a series of vertical timbers, predominantly oak, set further apart than those in the side walls. Most of the timbers were in individual post-pits. The intercutting of some of these features demonstrated that there had been a sequence of repairs or replacements of timbers. This is clearest in the east wall itself where the original structure appears to have comprised vertical timbers 10 and 48. The shape of the irregular wall trench suggests that there may have been at least one timber between 10 and 48. These were then replaced or augmented by timber 12, and then by timbers 9, 11, 159 and 160. Post 36 was also clearly secondary to 37, although they could have co-existed. Clearly other timbers may be secondary but, lacking horizontal stratigraphy, this cannot be proved. The overall impression is that the east end would have given a very open appearance with gaps of *c*.0.30–0.60m between the timbers. A larger gap, 1.20m wide, flanked by timbers 4, 6 and 49 on the east and timbers 32 and 34 on the west, gave the appearance of an entrance (Fig. 18). The gap of 0.80m between posts 3 and 6 is less convincing as an entrance but does seem emphasised by the outlying post 2. There may also originally have been a gap between posts 13 and 44 but this was later blocked by post 46.

The west end of the building had less topsoil cover and as a result may have suffered greater plough damage. Rabbits had also burrowed at the south end of the linear trench 53. Nevertheless the evidence suggests that the structure here had been far lighter or more ephemeral than at the east end of the building. Only the two posts which continued the line of the south wall (51, 75) were of a size comparable to the posts in the east wall. They were between 0.30m and 0.45m across and both had charred bases. The post-pits (55, 59) which continued the line of the north wall were smaller; both had a fairly humic fill but the lack of visible post pipes and of packing material suggests that these posts may have been removed rather than rotted *in situ*. The west wall itself was defined by a shallow trench (53) 3.4m long and 0.30–0.45m wide. The fill was of a loose, very dry, grey pebbly material with no visible evidence of timbers. It had been cut by a secondary post-pit (58) with a post-pipe *c*. 0.30m in diameter, the humic gravel backfill of which was similar to the fill of post-pits 55 and 59. Two much smaller posts (56, 57), 0.13–0.15m in diameter, were found to the north of the wall slot; both had rotted *in situ*. Small amounts of burnt material were found over the fills of all these features. Allowing for the greater disturbance at this end, there was clearly never a wall comparable to the one at the east end of the building. Indeed it appears probable that if a sill beam or any wall timbers had ever existed in the wall slot 53, they had been removed before the building was destroyed. It also appears possible that posts 55 and 59 had been removed, although the difference in fill between these and the wall slot suggests that this was a different event. Gaps in this rather vague wall line suggest possible entrances at each end (Fig. 18).

The internal partitions

The interior of the building was divided by a series of partitions which created two main central spaces and apsidal areas at either end (Fig. 12: Areas A–D). The position of the partitions and internal posts corresponded to the segments of the wall trenches of the north and south walls. Partitions 1 and 4 were set respectively *c*.1.8m and 1.4m back from the ends of the north and south walls, the projecting segments of the walls framing the axial pits. Partition 2 bisected the central area of the building. Partition 3 may have partially divided the western half. A series of posts projected from the inner faces of the north and south walls (167, 169, 92 to the north and 113, 141, 146 to the south). Two of these posts (167, 113) cut through the wall trench fills and were therefore secondary but this may have been simply a sequence of construction. The size of these posts ranged from round timber *c*.0.35m in diameter to *c*.0.80m × 0.40m split timbers. The regularity of their spacing suggests that they were weight-bearing and possibly related to roof support. Posts 141 and 169 were on the line of partition 2 and post 92 was in line with partition 3. Those projecting posts which were not on partition lines appear to have been augmented by freestanding posts just inside the wall line (114, 112, 87, 88 and possibly 143); these may have borne some weight which elsewhere was carried by partitions.

Most of the partition timbers (Fig. 15) were vertical split planks, with average thicknesses of 0.10–0.30m and widths of 0.20–0.40m. In a number of post-pits there were two or more abutting vertical planks (41, 140, 78 and 125). These internal planks were generally far smaller and more reduced than the split timbers in the outer walls.

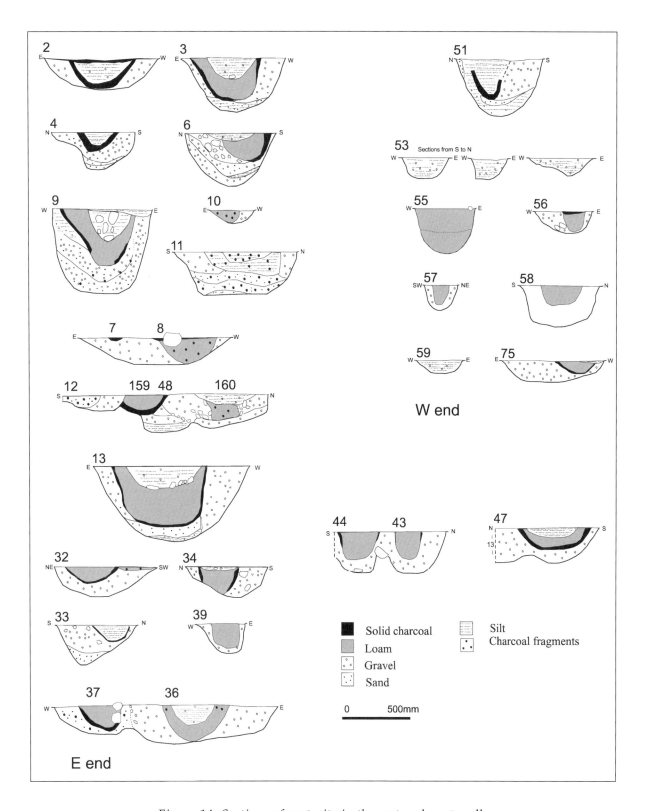

Figure 14. Sections of post-pits in the east and west walls

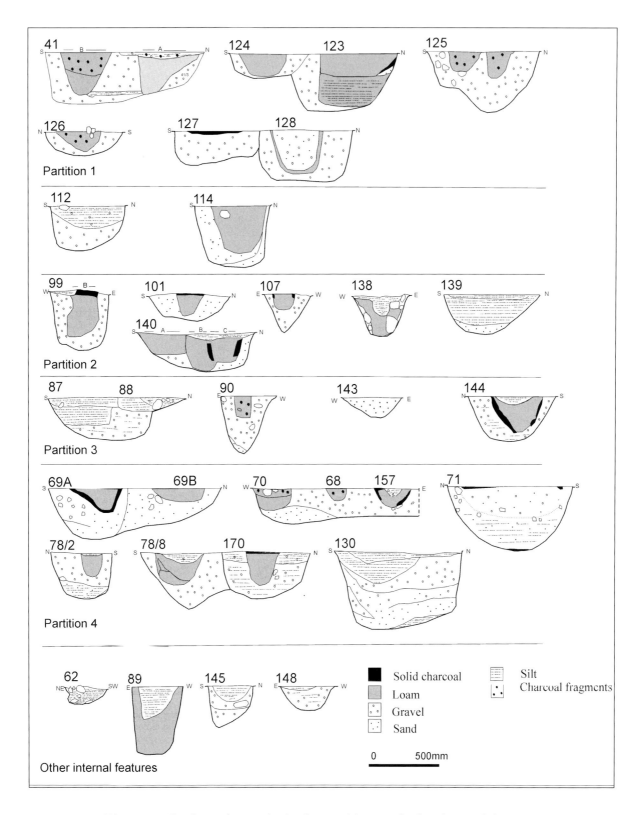

Figure 15. Sections of post-pits in the partitions and other internal features

Oak (125A) and willow/poplar (125B, 78/2) have both been identified.

Partition 1

Partition 1 extended between wall timbers 42 and 155, lying directly to the west of the massive timbers 38 and 31 at the ends of the north and south walls respectively. In its initial form the partition appears to have been composed of four sets of vertical split planks (41, 123, 125, probably 127). These form two groups on either side of a central gap 1.6m wide; the gaps between the other timbers and the side walls being *c.*0.60–0.80m. Post 127 was subsequently replaced by the larger split timber 128. Two vertical planks to the west of the partition appear related; one of these (124) is clearly secondary as it cut the post-pit of timber 123.

Partition 2

Partition 2 extended between wall timbers 141 and 169. It extended on either side of a central gap *c.*1.8m wide and was comprised of vertical planks (107, 140 and 99), a post-pit (139) and a round post (101). Another plank (138) stood on its W side, comparable to the position of 126 in partition 1. There is considerable similarity between partitions 1 and 2, both in their layout and use of planks.

Partition 3

Partition 3 is used to describe a series of features (87, 88, 90, 144 and 143) which extended into the interior between wall posts 92 in the north wall and 146 in the south wall. The irregular shallow gully 143 was filled with dry, grey, pebbly gravel with a little charcoal-rich material on the surface only. It may have held a horizontal beam, or light screen (wattle for example) but there was no direct evidence for this. It appears to have gone out of use before the end of the building's life as it seems to have been backfilled prior to the destruction of the building, since the fill was sealed by burnt material. There was no occupation debris in the fill.

The other features in this area demonstrate the dangers of interpretation based on plan alone. Context 89 (discussed below) was clearly a small pit containing a deliberate deposit: there is nothing to suggest it ever formed part of a partition. Similarly, 90, although apparently corresponding to 144, had a soft humic fill (90/1) containing a large concentration of burnt flint which may also have been a deliberate deposit (Warren, chapter 6.3). If this had replaced an earlier post, the post

would have been considerably smaller than post 144.

Partition 4

Partition 4 extended between timbers 172 and 81 in the north and south walls. A central gap *c.*1.4m wide was flanked by two post-pits (130, 71), both *c.*0.90m × 0.50–0.68m and between 0.45m and 0.51m deep, significantly larger than most of the internal post-pits. The lower fills of 130 were a series of redeposited sands and gravels; the steep angle of the deposits on the south side of the pit was suggestive of a primary timber having been removed and the pit backfilled. The upper, soft dark fill (130/1) appears to have been a recut but may in fact be the sinking of overlying layers over the disturbed area where a timber had been removed. There were no artefacts in these fills and a sample of the dark silt (130/7) in the base of the pit was archaeologically sterile apart from small amounts of charcoal. A single flint was recovered from the top fill 130/1. Pit 71 also appeared to have had any post removed and the fills were of similar gravely sands but with a greater humic content and inclusion of occupation material including pottery and flint throughout. As with pit 130, the basal fill incorporated a small amount of charcoal. These large pits were flanked by shallow wall slots, both of which turned to lie parallel to the inside of the western segments of the north and south walls. These wall slots held a series of vertical timbers, most of which were split planks (78/2, 78/3, 78/7, 78/8, 69B, 157, 68, 70). Two secondary timbers were additions or replacements on the main line of this partition (69A, 170).

Lacking horizontal stratigraphy, it is not clear if the sections of the north and south walls to the west of partition 4 coexisted with the inner plank walls running west from the partition, or if one replaced the other. It is however clear that the effect was an extension of the side walls beyond the partition, to frame or enclose pit 50.

The axial pits

Two very large pits (30, 50) were located on the longitudinal axis of the building, *c.*17m apart. Both ends of the north and south walls extended beyond the partitions and shielded these axial pits.

Pit 30

Pit 30 (Fig. 16) was 1.5m × 1.6m and *c.*1m deep with near-vertical sides. The initial cut of the

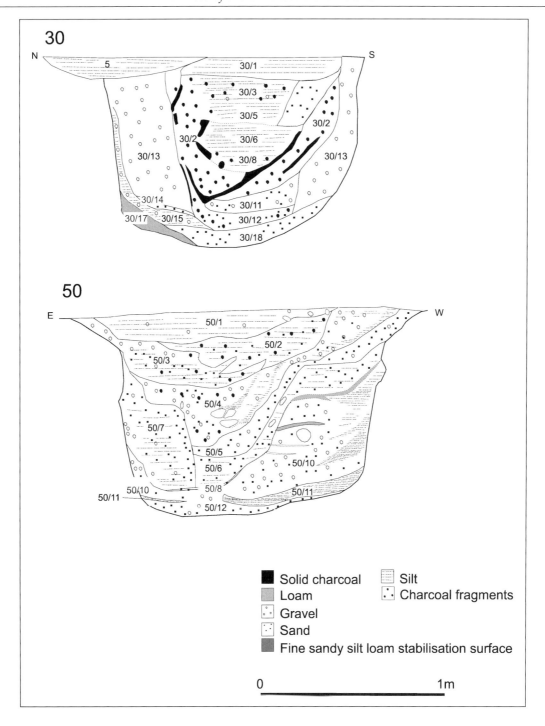

Figure 16. Sections of axial pits 30 and 50

pit appears to have been rapidly backfilled with redeposited sands and gravels (*e.g.* 30/13) mixed with original turf and topsoil. Below these fills there was a small silty deposit (30/17) which yielded carbonised grains of wheat and weeds of cultivation (Lancaster, chapter 3.2), indicating some level of activity in the area around the time the pit was dug. The very steep inner faces of these primary fills suggested that they had been thrown in against a solid vertical feature such as a large timber. Subsequently this timber appears to have been dug out from the south and east, in the process widening the hole that had held it. The resulting void partly filled with sands and gravels containing some charcoal, which may represent the disturbed primary fill going back into the hole (30/12, 30/11, 30/21, 30/22 and 30/23). Then the remaining hole was very rapidly filled with a thick layer of burnt material (30/2) covering the base of the hole and extending up the sides which still retained their near-vertical shape. This layer included small charred branches including hazel, birch, alder and willow/poplar, some of which were lying almost vertically against the sides of the pit recut. There was a large concentration of pottery, flint and carbonised fragments of a possible wooden vessel (Crone, chapter 6.4) jumbled in among the charcoal. Samples yielded significant quantities of grain and some hazelnut fragments (Table 3). During excavation of some of the burnt branches in 30/2 against the edge of the sand/gravel 30/13, it was observed that there was some apparent reddening of the underlying sand in a few places as if some of the branches had been thrown or had fallen into the pit while burning. However, the thin section analysis indicates that the burnt material is more likely to have been burnt and then dumped into the pit. Pollen from these fills records evidence for cereal-type plants and associated arable weeds and hazel (Davies, Tipping and McCulloch 2007 and Lancaster, chapter 3.2).

Pit 50
Pit 50 (Figs 16, 17) was 1.8m × 1.53m, and *c*.1m deep with near-vertical sides, although the very top of 50 was slightly splayed, possibly by erosion. Pit 50 also appears to have had a rapid initial backfilling of sands and gravels with interleaved lenses of possible turf or disturbed topsoil (50/12, 50/11, 50/10, 50/8 and 50/7) against the vertical pit sides. The near vertical edge of one of these fills (50/7) suggests that a solid vertical timber had been placed in the pit at this time. A recut appears to have dug this out. The lower fills in the recut (50/6, 50/5) were silt and sand, possibly from the disturbed primary fills, sloping in from the west and probably tipped in very rapidly as they retained the almost vertical edge of 50/7. The same applies to the higher fills (50/4, 50/3, 50/2) although these are differentiated by being very full of charcoal dust, though few charcoal pieces. The great contrast between pits 30 and 50 is in the absence in pit 50 of large charcoal fragments and the comparative paucity of artefacts. These comprise a number of small flint chips and flakes of flint, and two flakes of probable burnt pitchstone

from the upper fills 50/2 and 50/3 (Warren, chapter 6.3), but no pottery. Samples from pit 50 only yielded two burnt grains in contrast to 226 from pit 30 (Lancaster, chapter 3.2 and Table 3). Both pits yielded small quantities of hazelnut shell and rare tiny fragments of burnt bone.

Discussion of the pits
The primary function of both pits appears to have been to hold some form of large vertical object which was subsequently dug out. The vertical objects appear to have been solid and could have been of wood or stone. However, wood appears more likely to have been used because it can be argued that stones of this size, being heavier, would have created more disturbance when they were subsequently dug out. These vertical timbers would have been between *c*.0.30–0.40m in diameter (pit 50) and *c*.0.50m in diameter (pit 30), both were *c*.0.90m deep. They appear to have been set up when the primary fills were backfilled, very shortly after the pits were dug. The diameters of the pits were probably dictated by the practicalities of having enough space to dig to this depth, especially if short handled tools were being used. As larger diameter posts in the walls were set in far shallower pits, it may be postulated that the need for such deep pits was either to support very tall timbers or to support timbers which were top heavy. It is considered very unlikely that these posts held a ridge beam 17m long as there is an absence of evidence for other supports on the longitudinal axis. They were however focal within the building. It may be argued that they had a totemic role. The central timber at Seahenge (Holme-next-the-Sea), Norfolk (Brennand and Taylor 2003) although later in date, underlines the possibility of natural timbers being used as a totemic focus within prehistoric structures in Britain.

Both axial pits seem to have been dug early in the sequence of construction of the building as the primary backfill was of very clean gravels with an absence of the occupation material which might be expected if they had been dug through the floors of an existing building. Three grains from samples of the primary backfill of pit 30 (Fig. 3: 30/17 and 30/13 and Lancaster, chapter 3.2) and some very fine comminuted charcoal observed in the thin section of primary fill 30/13 may derive from activity in the vicinity during construction. These fills were very similar to the primary fills

Figure 17. Section of axial pit 50 during excavation (© Charles Murray)

of the wall trenches so it is possible that the axial pits and the wall trenches were dug at the same time. However, it is also possible that the axial posts were the first features to be set in place and that the building was planned around them.

The 'totem' in pit 30 appears to have been removed hours, or at most days, before the building was burnt, as the void had filled with burnt material before its sides had eroded. It could be argued that it was removed after the building was destroyed, but this seems less probable as it might be expected that this would have created more disturbance of the sides and greater mixing of the fills. The 'totem' in pit 50, as discussed above, also appears to have been removed and the void backfilled soon after. The quantity of charcoal dust in these fills (Fig. 16: 50/2, 50/3, 50/4) suggests that this also happened around the time of the destruction of the building.

The greater abundance of large pieces of charcoal in the post-destruction fill of pit 30 may be explained in a number of ways. It may indicate that there was more activity near pit 30, that the east end of the building had been roofed, or that the wind took most of the fire towards the east with only some drifting soot getting into the soils near pit 50. For both pits the evidence suggests that the process of post-destruction filling was very rapid, occurring within, at most, a few days of the 'totems' being removed. It is not possible to be certain if this filling was deliberate, or a result of the processes of collapse within the burning building. It has been argued above that the size of the pits may indicate that the 'totems' were either tall or top heavy. If the ends of the building were roofed, installation or removal of large or long timbers from these pits, although difficult, would have been possible by raising or lowering the timber along the longitudinal axis of the building. If, however, the ends of the building were unroofed, raising or removal of the posts would have been relatively simple. The apparent salvage or curation of these objects before the building was burnt emphasises their potential importance.

Other internal features

There were a small number of features (Fig. 15) which could not be related to the surviving structural evidence. Three of these (Fig. 12: features 62: Area D; 145: Area C; 148: Area B) were very small, fairly shallow pits with predominantly gravel fills. Only pit 145 had an upper fill which may have included post-destruction burnt material: this yielded several sherds of pottery. The small pit 89 (Fig. 12: Area C), however, appears to have held a structured deposit; the soft, dark, organic fill contained significant quantities of burnt flints (Warren, chapter 6.3), burnt grain (including bread/club wheat, naked barley and emmer), charred hawthorn leaf buds (which are edible) and fragments of hazelnut shell (Table 3). There were also numerous tiny fragments of burnt bone, a solid clump of which were clustered at the base of the pit as if originally wrapped together; one piece has been identified as either sheep or roe deer (Smith 2007 and Lancaster, chapter 3.2). It is noteworthy that the contents appear to represent both wild and cultivated resources. The inclusion of hawthorn buds might suggest that they were deposited in spring, although the grain and nuts represent the fruits of late summer and autumn. Pit 90 (Fig. 12: Area C), as noted above, held a similar, possibly deliberate, deposit of burnt flint but the other contents were far less varied, with only one grain of wheat and five fragments of hazelnut (Table 3).

Entrances, possible light sources

The roughly east northeast/west southwest orientation of the long axis conforms to the norm suggested by Topping (1996, 162) of many Neolithic buildings having a long wall facing south to absorb warmth. It may also be significant that both Warren Field and Balbridie (Ralston 1982) were orientated parallel to the adjacent river Dee, and Claish was parallel to the River Teith (Barclay, Brophy and MacGregor 2002). The same is true for other potential timber halls in Scotland, presently known only as cropmark sites. The rivers must have been major elements in the lives of the builders (Fraser, chapters 3.4 and 3.5; *cf.* Brophy 2007, 92–4).

The very clear evidence of the timbers at Warren Field shows that there were no doorways in the side walls and suggests that the entrances were at either end of the building (Fig. 18). One

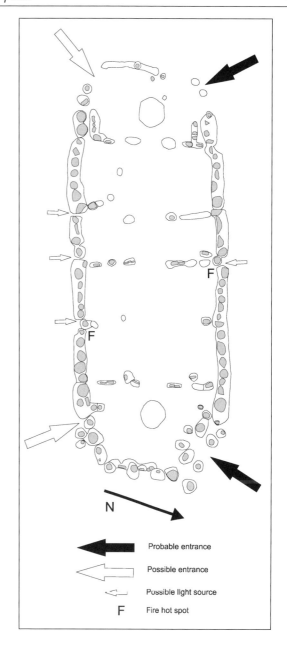

Figure 18. Plan of the Neolithic timber hall showing possible entrances, light sources and fire hot spots

entrance appears to have been at the northeast corner opening into the apse-like area at the east gable. The additional posts around this entrance give an impression that it was the main point of entry. There may originally have been another entrance from the southeast but if so this was later blocked by a secondary timber. At the west end of the building there were large gaps on either side of the shallow wall slot (53), both of which may have been entrances. The northwest gap is the more convincing as two post-pits (Fig. 12: 55 and 59) could be interpreted as door posts.

Consideration of light is obviously dependent on how much of the building was roofed, but the widely spaced posts in the east gable suggest that, whether this area was roofed or not (see Figs 26 and 27), considerable light may have penetrated through the entrance(s) and probably between the posts. The internal partitions as excavated do not appear to have been solid blocking walls, but it is possible that they formed a framework to support wattle panels, which would have excluded light from the interior. The timbers of the north and south walls were tightly set and probably originally contiguous; in the better preserved parts they had an average gap of 0.10m between timbers as excavated. Even if these had not been packed with a filler such as mud or moss, the gap would not appear to have allowed much light between the posts, but there were larger gaps of *c*.0.40m width on either side of the posts 113, 141 and 146 which projected in from the south wall, and similarly between posts 161 and 169 in the north wall. These could have let shafts of light into the building in Areas B and C, without allowing access (Figs 12, 18).

Immediate environs

In order to look at paths or other related features around the building, an area *c*.6m wide was excavated outside the walls (Fig 11). This revealed no contemporary post-pits or other features. Clearly, if stake or wattle fences had been in use it is unlikely that these would have penetrated the subsoil as the necessary depth for posts in a wattle fence is only *c*.0.20–0.30m. Geophysical survey was not undertaken outside this area as results over the outline of the building itself had been disappointing due to the underlying geology. There were very few artefacts outside the building and those found were in topsoil and may have been dragged from contexts within the structure by ploughing. The pollen from axial pit 30 did not include weeds that might be expected from trampled ground and suggests that the immediate vicinity of the building was in cereal cultivation (Davies, Tipping and McCulloch 2007 and Lancaster, chapter 3.2). However, the pollen samples were from a context regarded as accumulating directly around the time of the destruction of the building and may not reflect the situation throughout its total life and usage, particularly its early life.

The overall impression is that the Warren Field building stood in isolation within this cleared, cultivated area and that there was an absence of other structures around it. This conclusion is further supported by the lack of Neolithic artefacts either from field walking or from the excavation of Areas 8–14 (Fig. 1, chapter 4.1) in other areas of the field. This clearly has implications with regard to the function of the building and is in contrast to some other sites such as Parc Bryn Cegin, Llandygai, North Wales (Kenney, pers. comm.) where there were traces of a possibly contemporary but more ephemeral structure *c*.7m from an early Neolithic rectangular building, or many of the Irish sites with smaller rectangular Neolithic buildings regarded as houses where ancillary buildings, pits and other more domestic features are commonplace (for example Grogan 1996, 56–7). At Balbridie, sampling of a number of areas outside the building proved negative (Fairweather and Ralston 1993 and Ralston, pers. comm.), while a pit directly north of the Claish building is thought to be later (Barclay, Brophy and MacGregor 2002, 70–1). However, Neolithic pottery from the Crathes Castle Overflow Car Park site and from Milton Wood, both within a radius of 300m from the hall, although possibly slightly later (Sheridan, chapter 6.1), is a useful reminder that settlement may have extended around the periphery of the cultivated ground.

3.2 Palaeoenvironmental Synthesis

Stephen Lancaster

Introduction

The original consideration of the environmental evidence from Warren Field exists as a number of archive reports concerned with palynology (Davies, Tipping and McCulloch 2007), soil micromorphology supported by loss on ignition analyses (Lancaster 2007a; 2007b), analysis of charred plant macrofossils (Hastie 2004; Timpany 2006a; 2006b), and bone (Smith 2007). Fully integrating different forms of environmental evidence is not without its difficulties. The physical circumstances that allow sampling of environmental material for different techniques vary, as do the conditions that determine the survival of different forms of environmental evidence. Different techniques provide information at different spatial and temporal resolutions, although the analyses at Warren Field are characterised by methods that reduce these difficulties. As such, completely parallel sets of data are not often available, a consideration that affects Warren Field.

The geomorphological setting of the site has already been described (Tipping, chapter 1.2). The glacifluvial terrace forms a well drained parent material, and the soils that develop on this are consequently highly oxidised, well drained, and generally somewhat acidic. These conditions affect the type of environmental material that survives and the preservation condition of that material. Calcareous material does not generally survive, as reflected in the survival of only small fragments of burnt bone. Such conditions are not ideal for the preservation of pollen, and a number of contexts sampled for pollen were found to have either no surviving pollen or pollen in too poor a state of preservation to be interpretable. Plant macrofossils only survive through charring in these conditions. Moreover, sands and gravels do not aid the survival of charred plant material: any degree of transport around a site composed of such materials tends to rapidly crumble and abrade charcoal. The physical character of the soils and sub-soils is also significant: the deposits do not cohere well, making sampling for thin-section analysis difficult. The methods by which data were obtained are presented in each of the archived reports.

Soil micromorphology (Lancaster 2007a; 2007b)

Five thin-section samples were taken from pit 30, one of the axial pits in the timber hall. These were taken in parallel with pollen samples. Full descriptions of all thin-sections are given in Table 16 in Appendix 2. The sampled deposits largely comprise two components: an unsorted to poorly sorted coarse mineral component of sand with small stones, consisting of quartz, feldspars and fragments of metamorphic rock; and a fine, moderately sorted, organo-mineral component, composed of fine sand and silt sized particles of quartz and feldspar and humified organic matter, with finely comminuted charcoal intermixed throughout the fine material. The fine material has frequently formed as bacillo-cylindrical excrements, generally interpreted as being the product of enchytraeid worms (Bullock

et al. 1985). The compositional difference from deposit to deposit was largely explicable in terms of the variation in the proportion in these two main components. In addition to these components, the most common element comprises coarse (> 50 μm) charcoal fragments. This was observed in most of the contexts in pit 30. The charcoal fragments have eroded and rounded forms. There is no other evidence of heating in the samples, *e.g.* reddening of the fine fraction.

Despite the ubiquity of enchytraeid excrement throughout the deposits in pit 30, fragments of humified organic matter that have not been eaten by enchytraeids were noted in 30/12, 30/2, 30/5 and 30/6. This indicates that enchytraeid activity was relatively short lived.

The boundaries between deposits that were identified in the field are also clear and well defined at the microscopic scale of observation. Contexts are defined on the varying proportions of the two main components identified above.

Pollen analyses (Davies, Tipping and McCulloch 2007; Tipping et al. 2009)

Sixteen samples were taken from pit 30. Due to the soil conditions at the site, insufficient identifiable pollen survived in some of these samples. Rigorous analysis of the state of preservation (Tipping, Carter and Johnston 1994; Bunting and Tipping 2000; Tipping 2000) allowed the interpretation of twelve samples. Tables 17–18 in Appendix 3 show the pollen preservation and pollen concentration values for polleniferous contexts and tabulate the results of the tests applied to establish the veracity of pollen assemblages. Percentage pollen results are presented in graphical format in Fig. 8.

The samples from pit 30 are dominated by hazel (*Corylus avellana*-type), grasses (Poaceae anl D<8 μm), *cf.* dandelions (*Cichorium intybus*-type), buttercups (*Ranunculus acris*-type) and moonwort (*Botrychium lunaria*, a fern). There is relatively little variation in the types of pollen through the profile of the pit, with the exception of a change in the range of herb pollen types. In lower contexts (30/12 and 30/11) there are more buttercups, clovers/vetches/peas (Fabaceae) and *cf.* yarrow (*Achillea*-type), while in the upper contexts (30/6, 30/2 and 30/3), there is a consistently higher hazel representation among the tree pollen, more campions (Caryophyllaceae, *Silene vulgaris*-type), *cf.* daisies (*Solidago virgaurea*-type) and large grass pollen grains (Poaceae anl-D>8 µm), typically interpreted as cereal pollen (Appendix 3, Table 19). Microscopic charcoal is also present in higher quantities in these upper contexts.

Plant macrofossils (Hastie 2004; Timpany 2006a; 2006b)

The distribution of the charred timbers in the hall suggests that the main primary posts were made from oak (*Quercus*), particularly in the eastern half of the structure. Posts identified from the western half of the structure were largely of willow/poplar (*Salix/Populus* sp.) (Fig. 22 and Table 15).

The charcoal samples collected from the post-pits contained charcoal not only related to the posts but also to destruction material deposited in the tops of postholes and rotted posts. The charcoal recovered from these contexts and from pit 30 therefore relates not just to the wall timbers, but perhaps to other structural elements, such as roofing, and also to the use of the hall (Murray and Murray, chapter 3.3). These samples showed the presence of other wood species in addition to those identified from the walls, namely alder (*Alnus glutinosa*), birch (*Betula* sp.), hazel (*Corylus avellana*) and hawthorn/fruit trees (Pomoideae). Fragments of a possible carbonised wooden vessel recovered from pit 30 were of birch – a reminder of the wooden artefacts that may have been in use (Crone, chapter 6.4).

Cereals identified were principally bread/club wheat (*Triticum aestivo-compactum*), naked barley (*Hordeum vulgare var nudum*), emmer wheat (*Triticum dicoccum*), and a single oat grain (*Avena* sp.) (Table 3). Of the cereal grains that were recovered, 365 (approximately two thirds) could be identified to species level. Where identifiable cereal grains occurred, the assemblages were generally mixtures of bread/club wheat and naked barley, in no fixed proportion. While the grain tended to occur in particular concentrations, these concentrations occurred across most of the central and eastern end of the hall, including in post-pits associated with structural elements, one of the axial pits (pit 30) and another pit (89) which seems to have had a deliberately placed deposit (Fig. 19; Murray and Murray, chapter 3.1). The greatest number of grains was recovered from pit 30 (30/2). Within this context frequency was variable, with different samples from this context yielding from two to 153 grains. The impressions of cereal grains

Sample:	2004-01	2004-02	2004-03	2004-06	2004-07	2004-08	2004-09	2004-10	2004-12
Context:	38/01	08/02	30/01	11/02	49/01	11/05	30/02	11/06	30/02
Feature:	Post-pit	Post-pit	Pit	Post-pit	Post-pit	Post-pit	Pit	Post-pit	Pit
Taxa									
Betula sp. buds	–	–	–	–	–	–	–	–	–
Corylus avellana nutshell fragments	–	–	–	1 (<0.1g)	–	7 (0.2g)	5 (0.2g)	2 (0.1g)	5 (0.2g)
Crataegus sp. buds	–	–	–	–	–	–	–	–	–
Chenopodium sp. fruit	–	–	–	–	–	–	–	–	–
Stellaria media fruit	–	–	–	–	–	–	–	–	–
Rumex cf. acetosa fruit	–	–	–	–	–	–	–	–	–
Carex sp. (trigonus) nutlet	–	–	–	–	–	–	–	–	–
Cerealia cf. Avena sp. grain	–	–	–	–	–	–	–	–	–
Hordeum sp. grain	–	–	–	–	–	–	–	–	–
Hordeum vulgare cf. var nudum grain	–	–	–	–	–	–	–	–	–
Hordeum vulgare var nudum grain	–	12	–	7	–	4	2	8	32
Triticum aestivo-compactum grain	1	8	–	4	–	13	6	4	63
Triticum dicoccum grain	–	–	–	2	–	3	–	1	1
Cereal indet. grain	–	20	–	7	2	11	13	4	57
	–	–	1	3	225	22	57	60	56
Fungal sclerotia									

Sample:	2005–13	2005–22	2005–25	2005–28	2005–29A	2005–29B	2005–29D	2005–31	2005–35	2005–42	2005–43
Context:	50/03	114/01	59/02	90/01	30/02	30/02	30/02	89/01	89/02	99/01	140/02
Feature:	Pit	Post-pit	Post-pit	Post-pit	Pit	Pit	Pit	Pit	Pit	Post-pit	Post-pit
Betula sp. buds	–	–	–	–	–	–	–	–	–	–	–
Corylus avellana nutshell fragments	7 (0.4g)	7 (0.3g)	–	5 (0.1g)	–	–	3 (<0.1g)	19 (0.7g)	19 (2g)	–	4 (0.2g)
Crataegus sp. buds	–	–	–	–	–	–	–	–	3	–	–
Chenopodium sp. fruit	–	–	–	–	–	–	–	–	–	–	–
Stellaria media fruit	–	–	–	–	–	–	–	–	–	–	–
Rumex cf. acetosa fruit	–	–	–	–	–	–	–	–	–	–	–
Carex sp. (trigonus) nutlet	–	–	–	–	–	–	–	–	–	–	–
Cerealia cf. Avena sp. grain	–	–	1	–	–	–	–	–	–	–	–
Hordeum sp. grain	–	–	–	–	–	–	–	–	2	–	–
Hordeum vulgare cf. var nudum grain	–	–	–	–	–	–	–	–	–	–	–
Hordeum vulgare var nudum grain	–	7	–	–	6	2	4	5	5	1	8
Triticum aestivo–compactum grain	–	6	–	1	14	–	–	26	26	1	10
Triticum dicoccum grain	–	–	–	–	–	–	–	–	1	–	–
Cereal indet. grain	–	10	–	–	11	–	–	15	10	4	16
Fungal sclerotia	5	22	5	–	–	–	–	–	–	–	–

Sample:	2005–45	2005–48	2005–50	2005–54	2005–55	2005–56	2005–59	2005–60	2005–62	2005–64	2005–66
Context:	108/2	111/04	167/04	69/02	170/03	170/01	50/02	99/01	30/12	30/17	30/13
Feature:	Post-pit	Post-pit	Post-pit	Post-pit	Post-pit	Post-pit	Pit	Post-pit	Pit	Pit	Pit
Betula sp. buds	–	–	–	–	–	1	–	–	–	–	–
Corylus avellana nutshell fragments	–	–	–	2 (0.1g)	1 (0.2g)	–	4 (<0.1g)	15 (0.8g)	–	–	–
Crataegus sp. buds	–	–	–	–	–	–	–	–	–	1	–
Chenopodium sp. fruit	–	–	–	–	–	–	–	–	–	–	–
Stellaria media fruit	–	–	–	–	–	–	–	–	–	–	–
Rumex cf. acetosa fruit	–	3	–	–	–	–	2	–	–	–	–
Carex sp. (trigonus) nutlet	–	–	1	–	–	–	–	–	–	–	–
Cerealia cf. Avena sp. grain	–	–	–	–	–	–	–	–	–	–	–
Hordeum sp. grain	–	–	–	–	–	–	–	–	–	–	–
Hordeum vulgare cf. var nudum grain	–	–	–	–	–	–	–	–	1	–	–
Hordeum vulgare var nudum grain	–	–	1	–	–	3	1	8	1	–	–
Triticum aestivo–compactum grain	–	–	2	–	–	3	–	40	3	1	–
Triticum dicoccum grain	–	–	–	–	–	–	–	–	–	–	–
Cereal indet. grain	1	–	2	–	–	1	1	18	6	1	1
Fungal sclerotia	–	–	–	–	6	–	–	2	–	1	–

Table 3. Plant macrofossil identifications from the timber hall

were also noted on three pottery sherds (SF 75 and 227 from pit 30 and SF 189 from 71/2). All the impressions were of bread/club wheat (Fig. 43 and Sheridan, chapter 6.1).

Non-cereal plant macrofossils consisted of fragments of hazelnuts, buds of hawthorn (*Crataegus*) and birch, fruits of common chickweed (*Stellaria media*) and sorrel *(Rumex cf. acetosa)*, and a nutlet of sedge (*Carex* sp.). Numbers of macrofossils were low and restricted to single contexts, with the exception of hazelnut shell fragments, which were found in eight contexts. The macrofossils were mostly recovered from contexts that also contained cereal grains.

Bone (Smith 2007)

As noted above, soil conditions at Warren Field are unfavourable for the preservation of bone. What little bone was recovered had mostly survived as small calcined fragments. Little of the material could be identified beyond being of mammalian origin. A single larger fragment from context 89, a small pit containing a deliberate deposit (Fig. 12: Area C), was determined to be from a distal metapodial, probably from a sheep, although an origin from roe deer cannot be eliminated because of shrinkage and distortion caused by cremation.

Formation processes

The infilling of pit 30 contrasts with that of the pits in the pit alignment (Lancaster, chapter 2.2) as it was sufficiently continuous that no episodes of soil formation were observed. The unsorted to poorly sorted nature of the deposits points to individual fills having been deposited rapidly. The steep-sided cut of the pit would not have been stable for any length of time without revetting, for which there is no evidence. Nor is there evidence in the shapes of the deposits or interfaces for extensive slumping, which would have been the result of the instability of the pit wall. This suggests that the pit was very rapidly filled, either deliberately or through the collapse of the hall.

The pit deposits had generally undergone relatively little post-depositional modification. Although there had been enchytraeid activity, the survival of fragments of humified material suggests that conditions inimical to biological reworking, either through oxygen exclusion or drying, were rapidly established within the deposits (Didden 1993). The sediment reworking that has occurred will have been over a very small distance. The parallel sampling for pollen and thin-section micromorphology means that the stratigraphic security of the pollen can be assumed on the basis of these findings.

The charcoal component of the fills is composed of eroded and rounded fragments, indicating transport with other sediment. The fills are largely derived from local subsoils, and are mostly relatively homogenous. This suggests that the composition of the fills was not a significant consideration in their deposition. One possible exception to this was context 30/2, which contained much charred material, including grain and fragments of a possible wooden bowl. The distribution of material within this context is, however, random and chaotic, giving no suggestion of structured deposition, in contrast with, for example, pit 89. It would seem that the focus of activity at pit 30 was whatever contemporaneous object the fills of pit 30 supported, and that subsequent contexts only filled the void left by that object's removal (Murray and Murray, chapter 3.1).

Environmental reconstruction

Although the key component in reconstructing the early Neolithic environment is the pollen analysis, this is supplemented by evidence from other analyses. The relatively limited pollen source area for pit 30 reduces some of the problems of difference of spatial scale between palynological, stratigraphic and other palaeoenvironmental evidence.

Under normal pollen dispersal and deposition conditions, small catchment hollows like pit 30 primarily reflect local pollen production, up to a radius of *c.*100–400m, perhaps extending up to 1 kilometre (Sugita, Gaillard and Broström 1999; Bunting 2002; Broström, Sugita and Gaillard 2004; 2005). While the taphonomy of pit 30 is relatively complex it is estimated that the pollen source area encompasses the hall and the surrounding glacifluvial terrace on which it is constructed. In general terms, the samples were fairly homogenous except for a change in the range of pollen types and charcoal representation between the lower (30/12, 30/11) and upper contexts (30/6, 3/2 and 30/3). This change in pollen and charcoal representation coincides with the inferred burning of the structure, seen in the charcoal-rich context 30/2. It is tentatively suggested that the pollen-stratigraphic change reflects the increased representation of plants growing outside the hall after its destruction by fire, although the rapidity of infilling may mean that the period post-burning is very short. The main inference, therefore, is that the pollen derives primarily from local sources and that the local vegetation, over a range of a few hundred metres, is likely to have provided the most constant source of pollen. Defining the environment and land-uses around the structure remains complex but some interpretations can be made.

With the exception of hazel, there were few trees within the pollen source area. The early Neolithic radiocarbon dates for the pit were obtained from charcoal identified as alder (or in one case, alder/hazel), which is poorly represented in the pollen diagram (2.8–8.9% TLP) and was probably not present on the sandy soils of the terrace, but growing on the valley sides of the incised Coy Burn to the east, on the periphery of the pollen source area. Birch, pine (*Pinus sylvestris*), oak and elm (*Ulmus*) were rare and pollen from these trees may have drifted in from elsewhere, as the lime (*Tilia*) pollen must have done. Given the herbaceous pollen results (see below) it is evident that the hall was located in a cleared area, with most of the tree pollen reflecting a wooded area beyond. This contrasts with pollen evidence for the wider area from sites with much larger pollen source areas, such as Loch of Park, 4 kilometres to the northeast (Vasari and Vasari 1968), and the Red Moss of Candiglarich, 4.5 kilometres to the north (Clark 2002; Clark and Edwards 2004), which show a heavily wooded landscape. Plant macrofossils point to the presence of ash (*Fraxinus excelsior*), willow/poplar and hawthorn, probably in the vicinity of the hall, in addition to the oak, birch and alder noted in the pollen analysis. Given the relatively limited extent of the pit 30 pollen catchment, these need not have come from a great distance, perhaps no more than a few hundred metres. The presence of birch and hawthorn indicate a woodland edge/clearing habitat, perhaps the edge of the cleared area in which the hall was situated. The alder indicates wet woodland, such as could have been found by the Coy Burn.

Grassy ground cover was common, perhaps growing beneath or between hazel shrubs. There is little convincing evidence for grazing disturbance, as the main herbs, buttercups, *cf.* dandelions and *cf.* yarrow can grow in varied grass swards and only two grains of ribwort plantain (*Plantago lanceolata*), a classic grazing or mowing indicator, are recorded, both in a single sample (context 30/11). This absence of palynological evidence for pasturing needs to be considered in the light of the findings of the pottery lipid analysis, which demonstrate the use of animal products: this issue is discussed in greater detail below. The records of barley (*Hordeum* group), oats/wheat (*Avena/Triticum* group) and Poaceae anl-D>8 μm (large grass grains, too crumpled to meet all of the size criteria for barley or oat/wheat groups) are taken to indicate the presence of cereals (Appendix 3). Barley and wheat are also present in charred seed assemblages from the structure. Cereal pollen may have originated from cereal use or storage in the structure, or have been derived from crop growth in the surrounding area. The consistent occurrence of such cereal-type pollen records is considered as good evidence that crops were grown around the structure. Given the limited pollen dispersal from cereal crops (Hall 1989; Vuorela 1973), it is probable that they were grown on the dry, sandy soil on the glaciofluvial terrace, immediately around the hall. Many pollen types in the samples would fit into an arable context, either as crop weeds or on field edges. The abundance of moonwort is unusual, however. It is difficult to assess whether this represents the growth of this small fern in the open area that is thought to have surrounded the structure, or whether it was collected or present in other materials used in the hall.

Land use and resources

The pollen evidence from the site suggests cereal cultivation close by, perhaps extending over most of the terrace on which the site is situated. The evidence of the cereal remains indicates the consumption/storage of bread/club wheat, naked barley and emmer wheat. The single oat grain might be intrusive or represent a weed.

Pollen evidence from the wider area shows a heavily wooded landscape, indicating that the woodland had been cleared around the hall. The clearance of nearly all tree species, particularly oak, over this area early in the Neolithic is highly unusual. While such clearance might have provided a source of the timbers for the hall, this

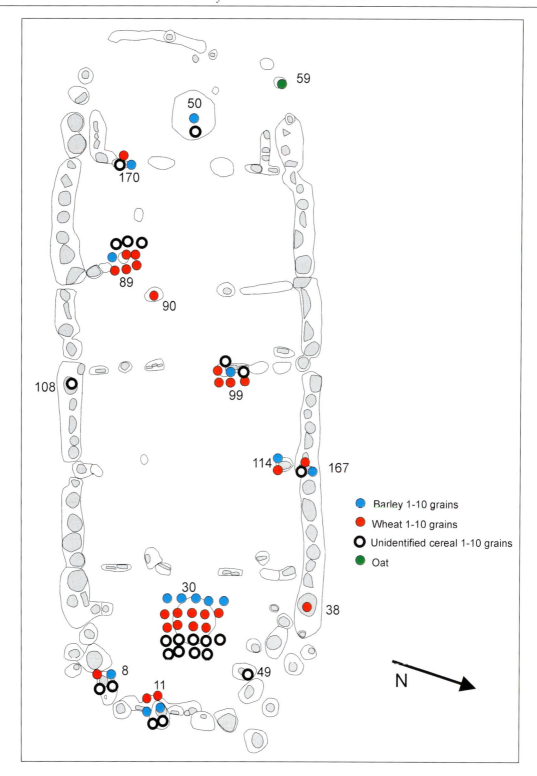

Figure 19. Plan of the Neolithic timber hall showing distribution of grain. The numbers refer to contexts

level of consumption would not account for the scale of clearance. The presence of hazel within the cleared area might imply conservation of this potential resource. The frequency with which hazelnut shells, generally in association with cereal grains, have been recovered from a variety of contexts within the hall suggests that the trees were a food source, the occasional finds of hazel charcoal suggesting use of the wood. Clearance would have created woodland edge environments in which ash, willow/poplar and hawthorn/fruit trees could have thrived. These trees figure in the construction of the hall, suggesting the use of the woodland edge environment as a resource. The finds of birch and hawthorn buds indicate gathering of material in the early spring. Whether the leaf buds were collected in their own right, or are the waste from the cutting of wood is unclear. Hawthorn leaf buds are edible, and could have formed a useful supplement to diet in the early spring. Birch leaf buds are edible, but strongly flavoured. They are reputed to have medicinal properties (Grieve 1931). Both trees produce flexible wood that might be useful in making lighter structural elements such as wattle.

The high frequencies of moonwort spores may relate to both the close proximity of a field edge habitat and the robustness of the spore in this soil. It should be noted, however, that the plant has a reputation as a vulnerary (*i.e.* useful in the healing of wounds; Grieve 1931). With this possible exception, there were no unusually high frequencies of particular pollen types in any sample to suggest that large quantities of specific, pollen-containing plant materials were used or stored in or around the structure.

The absence of a signal in the pollen analyses for grazed grassland is notable given the current emphasis on livestock in the Neolithic period (Ray and Thomas 2003), and the findings of the lipid analysis of pottery from this site. The extremely poor survival of bone means that it is difficult to comment directly on the animal economy of the site. The findings of the lipid analyses demonstrate, however, the availability of animal products. The majority of the lipids isolated were of ruminant dairy fat, with a single instance of porcine fat. The absence of a pasturing signal in the palynological evidence can be reconciled with the lipid evidence in a number of ways. The pollen catchment of the hall is sufficiently constrained that livestock could have been grazed further away, outside the pollen catchment, without being too far from the hall in practical terms. It is worth noting the absence of a pasturing signal in the regional pollen diagrams at this time: as with the inferred clearance for construction and cereal growing this demonstrates that local human impacts on the environment are simply of too small a scale to affect the larger scale environmental record. The porcine lipid need not indicate domestic livestock: the wooded environment of the wider area that both the pollen analysis from the hall and the regional pollen studies have demonstrated would have been a good habitat for wild boar.

The presence, and in some cases dominance, of bread/club wheat requires consideration: this variety of wheat is generally unusual across Scotland during the Neolithic. There has been some suggestion that the presence of bread/club wheat may indicate the status of the site, as it has generally only been found at hall sites (Barclay, Brophy and MacGregor 2002; Fairweather and Ralston 1993). It should be noted, however, that bread/club wheat has been found at a 'non-hall' Neolithic site, Garthdee, also in Aberdeenshire (Murray 2005). This site was a relatively small (approx. 11m × 8m) oval-shaped structure with a well-defined floor layer. The relationship of bread/club wheat to status may not, therefore, be clear cut.

The cereal grain assemblage at Warren Field is relatively large, at 365 grains identified to species level, compared to 40 at Claish and 75 at Garthdee, but is dwarfed in comparison to Balbridie, where approximately 20,000 grains were recovered. The same three cereal taxa were identified at these sites: naked barley, emmer wheat and bread/club wheat; Table 4 shows approximate percentages from each site.

Warren Field is unique in having bread/club wheat dominate the grain assemblage, although

Table 4. Percentages of different cereal grains from four Neolithic sites

Site	% Naked Barley	% Emmer Wheat	% Bread/Club Wheat
Warren Field	32	2	66
Balbridie	18	80	2
Claish	30	70	'a little bread wheat'
Garthdee	80	3	17

it should be noted that although as a percentage Balbridie produced relatively little bread/club wheat, one context was predominantly composed of bread/club wheat and given the size of the assemblage might contain more grains than the entire assemblage at Warren Field. The considerable variation in the quantity of grain throughout context 30/2 suggests that the process of charring might have been uneven across the original stocks of grain and subsequent deposition highly variable. The apparent dominance of bread/club wheat might therefore be an accident of preservation.

The amount of cereal grain recovered at Warren Field is consistent with the palynological evidence for cereal growing. No other parts of cereal plants were noted, however, and possible arable weed seeds were rare. This suggests that the grain within the hall had undergone all processing and cleaning elsewhere, though not necessarily distant from the hall, and that the hall itself was the site of storage and/or consumption. The absence of crop-processing waste has been noted at the three other sites discussed above, and in the case of the hall structures, has again been tentatively interpreted as reflecting the status of the site (Barclay, Brophy and MacGregor 2002; Fairweather and Ralston 1993). Given the inferred proximity of cereal fields at Warren Field it would seem likely that crop processing must, however, have occurred near to the hall. Combined with the absence of crop processing residues at other Neolithic settlements, *e.g.* Beckton Farm and Cowie Road (Pollard 1997; Rideout 1997), it would appear more likely that the clean nature of the grain assemblages reflects a functional distinction between processing and consumption/storage areas at the scale of individual structures rather than status distinctions between sites.

Conclusion

The Neolithic hall is an unusual monument type in Scotland, and the combined use of a variety of environmental techniques on such a site is unique. The direct identification of the wood species used in different elements of the hall is a valuable insight into Neolithic construction.

The storage/consumption of cereals, including bread/club wheat, evidenced by the presence of clean grain, is usual on the few Neolithic hall sites in Scotland. The association of pollen evidence of cereal cultivation with such a site is unusual. The

association of clean, processed grain, with pollen evidence of cereal cultivation suggests that the hall may have been part of a larger area of activity, so far unidentified and perhaps not preserved, where crop processing occurred.

Local crop growing was not demonstrated at Balbridie, despite the abundant evidence for grain, although Edwards (1989) reported that turves at Balbridie contained cereal-type pollen. Cereal remains were also reported at the comparable hall at Claish, near Stirling (Miller and Ramsay in Barclay, Brophy and MacGregor 2002), but local growth of cereals has not yet been demonstrated there. The level of activity at Warren Field, suggested by the pollen analysis, in terms of the size of the area largely cleared of trees and used for cereal cultivation (probably hundreds of metres across), is extraordinary for this date in the British Neolithic.

The absence of palynological evidence for pasturing is interesting in the context of the lipid analysis. Given the very poor survival of bone on the site, this has given a rare insight into the use of animal resources. The absence of an impact on the palynological record, both at the site level and the regional level, suggests relatively small-scale rearing of livestock, highly localised or thinly distributed across the landscape.

3.3 Discussion of the structure

Hilary Murray and Charles Murray

In the following discussion comparisons will be made with other early Neolithic buildings in Britain and Ireland, particularly with the buildings at Balbridie, Aberdeenshire (Ralston 1982; Fairweather and Ralston 1993), Claish, Stirling (Barclay, Brophy and MacGregor 2002) and Lockerbie, Dumfries and Galloway (Kirby 2006). Such comparisons do not necessarily imply that all the buildings fulfilled the same range of functions. They may however be regarded as showing contemporary methods of using timber and solving structural problems. Much of the Scottish evidence has been discussed at length by Barclay, Brophy and MacGregor in the Claish report and will not be repeated in detail. Balbridie, less than a kilometre away from Warren Field, is obviously of particular interest. Interpretation of the radiocarbon dates (Marshall, chapter 5) suggests that the two buildings probably coexisted, with Balbridie possibly continuing in use after the destruction of the Warren Field structure.

Even if the two structures were not in use at the same time there is likely to have been an awareness or memory of the earlier building. However, intervisibilty analysis shows that Balbridie would not have been visible from Warren Field (Fig. 20 and Winterbottom and Tipping 2007).

Plan

The total interior of the Warren Field building measured $c.176m^2$ (between the inner faces of the wall timbers). There were four distinct zones in the building: the east and west apsidal ends (Fig. 12: A and D) and the central space enclosed by the north and south walls which was divided by the partitions into two symmetric areas: Area B between partitions 1 and 2 and Area C between partitions 2 and 4. Each of these was $c.8m$ wide (north-south) and $c.6.8m$ long (east-west), with floor areas of some $54m^2$. Both Areas B and C appear to have been open spaces, although Area C had a partial and possibly temporary partition between post 144 and the north wall (partition 3).

It is argued below that Area B may have been constructed before Area C. It certainly had greater symmetry and more oak appeared to have been used in its construction. It was also nearer to the more imposing eastern end of the building. These differences might imply a functional distinction between the two areas. Without surviving floor levels this is difficult to prove but the differential distribution of flint and pottery (Fig. 36) may be indicative. There was far more pottery in contexts around Areas A and B and more flint from Area C, with some evidence to suggest that flint working took place there (Warren, chapter 6.3). There was a further, marked contrast, with far more artefacts from Area A compared to Area D. The distribution of grain (Fig. 19) shows it occurring in most sampled contexts in Areas A and B but far less in Area C, with the exception of the apparently structured deposit 89. In Area D there were only two cereal grains from pit 50. A single oat grain from Area D was considered possibly intrusive or may be a crop contaminant (Table 3). These distribution patterns reinforce the impression given by the structural evidence that the eastern end was a focal point and a thoroughfare, with the main entrance at the northeast corner, whereas the western end was an area of limited activity.

Interpreting this as implying lesser importance would be dangerous, however, especially as it is in the western end that there are one, possibly two, structured deposits (89, possibly 90) and pit 50, framed by the projecting ends of the north and south walls, appears to have held a possibly totemic post in the same way as pit 30. The rather insubstantial structure surrounding the western end does not give an impression of a strongly protected or even concealed area. However, it is feasible that there was a fence or that access to the area was restricted by taboo or tradition.

Comparison to the buildings at Balbridie and Claish (Fig. 21) indicates that the Warren Field building ($c.22.5m \times 8m$: $176m^2$) was smaller and narrower than Balbridie ($22m \times 11m$: $242m^2$), but very similar in both size and proportions to Claish ($24m \times 8.5$: $204m^2$). The building at Lockerbie which may also be as much as $27m \times 8m$ ($216m^2$) is a similar width to Warren Field but may be shorter if the asymmetric northern end is regarded as a separate structure. (In this comparison the measurements given are the internal dimensions of each building, measured between the inner faces of the wall timbers. Using the criteria used by Barclay, Brophy and MacGregor 2002, 133, note 4, citing the measurement between the centre of the post-pipes, the Warren Field building was $23m \times 8.5m$ and the internal area $195m^2$.)

The division of internal space at Balbridie and Claish appears more complex than at Warren Field, particularly at the ends of the buildings where both have some form of partition just inside the ends of the building. As, unlike Warren Field, these buildings had entrances in the centre of one or both gables, the inner partition may have screened the interior for practical or symbolic reasons. It is tempting to interpret the north end of the west gable at Balbridie as an entrance comparable to Warren Field but as this was the most heavily eroded area of the site the gap may be coincidental (Ralston, pers. comm.).

A common requirement for all these buildings appears to have been at least one fairly open area of around $50m^2$. At Balbridie, which was also orientated with the long axis lying east/west, Ralston (1982, 242) identified two main blocks of space in the building and, like Warren Field, the eastern area was the more open, with some internal posts in the western area. In contrast to Warren Field, the grain at Balbridie was concentrated in the western end of the central area (Barclay,

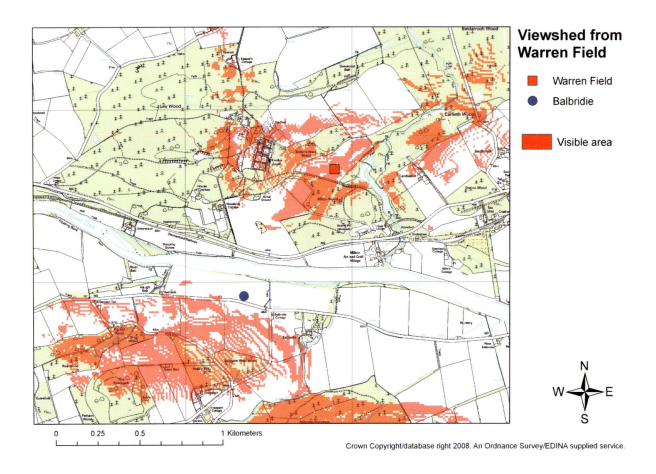

Figure 20. GIS viewshed analysis using ArcGIS 9.2 and the Ordnance Survey Landform Profile Digital Terrain Model (DTM), analysed by Sandy Winterbottom to test whether the Balbridie timber hall (blue dot) could be seen from the Warren Field timber hall (red square). The model used a DTM with a 10m resolution assuming a treeless landscape and a viewer 1.6m above the ground surface at Warren Field (Winterbottom and Tipping 2007). Unshaded areas could not be seen, indicating that even with no tree cover, Balbridie was below the shoulder of the glacifluvial terrace surface at Warren Field and could not be seen. (© Crown Copyright NTS licence No. 100023880)

Brophy and MacGregor 2002, 104), where it has been suggested that there might have been above-ground grain storage. Clearly the evidence for cereal growing around Warren Field shows that, at the least, storage over winter of seed grain would have been a necessity. However, there is no clear evidence to indicate that this took place in the excavated building as the quantities of grain found could have been from consumption rather than storage.

At Claish, which is orientated north/south, the excavators identified the equivalent open area in the northern part of the building (Barclay, Brophy and MacGregor 2002, illus 25: Area C). Like Warren Field, the pottery at Claish appears

to have been concentrated in this more open area, although this may be unrepresentative as there was less excavation in the southern area. The very small lithic assemblage from that site does not allow any spatial analysis. At Balbridie the distribution of pottery appears to have been from a wide range of contexts (Ralston, pers. comm.).

There is no exact parallel for the axial pits interpreted at Warren Field as holding totemic posts. However, at Balbridie there was a single large, freestanding post on the axial line at the western end of the building in a strikingly similar position to the Warren Field axial pits (Fairweather and Ralston 1993, Fig. 2). Two large pits near the axial line in the centre of the building at Claish

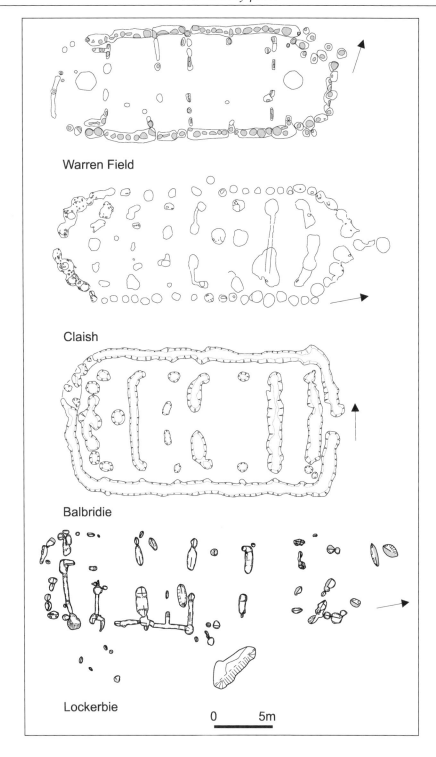

Warren Field

Claish

Balbridie

Lockerbie

0   5m

Figure 21. Comparative plans of the Neolithic halls at Warren Field, Claish (after Barclay, Brophy and MacGregor 2002), Balbridie (after Fairweather and Ralston 1993) and Lockerbie (CFA Archaeology Ltd)

do not appear to have held timbers although their original function is unclear (Barclay, Brophy and MacGregor 2002, 77–79: pits F15, F19).

There are similarities between the axial post-

pits at Warren Field and the axial timbers in later Neolithic contexts such as the possibly unroofed structure at Littleour, Perth and Kinross (Barclay and Maxwell 1998) and Balfarg structure 2, Fife

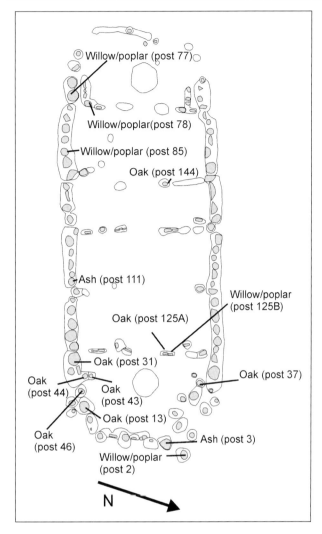

Figure 22. Plan of the Neolithic timber hall showing wood identifications

first and that the rest of the building could have been laid out in relation to them. They lay on the longitudinal axis of the building and were focal to the line of sight through the central gaps in the internal partitions, although clearly these may have had temporary screens or doors.

The north and south walls between partitions 1 and 2 were well built and symmetric to this axis. The primary form of partitions 1 and 2 also matched one another. In contrast, the north and south walls between partitions 2 and 4 were less carefully aligned, being skewed very slightly south of the axial line, and there was a greater mixture of timber varieties used. These differences may be viewed in terms of the relative importance of the two areas, or it could be argued that the eastern half (Areas A and B) had been built slightly earlier than the western half (Areas C and D) and that the building had been constructed in a series of modules. Such augmentation might simply reflect the work that could be achieved in a season. Modular construction has been observed in other large Neolithic structures in Scotland such as cursus monuments or post enclosures (Barclay 1995, 38) and has been suggested for another early Neolithic rectangular building at White Horse Stone, Kent (Hayden 2006).

Timbers for species identification were sampled throughout the building (Fig. 22 and Lancaster, chapter 3.2). They appear to show a greater use of oak at the eastern end, but with other timber such as ash and willow/poplar also being used for main wall timbers at the west end (posts 77, 85) and for posts in the multi-phase east wall (posts 2, 3). It is possible that the choice of timber was not dictated by species but by other factors such as proximity and size or by less mundane considerations such as the symbolism or associations of particular trees.

Some of the posts in the external walls were very large timbers in the round ranging up to 1m in diameter. However, the average was between 0.40m and 0.70m, suggesting that all parts of a felled tree were used. Some of the wall timbers were split, most appearing to have been halved, although a few (103, 175) may have been further converted. There appears to have been greater use of split timbers at the western end of the building.

In contrast most of the partition timbers appear to have been planks; where the evidence was clearest these appear to have been wedge-shaped

(Barclay and Russell-White 1993). Particularly striking is the axial pit in the enclosure at Douglasmuir, Angus (Kendrick 1995, 34–5, illus 5: pit BEA) which is very similar in size and profile to the Warren Field pits and also appears to have held a freestanding post. More general similarities between these structures and the large rectangular buildings have been discussed by Barclay, Brophy and MacGregor (2002, 122) who suggest the possibility of a shared symbolic tradition.

Construction and repair

As already mentioned there is some evidence at Warren Field to suggest that the axial pits and their possible totemic posts were positioned in section and are therefore likely to have been radially split. The conversion of timber by splitting appears to have been common in Neolithic Britain as a whole (Coles, Heal and Orme 1978; Noble 2006, 78–94) and there is ample evidence from Scotland, for example the use of squared timbers, possibly interspersed with planking on the long walls at Balbridie (Ralston 1982, 240), planks at Wardend of Durris, Aberdeenshire (Russell-White 1995, 15, 22–3) and the radially split oak, including narrow planks, found at the later Neolithic timber enclosure at Inchtuthil, Perthshire (Barclay and Maxwell 1991, 37).

There is clear evidence that there had been a number of repairs to the internal partitions and that the east end had been augmented or repaired on more than one occasion. Regardless of the lack of horizontal stratigraphy within the building, there were twenty instances where posts or post-pits were clearly cut through other features (shown blue on Fig. 12). While some of these, such as posts 113 and 167, may be no more than sequences within contemporary building operations, others, such as posts 9, 11, 12, 159 and 160 in the east end or post 128 in partition 1, were replacement or additional posts. It is clear that the west end was not built in the same form as the east end. It is also apparent that the very shallow western wall slot had been backfilled before the building was burnt, and possibly much earlier in the life of the building, as the backfill contained no charcoal or artefacts. It is even possible to speculate that this was perhaps only a marking of the line of a west end wall that was never fulfilled, or a demarcation in itself. It is perhaps significant that there is also some evidence that posts may have been removed from features at the west end of the building, specifically from post-pits 71 and 130, both in partition 4, and posts 55 and 59 in the west wall.

Similar evidence of repairs or modification of the original plan was observed at Balbridie (Ralston 1982, 244) and at Claish there were indications of post replacement although the speculative two-phase plan hypothesised for that site is less convincing (Barclay, Brophy and MacGregor 2002, 72–3 and illus 24). The evidence implies that all these buildings had a sufficient life for repairs or changes to have become necessary or desirable. The analysis of the radiocarbon dating (Marshall, chapter 5) suggests that the estimated probable lifespan of the buildings at both Warren Field and Claish was *1–50 years (68% probability)*.

Destruction

There is a wide acceptance (*e.g.* Thomas 2006, 237–8; Noble 2006, 45–58) that many of the oak-built early Neolithic structures in northern Britain, including lowland Scotland, were destroyed by fire, with parallels being drawn to the evidence and symbolism of burnt Neolithic houses in southeast Europe (Stevanovic 2002). Comparisons of the symbolic meaning of such practices are valid but it is necessary to examine the mechanism of the destruction in more detail as the structures and materials being burnt are not analogous. It is also essential to examine the role of fire throughout the life of the structure and not attribute all 'burning' phenomena to a single event.

The evidence of fire activity related directly to the structure at Warren Field includes two areas of fire-reddening of the subsoil, the charred sides and bases of timbers, and the widespread charcoal deposits overlying the fills of wall trenches and post-pits and sunk into rotted post cores. Other fire activity is shown by burnt grains, bone, flint and pottery. A high degree of efficiency in pyrotechnology is attested by the ability to fire high quality, fine-walled pottery.

Some of this activity can be related to deliberate events during the life of the structure, such as the structured deposition of burnt flint and foodstuffs in pit 89. It may also be inferred that some grains and artefacts may have been accidentally burnt in ordinary use, for example the charred grain in pre-destruction contexts such as 11/5, 11/6 and 71, and in the primary backfill of axial pit 30 (30/17). This can be supported by the considerable quantities of burnt flint (*c.*30%) and grain found around hearths in an apparently unburnt, contemporary, domestic Neolithic building at Garthdee, Aberdeen (Murray 2005). Other burnt grains and artefacts were found in post-destruction contexts at Warren Field and would have been in the building at the time of destruction.

Burning at construction

It is questionable if the charred sides and bases of the wall timbers below the contemporary ground surface at Warren Field can be attributed to the destruction of the building by fire (Figs 23, 24). Oak is fairly slow to ignite. Experimental burning illustrates that if flame is present the timber ignites and begins to char at *c.*300° C and continues to char at a steady rate, but it can take *c.*60 minutes to char the outer surface of structural oak timbers

Figure 23. Excavated section of post 13 with charring to base (© Charles Murray)

Figure 24. Post 31. After sectioning (Figure 13), the rotted core of the post was removed to reveal the thickness of the charcoal at the charred base and sides of the post (© Charles Murray)

above ground to a thickness of 30mm (Ware and Hattis 2000). At Warren Field, the very large oak timbers of the external wall would have been difficult to ignite, so the destruction of the building by fire, either accidentally or deliberately, would have required the primary ignition of more easily flammable materials such as roofing material and internal partitions, or gathered materials if the fire was deliberately augmented. By analogy with experimental house fires (Bankoff and Winter 1979; Neilsen 1966; Rasmussen 2007) one might postulate collapse of these elements within a very short period of time, making it unlikely that the external wall timbers would have been deeply charred or consumed by this primary fire. Even with the southeast European wattle buildings such as Opovo, where most timber used was 10mm in diameter and little was over 100mm in diameter, Stevanovic has argued that fuel must have been added to fully burn the buildings (Stevanovic 1997, 355–8, 381; 2002, 57). Total consumption of the large oak timbers at Warren Field would have necessitated refuelling for many hours or even days. Even if the fire was tended in such a way, experimental burning of posts (authors) show that it is very unlikely that the fire would have penetrated below ground and continued charring to the base of the timbers, especially as the underlying soils on the site are gravel rather than peat. Moreover, had this occurred in the outer walls, the far lighter timbers of the internal partitions might be expected to have been completely carbonised. Analysis of the 78 sectioned posts shows significant differences in the degree of charring. With two exceptions (42, 113) all sectioned posts in the north and south walls (92%) showed charring of the outer surface of the timber at the sides and base. At the east end of the building *c*.60% of sectioned timbers were clearly charred to the base, the exceptions being three split planks (10, 12, 160), a secondary post (36) and two others (8, 39). In contrast, only 19% of the generally lighter split timbers in the internal partitions showed any evidence of charring below the ground surface (five with charring, twenty-one without). It would appear improbable that in the course of a fire the larger wall posts were charred to the base, while the more flammable planks remained unburnt below ground level. Excavation of the reconstruction of an Iron Age house at Lejre in Denmark twenty-five years after it was destroyed by fire showed that no burning

of the oak uprights had penetrated below ground level; significantly the subsoil on that site was partly sand and gravel and partly clay (Rasmussen 2007, 94).

It is therefore suggested that this charring occurred either during felling or at the time of construction. Experimental work with stone axes shows that they were effective in felling hard and softwood trees up to *c*.0.35m diameter and that above that size, additional felling techniques such as ring barking or fire setting would have been necessary (Coles, Heal and Orme 1978, 26). As most of the timbers in the side walls of the Warren Field building were over 0.40m in diameter, some being as large as 1m in diameter, it is possible that some of the charring was due either to the initial felling of these larger trees or to 'cutting' them into the required lengths. A further strand of evidence is seen in the section of split timber 146 in the south wall as this shows charring on the outer face of the timber, but not on the inner (northern) split face. This would make sense as the timber would have been cut or burnt to lengths prior to splitting. However, it is also possible that charring may have been used as a preservative method to delay rot, a method which was considered potentially viable on a commercial scale as late as the nineteenth century (Scientific American 1885). Some experimental work at Lejre suggests that there is at least short term visible slowing of decay in oak timbers pre-treated by charring (Rasmussen 2007, 97). Alternatively it may have been considered to give structural strength as suggested by Semenov (1968, discussed in Stevanovic 2002, 56), or may even have had a symbolic significance. It must be stressed that the evidence is for charring of those parts of the timber which were below ground so it is not possible to assess any potential impact on the appearance of the building that would have occurred if the timbers had also been charred above ground.

This interpretation underlies the importance of distinguishing between different fire events in the life of a structure. Unless posts were set into a medium such as peat which would itself further the burning process, evidence that consists solely of the charring of the sides and base of posts below ground may represent timber preparation rather than destruction by fire (see also Rasmussen 2007, 97). This does not deny that destruction by burning may have taken place on many sites but does suggest that it may be only part of a more complex picture of fire in relation to buildings.

Burning at destruction

The widespread charcoal deposits in *post-destruction* contexts at Warren Field can, however, be used as evidence that the building was destroyed by fire at the end of its life. These deposits were ubiquitous in the top of all the negative features and account for the burnt debris fallen or placed in the secondary fills of pit 30. They included charcoal not only from oak, but also from hazel, birch and willow/poplar, including small diameter roundwood, which may have been used in internal features and in the roof framework. Experimental firing of buildings has shown that roof materials and freestanding small diameter timbers burn very quickly. The results of the experimental firing of the reconstruction at Lejre are useful (Nielsen 1966; Rasmussen 2007). The building had clay-daubed wattle walls and a thatched roof supported by larger vertical posts. Combustion was swift, causing collapse of the roof in 20 minutes; after 35 minutes only the larger vertical posts (considerably smaller than the Warren Field timbers) were standing, shown in photographs as heavily charred. The fallen debris continued to smoulder for two days, leaving a thick deposit of charred timber and ash. Temperatures in the core of the building reached 900° C, but near the external walls only *c.*700° C. Burning of another daubed wattle building in Serbia replicated these results, although perhaps significantly this example described some of the fairly small vertical timbers as having been ignited by fallen burning debris and reduced to ash-filled post-holes (Bankoff and Winter 1979, 13).

There is some evidence to suggest that the fire at Warren Field was a deliberate destruction rather than an accidental blaze. Following the investigative approach suggested by Tringham (2005, 102), the removal, directly before the fire, of the objects/totems set in the axial pits may be seen as analogous to the removal of family photographs observed by modern fire investigators in buildings destroyed by arson. Lacking floors, it is difficult to distinguish fire hot spots – another indicator of deliberate fire setting (Stevanovic 1997, 373). However, two areas of the interior (Fig. 18) had been sufficiently burnt that the underlying sand was reddened. Significantly, both of these are adjacent to gaps in the main walls which would have allowed a draft to stimulate fire within the

building. These are unlikely positions for hearths but quite possible as points of deliberate fire setting. As the finds analyses have shown, there was a high percentage of burnt flint (Warren, chapter 6.3) and some evidence of burnt pottery (Sheridan, chapter 6.1) from the post-destruction contexts. It would appear, therefore, that some objects were in the building at the time of destruction – although the relatively small assemblages compared, for example, to the far larger assemblage from the unburnt building at Garthdee (Murray 2005), could indicate some removal of building contents. If objects had been removed this would also suggest an intentional, planned fire.

The careful removal of the axial posts at Warren Field suggests that the building was deliberately destroyed by its users/owners rather than by hostile outsiders. The removal of structural elements before burning has also been observed at Parc Bryn Cegin, Llandygai (Kenney, pers. comm.) and Bradley (2005, 53) cites similar examples throughout prehistoric Europe, suggesting that such retrieval could create links between a destroyed building and structures that succeeded it.

The early Neolithic buildings at Balbridie (Ralston 1982, 239) and Claish (Barclay, Brophy and MacGregor 2002, 103) were also destroyed by fire, although there was no evidence for this at Lockerbie (Kirby, pers. comm.). Barclay, Brophy and MacGregor suggest that Claish may have been partially burnt and repaired before its final destruction by fire. There was no evidence to show if this fire was accidental or deliberate. A few other examples of burnt Neolithic structures in Scotland emphasize the difficulties in interpreting the evidence of burning during fieldwork and stress the importance of assessing the real extent of destruction that it represents. The enclosure at Inchtuthil had a wooden fence which had burnt *in situ* and fallen against the side of the enclosure ditch and some timbers are thought to have been burnt, replaced and burnt again (Barclay and Maxwell 1991, 33–5). The enclosure at Douglasmuir may also have burnt but the evidence of burning appears to have been restricted to a small number of posts (Kendrick 1995, 32–3). The evidence from the cursus monument at Dunragit is significant as it has been suggested that some posts had been removed or rotted and others which had been burnt had been pulled over, possibly before firing (Thomas 2001). (Incidentally, this would have allowed air into the post-pits so some burning below ground would have been possible.) Some of these sites perhaps indicate that, although there are a number of clear instances of deliberate destruction by fire, the firing in other cases may have been more limited than is sometimes suggested.

Deliberate fires are often considered to represent the ritual killing of a structure (Tringham 2005; Stevanovic 2002). In economic terms it was the consumption of huge resources of timber and labour used in the building. Whatever the motivation, the destruction would undoubtedly have been impressive. There is nothing at Warren Field to indicate the removal of charred timbers, the cores appearing to have rotted naturally. We may perhaps envisage a dramatic fire leaving stark and equally dramatic burnt timbers marking the site.

Reconstruction

Hilary Murray

Any reconstruction must inevitably remain hypothetical, but a failure to consider the three-dimensionality of the building would limit efforts to visualise it both as a structure and as a space within which people moved. Some attempt has therefore been made to suggest several possible reconstructions, two of which have been drawn (Figs 26, 27).

There has been some discussion whether these early Neolithic Scottish structures were roofed or unroofed (Barclay, Brophy and MacGregor 2002, 98; Fairweather and Ralston 1993, 315–6). At Warren Field the evidence strongly suggests that it was at least partially a roofed building. Specifically this can be argued from the symmetry of the plan and the juxtaposition of internal features, including possible roof supports, with elements of the outer walls.

Whilst agreeing with Barclay, Brophy and MacGregor (2002, 106) that it is not possible to be categorical about wall heights, it is valid to make some estimates. The average surviving depth of the posts in the north and south walls was only *c*.0.15–0.40m, allowing for some depredation by ploughing this might suggest an original depth in the range of 0.50–0.60m. A wall height of *c*.1.5–2m is possible, but much above this height stability would have been compromised. Many of the wall posts in the long side walls were set closely together and there was no evidence to suggest if gaps between them had been filled with moss or earth. No daub was identified. The posts at the

east end were more widely spaced. It could be argued that they were hung with skins or screened with wattle, but it is also possible that the spaces between them were left open to allow the 'totem' in pit 30 to be visible.

Allowing a roof pitch of at least 45° the apex of the roof would have been at a height of *c*.5.5m-6m. The massive timbers of the north and south walls could have carried much of the roof weight. The manner in which they had been set in the wall trenches, many with some loose gravel backfilled below them to allow for manoeuvrability, indicates the possibility that there was an aim to achieve a reasonably level wall top. Brunskill (1999, 24–5) describes this type of mass timber construction as typical of timber clearance stages of settlement and considers such walls to have had considerable load-bearing capacity. He suggests that coupled rafters at close intervals would be a likely form of roofing for such structures. The rafters would have needed to be jointed or tied at the apex and might have needed a bracing collar. It can be argued that the wide span (8m) would have required some internal support to avoid the roof becoming unstable longitudinally. Superficially the plan suggests this support existed, based on horizontal aisle timbers held by two rows of posts set in features 125, 99, 144, 71 to the north and 123, 140, 90 and 130 to the south. However, excavation showed that some of these features had held split planks as small as 0.20m × 0.08m and others (71, 130, possibly 90) appear to have had timbers removed during the life of the building. These features may simply have been part of a design to frame the views of whatever was in the axial pits and to divide space within the building.

The spacing of the posts projecting from the inner faces of the side walls (167, 169, 92 to the north and 113, 141, 146 to the south) gives another possible solution. These posts are set in roughly opposing pairs between 2.8m and 3.4m apart and between 3.2m and 3.8m from the end partitions (Fig. 12: partitions 1 and 4). If these had been naturally bent timbers they could have acted as primitive crucks, supporting a series of relatively short interrupted purlins, which would have given lateral stability to the rafters, while still leaving most of the roof load on the massive outer wall. The advantage of this reconstruction is that it explains the projecting posts and would also not have required many very long timbers. Ralston has suggested that similar posts projecting on the inner

Figure 25. Burnt remains of a reconstruction of a Neolithic hall with another reconstructed hall in the background. Archeon, Netherlands. 1996 (© Event Communications Ltd)

side of the wall line at Balbridie may have had a role in roof support (Fairweather and Ralston 1993, 315–6); Barclay, Brophy and MacGregor (2002, 106) interpret them as posts for doors or a link between wall and partition but as not all occur beside partitions (Ralston, pers. comm.) this appears unlikely. Both Balbridie and Claish have lines of aisle posts *c*.1m from the inner faces of the side walls which does not seem to have been true of Warren Field, although there are posts augmenting some of the projecting posts (114, 139?, 87, 112?).

There is little to indicate that the western end of the building was roofed and it is shown in the drawn reconstructions as an unroofed, fenced area. The posts at the eastern end could easily have supported a hipped roof (Fig. 26) although it would be possible to argue that it too was unroofed (Fig. 27).

Whatever the underlying structure of the roof, there is likely to have been a framework of smaller branches or wattle panels to hold the roof cladding. Small diameter roundwood such as hazel found in destruction contexts could have derived from such a framework or from internal partitions. The roof cladding could potentially have been thatch, turf or even wooden shingles. However, neither the charred plant remains nor the pollen data yielded evidence to suggest which was most probable. In support of wooden shingles,

it is clear that split oak was in common use in the structure. Thatch could have been of wild resources such as rushes, sedges, bracken, heathers etc. or of cultivated resources such as cereal straw, or indeed of a mixture of materials. While there may be an assumption that the burnt grain from post-destruction contexts was in storage or use in the building at the time of the fire, it is also possible that it represents occasional grains preserved in a thatch. The inclusion of some accidental grains among threshed straw used for thatch is well documented in the analysis of historic thatches (Holden 1998).

Visualisation

The impact of these large buildings must have been considerable. The visible consumption of so much hard won timber alone would have been impressive. The roof would have been around four times the height of a man and the choice of the slightly raised area on which the Warren Field building stood would have made it appear even taller. The careful alignment of the inner faces of the walls emphasises the importance of the interior. Entering the building from the northeast, a visitor would immediately be faced by the vertical timber in pit 30, possibly lit by light filtering between the posts of the eastern wall. A choice was necessary

Figure 26. Reconstruction of Warren Field Neolithic timber hall: variant 1 with east end roofed (Reconstruction by Hilary Murray. Drawing by Jan Dunbar)

Figure 27. Reconstruction of Warren Field Neolithic timber hall: variant 2 with east end unroofed (Reconstruction by Hilary Murray. Drawing by Jan Dunbar)

to walk either to right or left of this 'totem' before passing through the central opening in the first partition. Here the tight timber walls would have allowed little light through; it would have been dim, lit only by firelight and occasional shafts of light from the slit openings. Screens on the partitions may have separated different groups or activities from view. The wooden walls would have deadened sound and exaggerated the difference between the inside and the outer world.

Function

An increasing number of early Neolithic rectangular buildings have been found in recent years in Ireland (Armit *et al.*, 2003); others have been discovered at sites such as Yarnton, Oxfordshire (Hey, pers. comm.) and White Horse Stone, Kent (Hayden 2006) in England, and a hitherto unknown example was excavated in 2006 in the west of Scotland at Lockerbie, Dumfriesshire (Kirby 2006). It appears irrefutable that in the early Neolithic in Britain and Ireland there was a new tradition of building rectangular structures and indeed that this may have been more common than it might have appeared even a decade ago.

Arguments about the function and even the nomenclature of these rectangular buildings often appear to be polarised between those who describe them as domestic houses and others who seem to emphasise their ritual possibilities. For example, Grogan (1996, 57), discussing the Irish evidence of both rectangular and circular buildings, describes both as houses which 'formed the focal point for everyday domestic activity' on the basis of associated finds of domestic rubbish such as pottery, stone tools, personal items and food remains. Cross (2003), also referring to the Irish evidence, allows that some people may have lived in the rectangular buildings but interprets the evidence of bone (food debris), grain (possible alcohol) and pottery (serving vessels) as indicating that they had a community function as feasting halls. Topping (1996, 166), who describes Balbridie as 'some form of cult house with a regional significance', suggests that these buildings have to be seen as encompassing more than a purely residential role, introducing the phrase 'domestic ritual monument'. The term 'hall' initiated by Ralston and Reynolds (1981) to describe Balbridie when it was originally thought to be a Dark Age structure and discussed by Barclay, Brophy and

MacGregor (2002) in respect of Claish, is useful; it not only has some connotation of communal involvement or use, but also gives a sense of their impact within the landscape.

What is equally clear is that within the 'idea of rectangularity' there was a huge range of structural solutions, in walling, roof support systems and internal arrangements – in fact what we might expect if separate groups of people, using locally available materials (and possibly different sizes of group doing the building) constructed buildings that conformed to a remembered or described ideal. As Darvill (1996, 99) argued, 'superficially similar structures may play different roles yet embody common themes in their layout, structure and use'. There are some similarities between the large structures represented at sites such as Claish, Balbridie and Warren Field and the far smaller buildings on many of the Irish sites. Rather than trying to typologise these rectangular buildings it is perhaps preferable to accept that, regardless of size, they are different from earlier and contemporary traditions of round or ovoid buildings and it may be more important to ask why the rectangular plan was restricted to a very short timespan (Bradley 2003, 219; Whittle 2003, 158). The answers may help to understand their role.

In defining the Warren Field building it is worth comparing it with a very different contemporary early Neolithic settlement site excavated only *c.*20 kilometres away at Garthdee, Aberdeen, nearer the mouth of the river Dee, where a roughly oval turf-walled building, *c.*11m × 8–10m, can be dated to *c.*3800–3650 cal BC (Murray and Murray 2005b). Thick occupation deposits with hearths yielded large quantities of pottery, flint and carbonised grains, all very similar in nature to the far smaller quantities found at the hall at Warren Field. It would be inconsistent to accept the assemblage at Garthdee as reflecting everyday living but to interpret the same materials at Warren Field as indicating feasting, or to interpret grain on one site as food refuse and to suggest grain storage or curation of seed at the other. If we accept the artefacts and grain at Warren Field as showing that some people lived there, it is notable that, even allowing for the loss of floor levels and the possible removal of possessions prior to destruction, the quantity of artefacts was less than at the smaller Garthdee 'house'. This could suggest that only a small number of people lived at Warren Field or that they lived there for a shorter period or only for part of the year. The repairs to the structure make it unlikely that the building itself was only in existence for a very limited time, although as analysis of the dates shows (Marshall, chapter 5) its lifespan was probably fifty years or less. In contrast to this evidence for limited occupation, it is clear that the felling, conversion and movement of timber and the building of the structure at Warren Field would have needed more than a small group to achieve. The pollen evidence indicates an area of cleared ground used for cereal production around the building – this too suggests the involvement of a reasonable number of people, at least at times, for tasks such as ground clearance, sowing and harvesting.

It is also apparent that there was at least one deliberate structured deposit within the building and it has been argued that the large axial pits held timbers with a possible totemic role. Perhaps, as Bradley (2003, 221) concludes, 'there was no clear-cut division between ritual and daily life.' Or perhaps we should accept that while there are indicators of 'domestic life' at both Warren Field and Garthdee, there are also indications that Warren Field also had other more complex roles.

The close proximity of Warren Field and Balbridie needs some consideration; they are less than a kilometre apart on opposite sides of the river Dee, although Balbridie was nearer to the water and Warren Field set back on slightly higher ground. Both yielded a very similar range of artefacts and dates and they may have co-existed (Marshall, chapter 5 and Fig. 34), although Sheridan (chapter 6.1) uses the pottery evidence to suggest that Balbridie was built or continued in use later than Warren Field. While sharing the same 'idea of rectangularity', structure and proportions are very different and it is reasonable to argue that they were built by different groups of people, although that does not preclude contact between them. It is tempting to speculate that they reflect separate zones of influence, one on each side of the river. It is perhaps no coincidence that they were both situated on a major routeway at the interface between lower ground to the east and higher hill ground to the west.

3.4 The timber hall and the emergence of new ways of living
Shannon Fraser

Despite their seeming rarity, and the fact that until investigation of the structure at Claish Farm in 2001 only one example had been excavated, the chronological occurrence of the Scottish timber halls in the first quarter of the fourth millennium BC has meant that consideration of their function and role in society has been a recurring feature of the debate concerning the nature of the transition to agriculture in Britain. Interpretations have ranged from the exclusively ritual – the cult house, for instance (Topping 1996) – to the purely domestic, allowing for the embedded nature of symbolic behaviour within domestic, economic activity centered on the house structure (*e.g.* Rowley-Conwy 2004). A wide variety of the possibilities in between have been explored; Barclay, Brophy and MacGregor provide a useful discussion of a number of these (2002, 125–7; see also consideration of function by Murray and Murray in chapter 3.3). However, overarching discussions of the nature of timber buildings in relation to the establishment of new lifeways have tended to elide the detail of the Scottish hall sites, making broad assumptions which are not necessarily founded on the full evidence. This is partly a result of the fact that so many discussions are based on the restricted, interim data available from the meticulous excavations at Balbridie, which for so long remained unique. But it is also partly due to the fact that discussion of the transition to agriculture has seen the development of increasingly polarised views resulting in overly schematic arguments.

The last few years have seen increasing debate around a perceived consensus on the nature of the introduction of novel material elements into Britain in the centuries around 4000 cal BC. This 'consensus' view, developed in particular detail from the late 1980s, envisages indigenous communities drawing various elements from the lifestyle of agricultural communities on the Continent into existing ways of life, moulding them to fit localised traditions, with the ensuing internal developmental trajectory resulting ultimately in a new world view. Writers such as Julian Thomas (1991; 1999), arguing that the Atlantic Neolithic existed more in the symbolic realm than as integrated economic practice, see the transformation in economic behaviour as a process drawn out over a long period of time, contrasting with a rapid shift in the nature of social life. Thus, fourth millennium Britain has been interpreted by some as continuing traditional patterns of mobility, with cattle herding forming a key focus of seasonal routines in which dwellings were largely temporary, wild foodstuffs retained a prominent subsistence role, and ceremonial sites acted as places at which larger communities could come together (*e.g.* Thomas 1996; Whittle 1996; Pollard 2000).

There are difficulties here in the conflation of the mobility of pastoralists with that of hunters and gatherers, which are quite different in nature. But beyond this, many authors have noted that while this model was initially formulated to interpret the particular evidence of southern Britain, where it was difficult to catch traces of permanent, intensive settlement, it was in its wider application to the British Isles that it gained 'near consensus' status (Rowley-Conwy 2004, 83) and yet became increasingly problematic. Alternative views have been put forward by a number of scholars, often by those working with material outwith the south of England (*e.g.* Barclay 1996; 2003a; Cooney 1997; 2000; 2003). Indeed, it is debatable how far this vision of Neolithic beginnings ever formed a prevailing orthodoxy within the Scottish context. On the one hand, recognition of variability and regionalism embedded within the steadily-growing body of evidence for early Neolithic inhabitation of geographically disparate Scottish landscapes began to break down over-arching, all-embracing conceptions of the transition to agriculture – an issue highlighted by Ian Kinnes (1985) and explored in some detail by Gordon Barclay (1996; 2000; 2001; 2003a; 2003b; 2004). On the other hand, discontinuities across the Mesolithic-Neolithic transition in Scotland (beyond the introduction of domesticates, ceramics and monumental traditions) have been highlighted in a number of recent studies (*e.g.* papers in Shepherd and Barclay 2004). These include *inter alia* a new interest in the procurement and exchange of materials from distant locations; the introduction of new stone-working techniques; the loss of some tool forms and the introduction of others; settlement of some parts of the landscape with no known Mesolithic inheritance; and, in some areas, an apparent shift away from the exploitation of marine food resources to a diet in which terrestrial foods are predominant.

One of the key differences to the southern British case is that, although still limited, there is increasing evidence in different parts of Scotland for the use of settlement sites of at least a certain permanence in the earlier fourth millennium BC. Associated structures range widely in form, but are generally circular, ovoid or sub-rectangular structures of not more than about 10m in maximum extent, built of timber, stone and/or turf (*e.g.* Atkinson 2002; Johnston 1997; Murray 2005 and discussion above; Rennie 1984; 1985; possibly Alexander 2000; Marshall 1978). Some appear isolated, while other sites see a succession of lightly-built buildings and/or small agglomerations, sometimes with adjacent 'activity areas' of cobbling, hearths and pits. A domestic function (in its broadest sense) would certainly seem feasible for a number of these.

The relationship between this highly variable structural assemblage and the timber halls, which are of a completely different form and scale, and yet which are associated with the same types of pottery and often lithic forms, is as yet unresolved. Do they form part of an integrated settlement system, in which smaller houses are occupied by the same communities which use the timber halls, for a different purpose or at different times of the year? Are the timber halls places at which a number of different communities can come together in particular seasons, or are they residential loci for an integrated kin group? Are we seeing the separation of particular social groups, based on age/sex/genealogical relationships/knowledge-based authority? Or is this the development of different traditions by people of different genetic descent, with timber halls being more closely associated to incoming groups? Certainly, the timber and/or turf-built buildings in particular do display similarities with the more robust constructions of the Mesolithic in Scotland, as at Nethermills of Crathes (Kenworthy 1981), Ben Lawers, Perthshire (Atkinson, Donnelly and MacGregor 1997) and East Barns, Fife (Gooder and Hatherly 2003). Similarly, recognizing the variability of cereal quantities amongst early Neolithic settlement sites in lowland Scotland, Barclay (2003b, 81) has noted that we may be glimpsing differences in function or in regional economic strategies, some of which may have more connection to Mesolithic lifeways than others.

One of the many difficulties here is the spatially-restricted nature of excavations at timber hall sites, which prevents us from knowing whether contemporary, smaller buildings sat close by. A series of trial trenches around the Balbridie hall failed to reveal archaeological features, though Ralston and Reynolds (1981) noted the potential for settlement evidence buried under colluvium down-slope. A specific aim of the Warren Field excavations was to test for the presence of more ephemeral buildings among the wider cropmark complex around the building. Results from excavation, fieldwalking and pollen analysis provided little evidence for other occupation in the Warren Field. However, the discovery of truncated post-pits with early Neolithic pottery 300m uphill at the Crathes Castle Overflow Car Park site and a further sherd 200m to the southwest in Milton Wood, highlights the fact that settlement can easily extend across areas beyond the scale of excavations not connected with major development projects.

What certainly seems highly possible is that many more of these smaller, early Neolithic buildings remain to be discovered; equally, their relatively ephemeral nature means many more will have been destroyed, particularly in intensively farmed areas. The large timber halls, however, would appear to be genuinely rare. Despite the intensity of aerial photography in Scotland over the last thirty years, all of the halls identified from the air have been known since at least the 1970s. It may be argued that more may be revealed in pre-development fieldwork but, to date, the building at Lockerbie is the only possible early Neolithic timber hall to have been identified since archaeological evaluation became a routine part of the planning process in the mid 1990s. In terms of landscape location, scale and morphology, the likeliest unexcavated candidates number only four: Noranbank and Boysack in Angus, Newbiggins in Aberdeenshire, and Whitmuirhaugh in the Borders. Kenneth Brophy (2007) has noted the strong potential for a fifth site at Nether Kelly, Angus – a cropmark which is currently interpreted as a Neolithic mortuary enclosure. That the earlier building beneath the Anglian hall at Doon Hill, East Lothian may be of Neolithic date – a question first posed in the 1980s (Selkirk 1980; Hope-Taylor 1980; Ralston and Reynolds 1981) – remains a possibility as yet unresolved (*pace* Brophy 2007).

Another point of note is that the timber halls appear to occur within a tightly-defined span of time. Bayesian analysis of radiocarbon dates from Claish and Warren Field sets them within the period *c.*3800–3600 cal BC; Balbridie may have been built as early as 4000 cal BC, but, as Marshall notes (chapter 5), the nature of these

determinations means imprecision is greater. The ceramic assemblages at Lockerbie sit happily within this time frame. In contrast, smaller, sub-rectangular, oval and circular buildings continue to be built long after this (Ashmore 2004, 132–4). Post-built structures of similar scale to the halls follow on in the second half of the fourth millennium, but have been interpreted by their excavators as un-roofed enclosures (Barclay and Russell-White 1993; Barclay and Maxwell 1998; Barclay and Brophy 2004). Barclay, Brophy and MacGregor have postulated the development of some of the 'architectural vocabulary' of the timber halls in these new monuments (2002, 110; 131). But even if they were roofed buildings, their spatial organisation and constructional techniques appear somewhat different, and the precise relationship between the two traditions remains unclear. Brophy's recent hypothesis (2007) of an overt link between the burnt shells of the timber halls and features of the later structures is hard to sustain due to the considerable length of time which lies between them. Thomas has suggested a similar relationship between Scottish timber halls – viewed as communal monuments – and pit- and post-defined cursus monuments, in which the spatial order of the former is drawn upon in the latter in the 'symbolic transformation of the idea of the timber hall' (2006, 239). Here too there is a chronological issue: on present evidence the construction of these cursus monuments looks to begin slightly earlier than the buildings, while the evidence from the Warren Field of linear pit-digging in the Mesolithic, on an ultimately monumental scale, means some contribution from earlier traditions cannot be entirely discounted (see discussion of pit alignment, chapter 2.3).

The timber hall, as a novel, early material form, is thus caught up in the web of alternative interpretations of the emergence of new ways of living. Viewed in a framework of mobility or short-term sedentism, the hall becomes the focus of sporadic residence, the location for important social gatherings involving communal feasting, at which a whole series of social transactions might take place, from the exchange of goods and marriage partners to dispute resolution (*e.g.* Whittle 1996, 233–4; 1999, 63; Thomas 2006, 239). From a perspective which envisages settlement patterns based on permanent residential foci, with potential seasonal movement of some parts of the population, a view of the hall as a dwelling with regional significance emerges – something beyond the 'normal farmhouse', which may be the locus of political and/or symbolic activity relevant to a wider social entity (Barclay, Brophy and MacGregor 2002; Brophy 2007). A view in which cereal cultivation plays a primary and predominant role in the new lifeways of the fourth millennium, articulated by Peter Rowley-Conwy (2004), stresses a domestic, residential role of the hall as, in part, a 'cereal store' (cf. Cooney 1997, 27). While acknowledging the fact that the scale and nature of artefactual and environmental remains within the building is predicated upon the processes surrounding deliberate, seemingly non-aggressive burning, it is perhaps worth noting that in real terms the Warren Field and Claish halls produced extremely small numbers of cereal grains. Even the exceptional 20,000 grains from Balbridie would amount to about two kilograms – only enough to seed an area about the size of the hall itself (H. Murray, pers. comm.). Furthermore, evidence for the use of milk products obtained by analysis of organic residues in ceramics from Warren Field and the nearby Crathes Castle Overflow Car Park (Šoberl and Evershed 2008 and chapter 6.2) is an important reminder not to permit the scarcity of animal bone in the acidic soils of Scottish hall sites to influence our assumptions about the relative importance of different domesticated products, or of domesticated and wild resources.

Rowley-Conwy rejects the possibility of gradual economic transformation, instead postulating devastating upheaval of indigenous hunter-gatherers' traditional modes of life as an entirely new, domestic framework for living was introduced in the centuries around 4000 cal BC, predicated upon agricultural practice from the outset and involving predominant sedentism. Rather than being largely a matter of indigenous choice, Rowley-Conwy envisages these ideological and material transformations involving major and probably frequent movements of people. From the Scottish perspective, Alison Sheridan posits a similarly profound impact upon native populations occurring in the first three centuries of the fourth millennium BC, with the introduction of a 'Neolithic package' to large parts of Scotland by small farming groups from northern and northwestern France (Sheridan 2000; 2003; 2007b and chapter 6.2). In this view, the timber halls are part of colonists' varied responses to their new circumstances, with the groups arriving in northern Britain perhaps being large enough to

create monumental houses requiring substantial communal labour to erect (Sheridan 2007b).

In the Warren Field hall we see a timber structure that has no *direct* parallels, either in Atlantic Europe or amongst its excavated comparators in Scotland, although it does display strong links with the latter. Its inhabitants have already identified the regional flint sources utilised throughout the Mesolithic, while their procurement through long-distance exchange of Arran pitchstone, previously circulating only within the Firth of Clyde area, has already been established. They utilise new forms of lithic technology alongside those difficult to distinguish from earlier traditions. They have already begun to craft leaf-shaped arrowheads which hint at a shifting emphasis in the use of the bow, while being relatively uncommon in western Europe (Kinnes 2004, 139). Given the ambiguity of the evidence they may be hunting wild boar and roe deer; they may be engaged in raising domestic pigs and sheep. Their animal husbandry certainly encompasses the sophistication of dairying processes, with its implication of the time which must have elapsed for the breeding of mature dairy ruminants, be these cattle or sheep/goats. These people make pottery which involves advanced technological practices and which conforms to a stylistic tradition widespread over much of Scotland and Ireland, with relationships to northern French ceramic styles yet with no precise point of origin yet identified. The ground around the building seems to see the cultivation on a reasonable scale of a suite of cereal types with affinities to those found in northern and western Europe (Lancaster chapter 3.2; Fairweather and Ralston 1993; Fairbairn 2000; McLaren 2000). All of this is carried forward in a place which bears the signs of previous inhabitation, the resonance of which is formally acknowledged. This hints at the complexity of the relationships involved in the transition to agriculture both along the Atlantic facade and within Britain and Ireland. But further, in my opinion, it does not much resemble the very first settlement of incoming farmers. Rather, it looks more like the result of a certain passage of time in which perhaps quite complicated and varied interactions among native populations and more recent arrivals have taken place, which might include intermarriage, exchange of knowledge and resources, perhaps in some cases hostility.

The difficulty inherent in an issue upon which such different perspectives are brought to bear is that the common ground among the range of interpretations is played down, as are the refinements of the most strongly polarised arguments; thus the nature of the earliest Neolithic in Scotland risks becoming characterised as the product either of indigenous cultural impetus or of external economic introduction. In reality, the processes unfolding across the early centuries of the fourth millennium are likely to have involved extremely complex interactions among indigenous communities and groups of people arriving from different parts of northwestern Europe, with a whole range of social strategies being carried forward and interwoven, to a greater or lesser extent, in landscapes of widely different character. These are human engagements which take place in specific times and places, among specific communities with their own individual histories – as such, we should expect a 'bricolage of re-forming identities' (Barrett 2005, 122). And there is certainly time for this to happen: we may see the transition as rapid from the chronologically imprecise perspective forced upon us until very recently by radiocarbon technology, but as Rowley-Conwy notes (2004, 106), in terms of human generations and communal memory, two or three hundred years is a long expanse of time. We would be naïve to expect that the evidence currently at our disposal – despite the considerable augmentations of recent years – yet allows us to tease out all the intricacies of these human histories.

3.5 Biographies of people and place

Shannon Fraser

Ethnographic studies of human dwellings illustrate the vast complexity of ways in which a structure can both enfold within itself and perpetuate a cosmological framework in which people, landscapes both animate and inanimate, spiritual forces and notions of time all find their proper place. Whether a tent (*e.g.* Humphrey 1995) or a substantial, permanent building (*e.g.* Hugh-Jones 1979; 1996; Bloch 1995), in their materiality and the organisation of activity within and around them, these structures can express a symbolic universe. Whether we envisage the Warren Field building to have been a permanent dwelling, a periodic meeting place or a combination of the two, it is likely to have been anchored in a social framework of meaning connecting its inhabitants with the physical and metaphysical world around them.

The positioning of the building, with the ground falling away locally to east, south and west, would seem chosen to accentuate its mass and monumentality and its visibility from a distance, particularly in a relatively open landscape of hazel scrub and cultivated areas. If the palaeochannel curving round the hall to north and west had greater definition in the fourth millennium BC, as Tipping suggests (chapter 1.2), this effect would have been even more marked. But the near east-west orientation of the building – which it shares with the hall at Balbridie – may be tied in to a wider world. At a general level, the sun and moon traverse the sky each day from east to west, from the sea to the mountains, tracing the passage of the seasons. Around midsummer, light from the rising and setting sun might have penetrated the possible entrances in the northeast and northwest corners of the building.

If the speculated sequence of construction is correct (Murray and Murray chapter 3.3) – that the two axial posts within the building, of probable symbolic nature, may have been erected before the rest of the structure was raised – they provide a measurable alignment against the horizon. It was thus possible to test for a more specific reference to celestial movements embodied in the hall. Using the same search methodology outlined with reference to the pit alignment (chapter 2.3), with the azimuths of the axial post alignment at 72.3°±1.0° and 252.3°±1.0° with respect to astronomical north, Smith and Higginbottom (2008) determined that the hall's axis was not established with reference to any significant phenomena that we can recognise.

The materiality of the hall may have been linked to other natural cycles. Just a few minutes walk away, the river Dee flows from its source in the west, eastwards to the sea. It has its own seasonal rhythms, of spate and low water, of the salmon and sea trout which travel westwards to its high reaches and back down to the sea through spring, summer and autumn. Stretching back into later prehistory, the early or pre-Celtic root of the river's name is *deua*, referring to a female divinity. The Dee may have had symbolic attributes in even deeper antiquity, which may also have played a part in frameworks of reference encapsulated within the building.

Referring to the southern part of the hall at Claish Farm, Ian Ralston likened the effect of the density of posts to that of a forest with a roof (Barclay, Brophy and MacGregor 2002, 104). It is certainly possible that metaphorical links existed among the timbers used in the Warren Field building – structural, decorative and symbolic alike – and living trees in the surrounding woodlands. The form, characteristics and properties of different species may have had symbolic as well as practical values, both of which will have been drawn upon in the choice of wood for particular elements of the building and objects used inside it, and which will have contributed to the meanings embedded within it. Even today, trees such as the rowan and the hawthorn are considered by some to have protective qualities; the early Neolithic may have seen more multi-layered symbolic relationships among trees and people.

Some of these relationships were new and likely caught up in the complex interactions among indigenous communities and potential incomers. For example, the extent of interference in the woodland in the creation of the buildings at Balbridie and Warren Field was certainly entirely unprecedented – at most only a handful of trees would ever have been converted into structural timber before this time. And as the

pollen evidence indicates, clearance around the hall was of a much greater scale than that required for construction, producing an open landscape which, to date, has no contemporary regional parallels at all (Lancaster, chapter 3.2; Davies, Tipping and McCulloch 2007; Tipping *et al.* 2009). The management of domesticated cattle or sheep/ goats will have introduced further new elements into the woodland context: they may have grazed in the open hazel woods at the margins of this cleared area, or perhaps even further afield, given the scarcity of clear grazing indicators amongst the herbaceous pollen. Other areas of woodland may have been opened up to provide pasture.

We may also catch a glimpse of the metaphorical links among the building, its inhabitants and the moral and physical universe in which their lives were carried forward, for example in the formal deposit in pit 89, towards the western end. Here we see the burning and deposition of lithic and plant resources – the latter both wild and cultivated – which represent the activities of varied seasons and places (discussed in chapter 3.1). The meanings embedded within the hall are caught up

Figure 28. The timber hall during excavation in 2005, looking south. (© Charles Murray)

in a network of places near and far: locations for fishing; for obtaining stone and clay; for cultivating cereals; for hunting or for gathering foodstuffs; for grazing and for milking stock; for meeting other people, exchanging news and materials from further afield; for obtaining guidance from ancestral or spiritual sources. Included among these are temporary campsites, small settlement sites like that at Garthdee, monumental long cairns, timber enclosures and cursus monuments. Similarly, the act of constructing and maintaining the hall would have drawn on the activities of people of different age and sex, perhaps of different lineage, in different parts of the landscape – obtaining, working and setting up the timbers, collecting the materials for and creating the roof and partitions, perhaps filling the gaps between timbers or decorating the building.

All of these contributions would serve to define and sustain people's different roles in society and community, embodied in the physicality of the building (*cf.* Edmonds 1999; Finlay 2000). So too the hall as a 'theatre of experience' (Barrett 2006) will have contributed to the creation, constraint and elaboration of people's understanding of how the world is. That different possibilities were available, for example, in the direction of movement around the symbolic posts at both ends of the building, before entry into the central areas, has been noted above. Precise routes of movement into the building, within it and out again, may well have depended on who you were – your age, sex and status, your kinship, your particular role in the community – and the nature of activities that might be underway at a particular point in time, from routine to ceremonial. A similar framework of social convention would govern the location of various activities within the building, their timing, and the composition of the groups that undertook them. Interwoven with the metaphorical links to other aspects of the lived world embodied within the building, this will have expressed the identity of groups and individuals as participants in a recognised 'order of things'.

The hall itself will have had its own identity, perhaps its own name. Given its potential longevity (Marshall, chapter 5) and indeed its novelty in this landscape, it would be woven into the stories about the history of the land and its people. In another time and place, the epic of Beowulf describes Heorot, the hall of Hrothgar, thus:

> The hall towered,
> its gables wide and high and awaiting
> a barbarous burning. That doom abided,
> but in time it would come... .
> *Beowulf*, lines 22–5 (trans. S. Heaney)

In a different way, being a probable act of its inhabitants rather than the product of accident or aggression, the deliberate burning of the Warren Field hall may also have been implicit in its biography from its conception. Fitting into a pattern of conflagration at timber structures of monumental scale in the Scottish early Neolithic, this may have marked the transition from one kind of place to another, recognised from the very beginning as a stage through which it would pass when the appropriate time arrived. References to the transformational nature of fire appear already to have been incorporated into the fabric of the building – in the pre-construction burning of timbers which, as well as a functional aspect, may have had symbolic resonance; in the burnt materials placed in pit 89; and, perhaps, in the burnt flint and pitchstone deposited in pit 90.

As part of the story of the place and its meaning, therefore, the 'afterlife' of the hall may have been a part of people's lives for some time to come. That the hall ceased to be a vessel for physical activity does not necessarily signify the end of a human connection to the site, a point brought sharply into focus by the history of the adjacent pit alignment. The possibility that elements removed before burning carried the essence of the hall into the fabric of new structures – the axial posts, or perhaps other features – has been considered above, as has the substantial nature of what may have remained of the hall after burning. The identity of the place may thus have been drawn forward in the physicality of what, for a time, remained *in* place and that which took on a new role elsewhere. At the same time, memories of the hall, its relationship to what had gone before, and its dramatic end will have been woven into communal history.

Chapter 4

The local context: other sites on the Crathes Castle Estate

4.1 Other features in the Warren Field

Hilary Murray and Charles Murray

The project design included evaluation of the wider environment between and near the timber building (Fig. 1: Area 1) and the pit alignment (Area 3, incorporating Areas 2–7). In total seven other trenches (Areas 8–14), with a total area of 387m² were excavated, each targeted on anomalies that were visible on the 1976 aerial photographs (Fig. 2). The results showed that some of these anomalies were natural features, others were modern pits. Only in Area 10 were there possible early prehistoric features. However, these could not be dated and there were no artefacts. This lack of apparent prehistoric activity was also reflected in the negative results of fieldwalking in 1991 (Begg and Hewitt 1991). However, the pollen results (Davies, Tipping and McCulloch 2007) suggest that much of this area may in fact have been cultivated ground during the early Neolithic and further settlement might be expected to be beyond this. A small site at Crathes Castle Overflow Car Park and a pottery find in Milton Wood have yielded some evidence for such settlement.

Area 8

A trench 2.5m × 25m was excavated to investigate a large anomaly on the 1976 aerial photographs. This proved to be sediment in a dip in the natural ground surface, 0.10m deep and c.4.7m east/west across the trench. It appeared to be a natural feature.

Area 9

A trench 2.5m × 25m was excavated to investigate several small anomalies on the 1976 aerial photographs. One of these proved to be a small modern pit with a fill of plough soil containing a sherd of twentieth century china. A small, apparently natural dip filled with fine brown silt was also sectioned.

Area 10

A trench 25m long and varying in width between 2.5m and 4.5m was excavated to investigate several anomalies on the 1976 aerial photographs. A line of five post-pits extended almost 10m across the trench from northwest to southeast. They were spaced between 2m and 2.5m apart. With the exception of one which had been damaged by burrowing, they were between 0.50m and 0.70m in diameter and between 0.15m and 0.33m in surviving depth. Three had stone packing but only one had a post shadow, c.0.13m in diameter. There was no datable material in the fills and no associated artefacts. However, they are unlikely to be modern fencing as the posts had been dug in, not driven. By analogy with the small post-pits beside the pit alignment and the post-pits of Neolithic date from the Crathes Castle Overflow Car Park site (chapter 4.2), these could be prehistoric, but this cannot be proved. Apart from burrow damage, the top of one post-pit had a plough furrow mark running across it, emphasising the vulnerability of these smaller features.

Area 11

A trench 2.4m × 15m was excavated to investigate several small anomalies on the 1976 aerial photographs. No features were observed.

Area 12

A trench 2.2m × 15m was excavated to investigate several small anomalies on the 1976 aerial photographs. No features were observed.

Area 13

A trench 2.3m × 12m was excavated to investigate several small anomalies on the 1976 aerial photographs. Some appeared to be the result of extensive animal burrows. A small oval pit 1.05 × 0.65m was excavated. The full depth was *c.*0.60m, with the basal 0.10m sealed by a flat boulder which almost filled the pit and which appeared to have been wedged in position by several smaller stones and a lump of vitrified matter. The lower fill included charred cereal grains identified as hulled barley and oats (Timpany 2006b). Hulled barley, rye and possible emmer wheat grains were identified with other degraded grains among abundant charcoal fragments and a small number of unidentifiable burnt bone fragments from the upper fill above the blocking stone. Two of the grains from the basal fill were radiocarbon dated, giving conflicting dates (SUERC-12267: 370–110 cal BC and SUERC-12268: 1290–1410 cal AD). As there was some disturbance of the upper fill by burrowing there is a strong possibility of later material having been introduced into an earlier context so the date of the pit must remain uncertain.

Area 14

A trench 2.3m × 12m was excavated to investigate several small anomalies on the 1976 aerial photographs. One of these was a small pit 1.4m × 1m and 0.15m deep. The fill was slightly organic in content and included a sherd of nineteenth or early twentieth century white-glazed pottery and fragments of coal. A very large, deep pit, over 3.5m × 2.3m was not fully excavated. It appeared to have been machine dug and may have been a livestock burial or similar.

4.2 Neolithic features on the Crathes Castle Overflow Car Park site

Hilary Murray and Charles Murray

In March 2005, a new car park was created on rising ground *c.*300m north of the Warren Field (Fig. 1). Archaeological observation of the topsoil stripping of an area 25m × 51m revealed a number of very truncated features close to the crest of the hill. Six of these contained flint (Warren, chapter 6.3) or early Neolithic pottery (Sheridan, chapter 6.1) in a charcoal-rich, silty fill; another feature with a similar fill was probably contemporary. They ranged in size between *c.*0.83m in diameter and 0.28m surviving depth and *c.*0.40m in diameter and 0.13m surviving depth. A small number of other features lacked the charcoal-rich fill and may or may not be associated. The very truncated nature of these features makes interpretation difficult; they may have been post-pits but the evidence is insufficient to suggest if they had formed part of a structure.

This indication of previously unknown, early Neolithic activity in close proximity to the Warren Field sites is extremely important. The pottery, which includes part of a modified carinated bowl, suggests that these traces of settlement may be marginally later than the Warren Field timber hall (Sheridan, chapter 6.1). However, the site serves to highlight the fact that the apparent isolation of early Neolithic timber halls in Scotland may be a product of the restricted geographical focus of previous excavations, particularly as such slight, truncated features are not revealed as cropmarks, even in the best conditions.

4.3 Milton Wood

The possibility of other foci of Neolithic activity in the vicinity has been further emphasised in 2008 by the find of a single early Neolithic pottery sherd some 200m southwest of the timber hall during the observation of tree planting pits in Milton Wood (Fig. 1) on another part of the Crathes Castle Estate (Murray and Murray 2008).

Chapter 5

Radiocarbon dating

5.1 The radiocarbon dating of the pit alignment and the timber hall

Peter Marshall

Introduction

Thirty-eight radiocarbon age determinations have been obtained on samples of carbonised wood and charred plant remains from Warren Field, Crathes. A more extensive report is in archive (Marshall 2007).

Methods

The samples were submitted to the Scottish Universities Environmental Research Centre, East Kilbride (SUERC) and pre-treated following standard procedures, graphitised following the methods outlined in Slota *et al.* (1987), and measured by Accelerator Mass Spectrometry according to Xu *et al.* (2004).

The laboratory maintains a continual programme of quality assurance procedures, in addition to participation in international inter-comparisons (Scott 2003) which indicate no laboratory offsets and demonstrate the validity of the precision quoted.

Results

The radiocarbon results are given in Tables 5 and 6, and are quoted in accordance with the international standard known as the Trondheim convention (Stuiver and Kra 1986). They are conventional radiocarbon ages (Stuiver and Polach 1977).

Calibration

The calibrations of the results, relating the radiocarbon measurements directly to calendar dates, are given in Tables 5 and 6, and in Figures 29 and 31. All have been calculated using the calibration curve of Reimer *et al.* (2004) and the computer program OxCal (v3.10) (Bronk Ramsey 1995; 1998; 2001). The calibrated date ranges cited in the text are those for 95% confidence. They are quoted in the form recommended by Mook (1986), with the end points rounded outwards to 10 years. The ranges quoted in italics are *posterior density estimates* derived from mathematical modelling of archaeological problems (see below). The ranges in plain type have been calculated according to the maximum intercept method (Stuiver and Reimer 1986). All other ranges are derived from the probability method (Stuiver and Reimer 1993).

Methodological approach

A Bayesian approach has been adopted for the interpretation of the chronology from this site (Buck, Cavanagh and Litton 1996). Although the simple calibrated dates are accurate estimates of the dates of the samples, this is usually not what archaeologists really wish to know. It is the dates of the archaeological events, which are represented by those samples, which are of interest. In the case of Warren Field, it is the chronology of the use of the hall and the pit alignment that is under consideration, not the calibrated dates of the individual samples (Bayliss *et al.* 2007). The dates of this activity can be estimated not only using the absolute dating information from the radiocarbon measurements on the samples, but also by using the stratigraphic relationships between samples.

Fortunately, methodology is now available which allows the combination of these different types of information explicitly, to produce realistic estimates of the dates of archaeological interest. It should be emphasised that the *posterior density estimates* produced by this modelling are not absolute. They are interpretative *estimates*, which can and will change as further data become available and as other researchers choose to model the existing data from different perspectives.

The technique used is a form of Markov Chain Monte Carlo sampling, and has been applied using the program OxCal v3.10 (http://www.rlaha.ox.ac.uk/), which uses a mixture of the Metropolis-Hastings algorithm and the more specific Gibbs sampler (Gilks, Richardson and Spiegelhalter 1996; Gelfand and Smith 1990). Details of the algorithms employed by this program are available from the on-line manual or in Bronk Ramsey (1995; 1998;

2001). The algorithm used in the model described below can be derived from the structures shown in Fig. 32.

The pit alignment
Samples and sequences (Fig. 29 and Table 5)

Pit 19
A single sample (SUERC-10075) came from 19/5, a black charcoal-rich deposit at the base of the pit that is interpreted as a 'single-event' deposit (Fig. 3).

Pit 18
A single sample (SUERC-10077) came from 18/3,

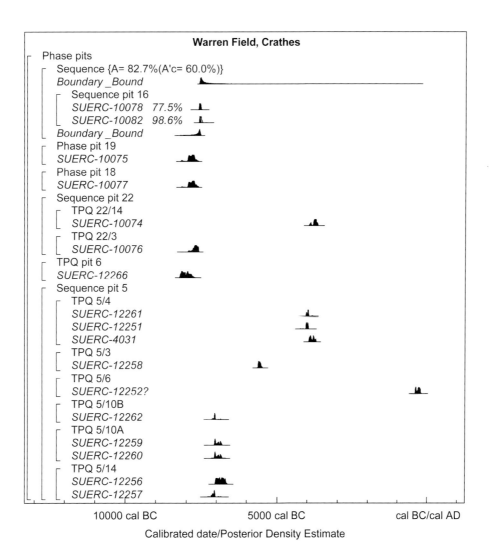

Figure 29. Probability distributions of dates from Warren Field pit alignment. Each distribution represents the relative probability that an event occurred at a particular time. These distributions are the result of simple radiocarbon calibration (Stuiver and Reimer 1993)

Table 5. Radiocarbon dates from the pit alignment

Laboratory Number	Context	Context Interpretation	Sample type	Radiocarbon Age (BP)	δ¹³C (‰)	Calibrated date (95% confidence)	Posterior Density Estimate (95% probability)
SUERC-10077	18/03	primary fill pit 18	Charcoal; hazel	8765±40	-25.9	7970–7610 cal BC	-
SUERC-12262	05/10B	early fill pit 5	Charcoal; birch and hazel	8080±35	-23.6	7180–6830 cal BC	-
SUERC-12257	05/14	primary fill pit 5	Charcoal; alder	8100±40	-24.1	7260–6840 cal BC	-
SUERC-12258	05/03	upper fill pit 5	Charcoal; oak	6635±35	-26.0	5630–5490 cal BC	-
SUERC-12259	05/10A	primary fill pit 5	Charcoal; birch	8040±40	-23.8	7080–6810 cal BC	-
SUERC-12252	05/06	rabbit burrow from behind section?	Charcoal; oak	2245±35	-24.7	400–200 cal BC	-
SUERC-12260	05/10A	primary fill pit 5	Charcoal; willow/poplar	8040±40	-24.3	7080–6810 cal BC	-
SUERC-12261	05/04	final fill pit 5	Charcoal; oak	5170±35	-25.2	4050–3810 cal BC	-
SUERC-12256	05/14	primary fill pit 5	Charcoal; alder	7945±40	-24.2	7040–6690 cal BC	-
SUERC-12266	06/11	primary fill pit 6	Charcoal; willow/poplar and hazel	8850±40	-26.1	8210–7790 cal BC	-
SUERC-10074	22/14	final fill pit 22	Wheat	4975±45	-22.6	3940–3650 cal BC	-
SUERC-10076	22/03	primary fill pit 22	Hazelnut	8710±40	-28.4	7940–7590 cal BC	-
SUERC-10078	16/03	primary fill pit 16	Charcoal; alder/hazel	8530±40	-24.6	7600–7525 cal BC	7590–7510 cal BC
SUERC-10082	16/06	primary fill pit 16	Charcoal; hazel	8460±40	-27.3	7590–7480 cal BC	7590–7530 cal BC
SUERC-12251	05/04	final fill pit 5	Charcoal; oak	5200±35	-25.4	4160–3950 cal BC	-
SUERC-4031	05/04	final fill pit 5	Charcoal; oak	5025±35	-25.8	3950–3700 cal BC	-
SUERC-10075	19/05	primary fill pit 19	Charcoal; alder/hazel	8755±40	-25.1	7960–7610 cal BC	-

a black charcoal-rich layer up to 100mm thick that had either been deposited as a single event or slipped in from the northern edge of the pit (Fig. 3).

Pit 16

The two samples (SUERC-10082 and SUERC-10078) came from 16/6, a black charcoal-rich deposit at the base of the pit, and (16/3), a similar, stratigraphically later deposit (Fig. 3). The radiocarbon results are in good agreement with the stratigraphy ($A_{overall}$=82.7%).

Pit 22

Two samples were submitted from this pit, from 22/3, a silty layer towards the base (SUERC-10076) and from 22/14, a smaller pit that cut pit 22 (SUERC-10074) (Fig. 3). Given the lack of a direct functional relationship between the samples and the contexts from which they came (*i.e.* they are not from discrete dumps or single event deposits (such as those from pits 16, 18 and 19) they only provide *termini post quos* (*tpq*) for their contexts.

Pit 6

A single sample (SUERC-12266) was dated from 6/11, a primary fill of the pit (Fig. 3). Given the charcoal could be residual the result provides a *tpq* for the subsequent infilling and recutting of the feature.

Pit 5

Ten samples were dated from pit 5 (Fig. 3). The two measurements from soil 5/14 are not statistically consistent (T'=7.5; ν=1; T'(5%)=3.8; Ward and Wilson 1978) and therefore represent material of different ages, however, given the 'soil' would probably have taken a considerable period of time to develop this is not surprising. Given the possibility that the charcoal may have been residual, the measurements only provide *tpq* for the context. The two measurements (SUERC-12259 and SUERC-12260) from a sandy gravel, interpreted as slippage from the upcast of the pit are statistically consistent (T'=0.0; ν=1; T'(5%)=3.8; Ward and Wilson 1978) and could therefore be of the same actual age. However, given the possibility that the charcoal may again be residual the results only provide *tpq*.

The measurements from 5/10B (SUERC-12262), 5/6 (SUERC-12252), 5/3 (SUERC-12258) and 5/4 (SUERC-4031, SUERC-12251 and SUERC-12261) also only provide *tpq* for their contexts. The charcoal from 5/10B is from upcast gravel that slipped into the pit and could therefore be residual, while all the other samples are oak and could therefore have an unknown age at death offset.

Interpretation

The three measurements on primary fills that are interpreted as not being *tpq* (*i.e.* pits 16, 18 and

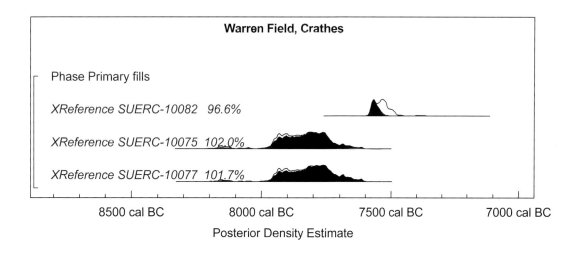

Figure 30. Probability distributions of dates from Warren Field pit alignment (primary fills of pits 16, 19 and 18): each distribution represents the relative probability that an event occurred at some particular time. For each of the radiocarbon measurements two distributions have been plotted: one in outline, which is the result of simple radiocarbon calibration and a solid one, which is based on the chronological model used. The distributions are derived from the model defined in Figure 29

19) are not statistically consistent (T'=39.5; ν=2; T'(5%)=6.0; Ward and Wilson 1978), however, those from pits 18 and 19 are (T'=0.0; ν=1; T'(5%)=3.8; Ward and Wilson 1978). This strongly suggests two chronologically separate periods of pit digging (Fig. 30) in the first half of the eighth millennium cal BC. Further analysis estimates that the interval between the episodes is *70–610 years (95% probability)* and most probably *190–370 years (68% probability)*.

The best estimates for digging on pits 5, 6, and 22 (all *tpq*) are:

Pit 5; 7040–6690 cal BC (SUERC-12256)
Pit 6; 8210–7790 cal BC (SUERC-12266)
Pit 22; 7940–7590 cal BC (SUERC-10076).

Although the recuts with Neolithic dates from pits 5 and 22 might be evidence of re-use by people using the hall, we cannot be certain of this given the dating evidence available. The three samples

from pit 5 are all identified as oak (and therefore could be effected by an unknown age at death offset), while the cereal grain from pit 22 could, given its size be intrusive, or given its context residual.

The timber hall

Samples, sequence and results (Fig. 31 and Table 6)

The three oak samples (SUERC-4044, SUERC-4048–4049) submitted in 2004 (posts 3, 43 and 46) were not taken from the outside of the posts and therefore may have a considerable age at death offset (Bowman 1990). For this reason they only provide a *tpq* for their use.

Samples submitted in 2005 from posts 13, 144 (north and south side) and 11 (SUERC-10084, SUERC-10087–10088, SUERC-10092) were also

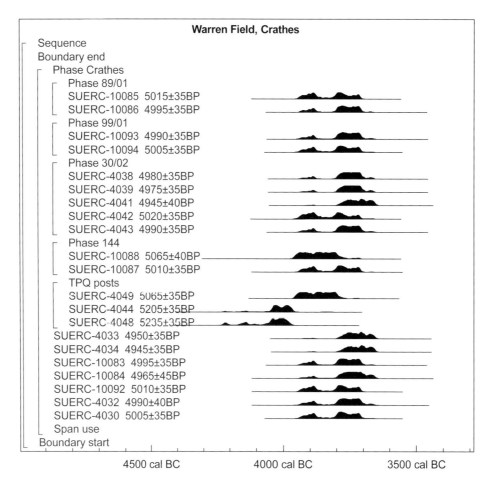

Figure 31. Probability distributions of dates from Warren Field timber hall. Each distribution represents the relative probability that an event occurred at a particular time. These distributions are the result of simple radiocarbon calibration (Stuiver and Reimer 1993)

Table 6. *Radiocarbon dates from the timber hall*

Laboratory Number	Context	Context Interpretation	Sample type	Radiocarbon Age (BP)	δ¹³C (‰)	Calibrated date (95% confidence)	Posterior Density Estimate (95% probability)
SUERC-10085	89/01	upper fill post-pit	Wheat	5015±35	-24.1	3950–3700 cal BC	3800–3710 cal BC
SUERC-10084	13	post 13 external wood	Charcoal; oak	4965±45	-25.5	3940–3640 cal BC	3800–3710 cal BC
SUERC-4049	46/02	post 46. Not external wood?	Charcoal; oak	5065±35	-25.0	3960–3780 cal BC	–
SUERC-10086	89/01	upper fill post-pit	Wheat	4995±35	-24.1	3940–3660 cal BC	3800–3710 cal BC
SUERC-10087	144	post 144 N side. External wood	Charcoal; oak	5010±35	-26.1	3950–3700 cal BC	3800–3710 cal BC
SUERC-10088	144	post 144 S side. External wood	Charcoal; oak	5065±40	-25.9	3970–3770 cal BC	3810–3710 cal BC
SUERC-10092	11	post 11 external wood	Charcoal; ash	5010±35	-24.8	3950–3700 cal BC	3800–3710 cal BC
SUERC-10093	99/01	infill of post pipe	Barley	4990±35	-23.5	3940–3660 cal BC	3800–3710 cal BC
SUERC-10094	99/01	infill of post pipe	Wheat	5005±35	-25.9	3950–3700 cal BC	3800–3710 cal BC
SUERC-4030	8/02	infill of post pipe	Barley	5005±35	-25.0	3950–3700 cal BC	3800–3710 cal BC
SUERC-4044	3/02	post 3. Possibly not external wood	Charcoal; oak	5205±35	-26.8	4220–3950 cal BC	–
SUERC-10083	50/03	secondary fill axial pit	Hazelnut	4995±35	-24.6	3940–3660 cal BC	3800–3710 cal BC
SUERC-4032	11/02	infill of post pipe	Emmer	4990±40	-22.7	3940–3660 cal BC	3800–3710 cal BC
SUERC-4048	43/04	post 43. Not external wood?	Charcoal; oak	5235±35	-25.4	4220–3960 cal BC	–
SUERC-4043	30/02	destruction fill axial pit 30?	Charcoal; alder	4990±35	-26.4	3940–3660 cal BC	3800–3710 cal BC
SUERC-4042	30/02	destruction fill axial pit 30?	Charcoal; alder	5020±35	-27.4	3950–3700 cal BC	3800–3710 cal BC
SUERC-4041	30/02	destruction fill axial pit 30?	Charcoal; alder/hazel	4945±40	-25.7	3800–3640 cal BC	3790–3710 cal BC
SUERC-4039	30/02	destruction fill axial pit 30?	Charcoal; alder	4975±35	-26.1	3910–3650 cal BC	3800–3710 cal BC
SUERC-4038	30/02	destruction fill axial pit 30?	Bread/club wheat	4980±35	-24.3	3940–3660 cal BC	3800–3710 cal BC
SUERC-4034	11/06	backfill of post-pit	Barley	4945±35	-23.8	3790–3650 cal BC	3790–3710 cal BC
SUERC-4033	11/05	backfill of post-pit	Emmer	4950±35	-24.5	3800–3650 cal BC	3790–3710 cal BC

oak, but were taken from the outside of the posts, and probably represent sapwood from just below the bark. The two measurements from post 144 (SUERC-10087–10088) are statistically consistent (T'=2.8; v=1; T'(5%)=3.8; Ward and Wilson 1978) and could therefore be the same age.

The remaining samples came from the fills of post-pits (8, 11, 89 and 99) and axial pits (30 and 50). Charcoal from the fill of post-pits is interpreted as relating to the use of structures rather than its construction, as suggested by experimental archaeology (Reynolds 1995). If possible, duplicate samples from these contexts were submitted to test

the assumption that the material was of the same actual age.

The following duplicate measurements are statistically consistent and could therefore be of the same actual age.

Post-pit 89 (SUERC-10085 and SUERC-10086); (T'=0.2; v=1; T'(5%)=3.8; Ward and Wilson 1978). Post-pipe 99 (SUERC-10093 and SUERC-10094); (T'=0.1; v=1; T'(5%)=3.8; Ward and Wilson 1978). Axial pit 30 (SUERC-4038–4043); T'=2.1; v=4; (T'(5%)=9.5; Ward and Wilson 1978).

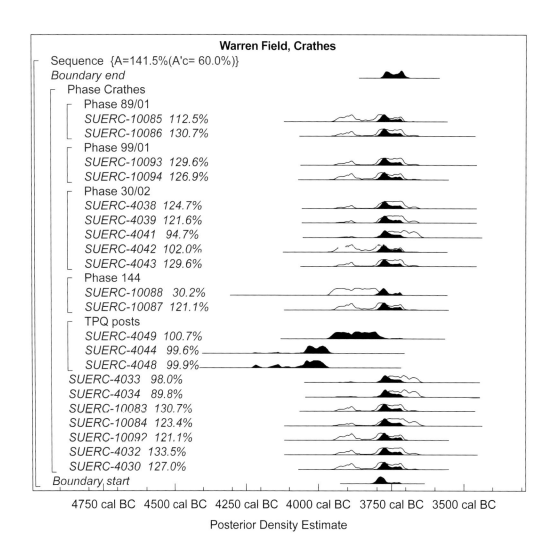

Figure 32. Probability distributions of dates from Warren Field timber hall. Each distribution represents the relative probability that an event occurred at some particular time. For each of the radiocarbon measurements two distributions have been plotted: one in outline, which is the result of simple radiocarbon calibration and a solid one, which is based on the chronological model used. The other distributions correspond to aspects of the model. For example, the distribution 'Boundary start' is the estimated date for the start of use of the hall. The large square brackets down the left hand side along with the OxCal keywords define the overall model exactly

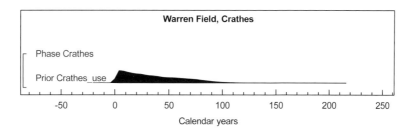

Figure 33. Probability distribution of the number of years during which the Warren Field timber hall was in use. The distribution is derived from the model defined in Figure 32

Table 7. Posterior density estimates of archaeological events and spans of use for three Neolithic halls

Site	Estimated start (95% probability)	Estimated start (68% probability)	Estimated end (95% probability)	Estimated end (68% probability)	Estimated span (95% probability)	Estimated span (68% probability)
Crathes	3820–3720 cal BC	3810–3760 cal BC	3780–3690 cal BC	3780–3700 cal BC	1–90 years	1–50 years
Balbridie	4000–3480 cal BC	3810–3590 cal BC (57%)	3730–3310 cal BC	3730–3310 cal BC	1–350 years	1–190 years
Claish	3770–3650 cal BC	3720–3670 cal BC	3700–3620 cal BC	3680–3640 cal BC	1–100 years	1–50 years

All the measurements from the hall, apart from those not taken from the outside of structural posts (SUERC-4044, SUERC-4048–4049) are statistically consistent (T'=13.5; ν=17; T'(5%)=27.6; Ward and Wilson 1978) which might mean that all the dated samples are exactly the same age. However, it is possible that if all the activity that resulted in them took place over a relatively short period of time such a group of results could be produced.

The model shown in Fig. 32, based on the assumption that the hall was in continuous use for a period of time (Buck, Cavanagh and Litton 1996), shows good agreement ($A_{overall}$=141.5%) between the radiocarbon results and stratigraphy (in this case the hypothesis that all the measurements come from a single phase of activity). An overall agreement index of 60% is recommended as the threshold for showing consistency between the prior information and the radiocarbon results (Bayliss *et al.* 2007; Bronk Ramsey 1995).

The model (Fig. 32) provides estimates for the start of the use of the hall of *3820–3720 cal BC (95% probability; Boundary start)* and very probably *3810–3760 cal BC (68% probability)* and the end of use of *3780–3690 cal BC (95% probability; Boundary end)* and very probably *3780–3700 cal BC (68% probability)*. The span of use of the hall (Fig. 33) is estimated at *1–90 years (95% probability)* and probably *1–50 years (68% probability)*. Given the

shape of the probability distributions for the start and use of the building (they both have pronounced tails), I as stated above believe the 68% probabilities given are probably the best estimates for the date of construction and duration of use of the hall.

Chronology of Scottish timber halls
Figures 34–35 and Table 7 summarise estimates for the start, end and span of use of the Neolithic halls from Warren Field, Balbridie, and Claish obtained by mathematical modelling.

Analysis shows that the hall at Warren Field almost certainly went out of use before the construction of that at Claish (*82.5% probability*), and therefore it is unlikely that they were contemporary. On the basis of the published results from Balbridie, analysis suggests a *72.9% probability* that the hall there was constructed before the one at Warren Field, however, submission of a more reliable suite of short-lived, single entity samples for radiocarbon dating are required to confirm this preliminary hypothesis (Ashmore 1999).

The halls at Warren Field and Claish had very short spans of use (estimated at *1–50 years; 68% probability*) and this parallels evidence from Parc Bryn Cegin, Llandygai (Fig. 35) where the Neolithic building was probably in use for *40–110 years (68% probability)* (Marshall *et al.* 2007).

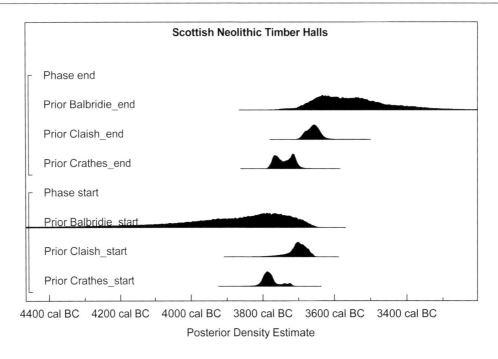

Figure 34. Probability distributions of dates for three Scottish Neolithic halls (start and end of use). Note the tails on the Balbridie distributions have been truncated to enable detailed examination of the highest areas of probability

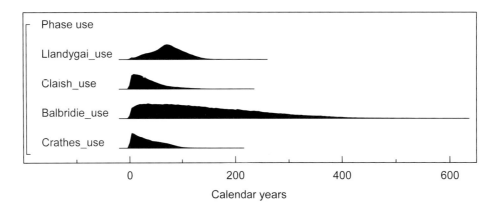

Figure 35. Probability distribution of the number of years during which four Neolithic halls were in use

Chapter 6

The finds

The following reports include the finds from all the sites considered in this volume. Most of the finds, including pottery and lithics, were from the timber hall; these were all plotted on site and their distribution is shown on Fig. 36. No pottery was found in the excavated pits of the pit alignment and lithics were only found in alignment pit 5. No prehistoric finds were associated with any of the smaller Warren Field sites (Murray and Murray, chapter 4.1). Pottery and lithics from the Crathes Castle Overflow Car Park site (Murray and Murray, chapter 4.2) and the single sherd of pottery from Milton Wood (Murray and Murray, chapter 4.3) are discussed here. A discussion of the results of the organic residue analysis of selected pottery samples from both the Warren Field timber hall and the Crathes Castle Overflow Car Park site follows the report on the pottery.

Throughout all reports the contexts are identified as 5/1 (etc) and small finds as SF 123 (etc).

All finds have been deposited in Marischal Museum, University of Aberdeen.

6.1 The pottery

Alison Sheridan

Introduction

The Warren Field pottery (which was all found inside or near the timber hall, Fig. 36), is a small assemblage, comprising just 133 sherds and six fragments (*i.e.* pieces less than 10mm × 10mm in size) and weighing only *c.*550g; the size of the sherds is also small, the largest being only 87mm × 51mm. Nevertheless, it is clear that numerous vessels are represented. The homogeneity in fabric, finish and colour and the small sherd size make

it hard to arrive at a definitive estimate of the total number of vessels, but a tentative estimate of between 45 and 52 can be proposed. In almost every case less than one-twentieth of the vessel is represented. This assemblage can be attributed to an early stage of the Carinated Bowl (henceforth, CB) tradition.

The Crathes Castle Overflow Car Park assemblage is much smaller, consisting of just eight sherds from two vessels, weighing *c.*145g overall. These vessels can also be ascribed to the overall CB tradition, but they constitute an early variant (as seen at Balbridie) – Henshall's so-called 'northeast style' (henceforth CBNE).

During archaeological observation of tree planting pits in Milton Wood near the Warren Field building in 2008 (Murray and Murray 2008 and chapter 4.3), a single sherd of CB pottery was found in a planting pit. Whether this belongs to the early stage of the CB tradition, or to CBNE (or indeed to a later development of the tradition), will be discussed below.

The pottery from the timber hall will be described first, then the Crathes Castle Overflow Car Park material, and finally the Milton Wood sherd. The discussion will cover all the material.

The Warren Field assemblage

Vessel forms, sizes, fabric, finish
and manufacture

A detailed, vessel-by-vessel description of the assemblage is presented in archive (Sheridan 2007a). Despite the small number of 'feature' sherds (such as rimsherds) present, it is clear that both carinated and uncarinated vessel forms are represented, with all but three vessels likely to fall

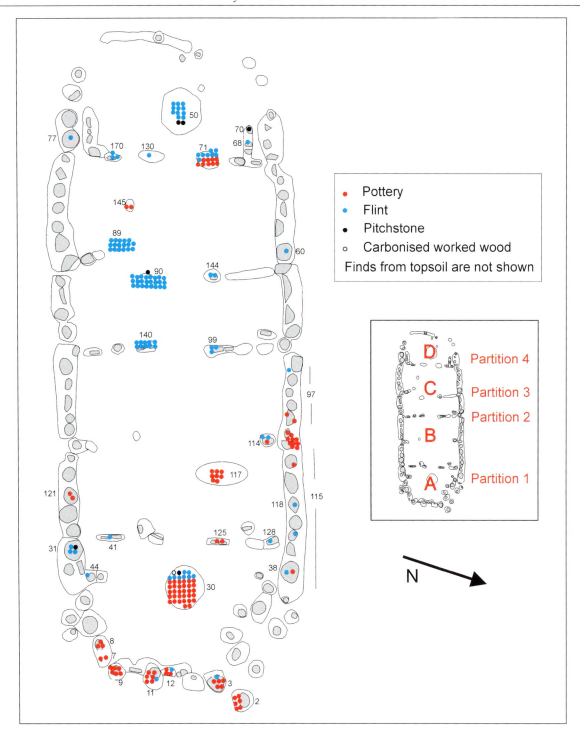

Figure 36. Plan of the Neolithic timber hall showing the distribution of finds. Letters A-D denote areas of the building. The numbers refer to contexts

into the former category. The uncarinated vessels (Pots 23–25) are described below.

Figures 37–41 show the rim profiles and, where reconstructable, the overall body profiles of the carinated bowls. The latter are based on careful examination of sherd profiles and on diameter estimation; rim forms are extrapolated from the range of extant rim forms as shown in Fig. 37, and neck lengths on Pots 12–15 and 18–19 have been extrapolated from similarly-shaped

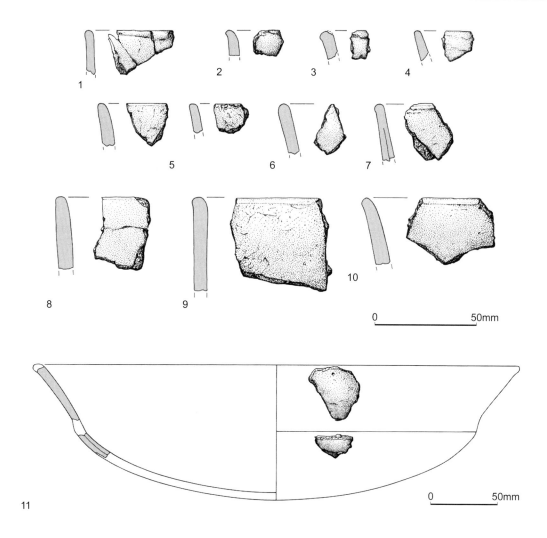

Figure 37. Warren Field: rim profiles for Pots 1–10, and reconstruction of Pot 11 (by Marion O'Neil)

carinated vessels from other 'traditional CB' Scottish assemblages. These vessel reconstructions are likely to encompass the full range of carinated bowl forms present in the assemblage. No example was found of the collared jar form that has been noted as a rare element in comparable assemblages elsewhere (*e.g.* at Claish, Stirling and Biggar Common, South Lanarkshire: Sheridan 2002, illus 19; 1997, illus 17.3).

The vessel forms (which are all round-based) range from shallow-bellied to deep-bellied bowls, with necks that are either virtually upright or that splay, to varying degrees (with Pot 11 having the widest-splaying neck). Rims are simple and rounded, and straight or minimally everted; all would have been shaped by smoothing from the interior outwards, and on Pots 1–3 this has left a

very slight ridge on the exterior. The necks are straight or minimally curving and, in the case of the most widely-splaying examples (*i.e.* Pots 11, 16 and 17), are long and tall in proportion to the belly: the neck of Pot 11 occupies half of the overall estimated height of the vessel. Carinations are very gentle and, in some cases, near-imperceptible; with Pot 14 it would be more accurate to describe the vessel shape as S-profiled. Vessel size, as based on estimated rim diameter, ranges from *c.*140mm (Pot 2) to *c.*360mm (Pot 11), with most vessels falling within the range 170–260mm: in other words, these are medium-sized to large pots. They are also consistently thin-walled – in some cases (as with Pot 1, at just 4.9mm), very thin indeed; if one excludes one anomalous sherd (Pot 22, discussed below), the overall range is 4.3mm to 10.4mm,

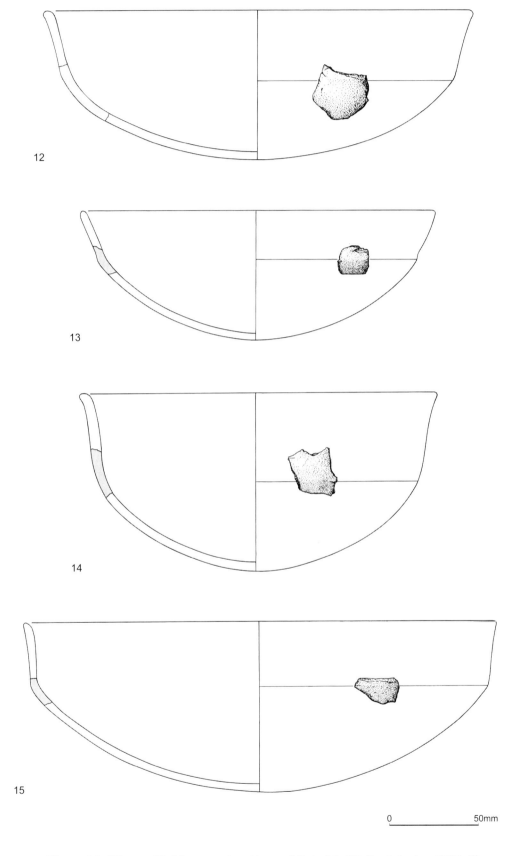

Figure 38. Warren Field: reconstructions of Pots 12–15 (by Marion O'Neil)

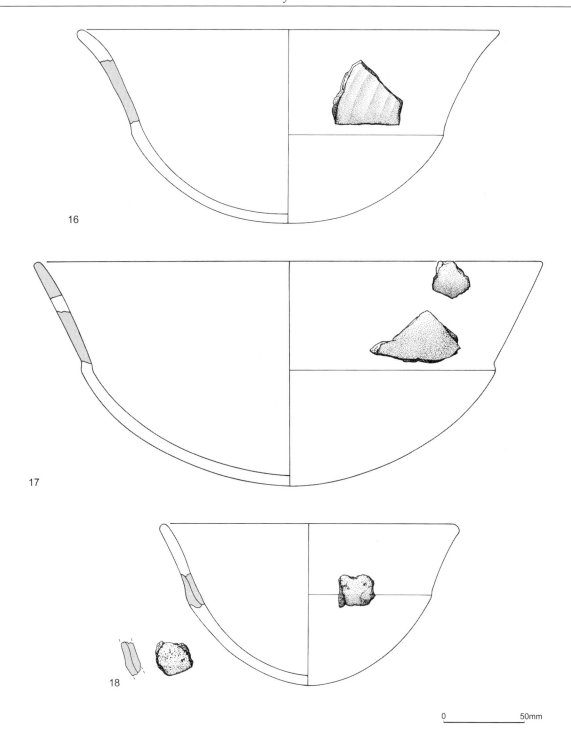

Figure 39. Warren Field: reconstructions of Pots 16–18 (by Marion O'Neil)

with most sherds falling within the 5–8mm range. One feature that has also been noted in other assemblages of the CB tradition (*e.g.* Easterton of Roseisle, Moray; Claish, Stirling; and Eweford, East Lothian: Henshall 1983, 20–22; Sheridan 2002, illus 17.36; Sheridan 2007c) is that sometimes, with a long, splaying neck (as in Pots 11, 16 and 17), the wall thickness decreases towards the bottom of the neck. While this may give weight and stability to a long neck, it also makes for a weak point at, or just above, the carination; and it is here where the pots in question have broken. Notwithstanding

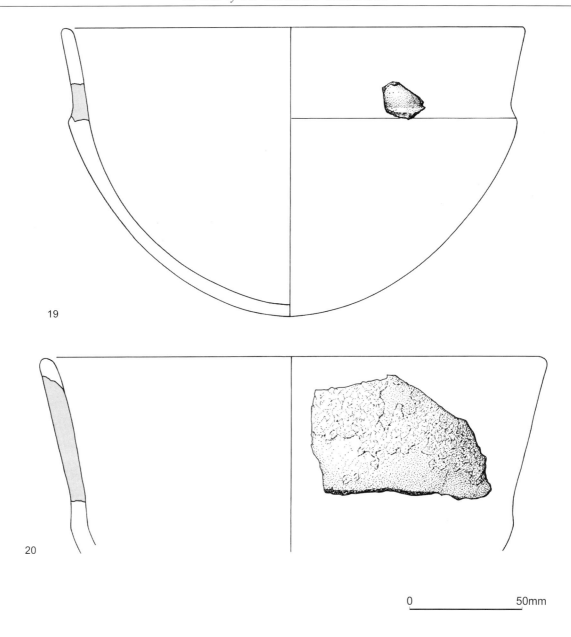

19

20

0 _____ 50mm

Figure 40. Warren Field: reconstructions of Pots 19–20 (by Marion O'Neil)

this design weakness, it is clear that considerable skill has been involved in the manufacture of this pottery: to make a large (or even medium-sized) thin-walled bowl requires experience and *savoir-faire*. It may be that the technique of 'paddle and anvil' had been used in the process: here, a smooth stone is struck against the inside of the pot while a paddle is held against the outside, to thin and extend the wall and to achieve a smoothly-curving wall. The absence of the relevant tool-marks from the Warren Field assemblage may simply mean that they were successfully eradicated; traces

have been noted in the CBNE assemblage from Balbridie (Cowie and Greig forthcoming).

As regards fabric, once more the assemblage shows a marked consistency (excepting Pot 22): it is very fine, with lithic inclusions generally no larger than 2mm × 2mm and at a density of 3% or less. They mostly comprise angular and subangular fragments of a speckly crystalline rock, which has been identified by geologist Fiona McGibbon (pers. comm.) as diorite, and also fragments of its constituent minerals – quartz, feldspar and amphibole. Given the abundance of diorite in

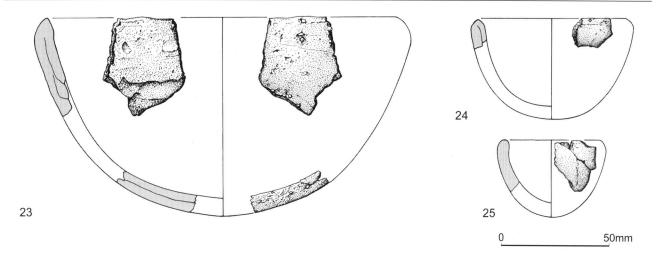

Figure 41. Warren Field: reconstructions of Pots 23–25 (by Marion O'Neil)

Aberdeenshire (with the Insch granite-diorite complex outcropping not far to the northeast of Crathes), this material could well have been obtained locally. Some of these inclusions probably represent material that had been deliberately crushed and added as filler to clay that had probably been refined through levigation; but the smallest fragments may well have been present naturally in the clay, and suggest that the clay is from an area rich in degraded diorite; once more a local source is likely. Regarding finish, with the exception of Pot 22, the surfaces have all been very carefully smoothed and in many cases they have a slip-like appearance, but this could have been produced through careful wet-smoothing, combined with rubbing with a material such as animal skin while the clay was leather-hard, rather than by the application of an actual slip. This treatment may well have produced the low surface sheen noted on the interior and exterior of many sherds (*e.g.* SF 165, Pot 9: Fig. 37); and the occasional presence of tiny mica platelets (once more probably of local origin) lends the surfaces a slightly glittery appearance. In a few cases, a more enhanced surface sheen was achieved through burnishing, at the leather-hard stage, using a pebble or a round-ended spatula of bone or wood. The burnisher used on the exterior of the thin-walled Pot 1 had left traces in the form of indistinct, roughly vertical facets where it had been rubbed up and down, while on Pot 17 (a large bowl with splaying neck), and on a belly sherd SF 184, the burnisher had produced a more

diffuse set of subtle undulations (Fig. 42). On Pot 21 (not illustrated) – another large bowl, probably with a splaying neck – the potter had produced a decorative effect by rubbing the burnisher up and down the neck and deliberately leaving the vertical flutings thus produced clearly visible. This feature is echoed in Pot 16 – yet another bowl with splaying neck – where a similar, but matte, effect (called 'fingertip fluting') has been achieved by running a fingertip up and down the neck while the surface was still malleable (Fig. 39). Some correlation would therefore seem to exist between splaying-neck bowls and special surface treatments, but this relationship is not exclusive.

As regards the firing of the carinated bowls, the occasional presence of a dark core (indicating incompletely burnt-out natural organic matter in the clay) suggests rapid firing; but in most cases, the fabric is the same colour throughout, indicating that the pots had been evenly fired. Most of the pots are medium to dark brown in colour; several are black, with these colours having been produced during the firing process.

Four carinated bowl sherds (SF 75 and 227 from axial pit 30, SF 189 from post-pit 71/2 and SF 115 from the topsoil) have cereal grain impressions (Fig. 43), whose species has been identified as bread wheat (Timpany, pers. comm). These were accidental inclusions, whose presence could be taken to indicate that pottery manufacture was carried out within the domestic context.

Before discussing the uncarinated vessels, it is necessary to mention Pot 22 (not illustrated),

Figure 42. Pot 17 (sherd SF 254) showing diffuse burnish marks (© National Museums Scotland)

Figure 43. Pottery sherd SF 189 with grain beside socket of grain impression (© National Museums Scotland)

which is represented by a single belly sherd (SF 107, a topsoil find) from a large vessel which is thicker (at *c*.15mm), coarser-textured and less carefully finished than the rest of the assemblage of carinated bowls. While the vessel's overall shape cannot be reconstructed, it is nevertheless possible that it comes from a carinated bowl; its lithic inclusions are the same as in the other pots, and there is no need to doubt that this had originally been part of the early Neolithic assemblage. Similar, slightly coarse vessels are occasionally encountered as rare elements in other assemblages of traditional CB pottery (*e.g.* at Biggar Common, South Lanarkshire: Sheridan 1997, 203).

The uncarinated vessels comprise a small bowl (Pot 23) from pit 30, a smaller bowl or cup (Pot 24) from post-pit 116/1 (=117), and a tiny cup-like vessel (Pot 25) from post-pit 131 (Fig. 41). Around a third of Pot 23 is present; it has an estimated rim diameter of *c*.160mm and wall thickness of *c*.10mm and, like Pot 22, its surfaces have not been as carefully smoothed as those of the fine carinated bowls. Wipe marks are clearly visible on the interior, and one of the rim-and-body sherds has broken along a ring joint line, indicating an unevenly-shaped ring joint. The inclusions are of the same rock type as those seen in the rest of the assemblage, but they are larger (ranging up to *c*.4mm in length) and slightly more abundant (3–5% density). Pot 24 is represented only by a single rim sherd, but enough survives to suggest a rim diameter of 70–80mm. The sherd is thinner-walled (6.2mm) and finer in fabric than Pot 23. Pot 25 is a tiny thumb-pot, just 50mm in its rim diameter and *c*.35mm deep, its uneven walls (*c*.6mm thick) reflecting the fact that it had been formed by manipulating a lump of clay. Its

inclusions are the same as those seen in the rest of the assemblage, ranging up to 3mm in size, and are at a density of *c*.3%.

Function

Clues as to the vessels' functions are provided by their shape, size, and evidence for organic encrustations and absorbed lipids (Šoberl and Evershed, chapter 6.2). The uncarinated vessels – or at least, Pots 23 and 24 if not also the tiny cup Pot 25 – may well have been used as drinking vessels, while some of the carinated bowls had probably been used for serving, and others for cooking, foodstuffs. Some could have been used as storage pots, albeit not for large amounts. The special surface finish accorded to some of the widely-splaying bowls suggests an emphasis on display, and hence their probable use as serving vessels. Evidence for cooking is arguably provided by very occasional (and mostly very thin) blackish-brown organic encrustations, seen mostly on the interior surface but occasionally on the exterior (or on both surfaces). It is assumed that this represents the burnt-on remains of the vessels' former contents, with exterior encrustations indicating spillage (rather than sooting from a hearth). Encrustations were noted on eight sherds, in six cases (SF 25, 54, 59, 80, 104 and 195) occurring on the belly (and being present on the exterior as well as the interior in the case of SF 54 and 80). A relatively thick, crusty deposit covers much of the exterior of the large neck sherd SF 186 (Pot 20, Fig. 40), and rim sherd SF 45 (Pot 6, Fig. 37) has a very thin patch on its exterior surface. The lipid analysis undertaken by Šoberl and Evershed confirms that some of the Warren Field pots (and the Crathes

Castle Overflow Car Park pots) had indeed been used for cooking, with traces of ruminant dairy fat and of porcine fat being detected. Whether the ruminant dairy fat in the four samples that showed evidence of heating above 300° C had resulted from the practice of sealing pots with milk while still hot from their initial firing, or from subsequent cooking using dairy fats – timber in a hearth would ignite around 300° C – is hard to prove, but the latter seems likely. The presence of the pig adipose fat – interestingly in the slightly distinctive pot 22 – provides excellent evidence for the use of the pots for cooking.

The evidence for burning of some of the pottery, and its likely cause, is discussed in the next section; suffice it to say here that the use of vessels for cooking is unlikely to have produced the burning-related features that were noted.

Spatial and contextual distribution; taphonomy

As discussed below and elsewhere in this volume (Murray and Murray, chapter 3.3) this pottery relates to activities undertaken during the occupation of the building. Most of the assemblage will probably have found its way into its contexts of discovery around the time of the building's destruction.

The pottery was unevenly distributed (Fig. 36), with around a third of the assemblage (by sherd number; *c.*140g by weight; around an eighth by estimated vessel number) coming from the axial post pit 30, having arrived there after what has been interpreted as the extraction of a massive post. Most of the rest comes from the post-destruction fills of the post pipes and wall slots of the perimeter walling, especially in the eastern part of the structure, with only a few sherds coming from interior features other than pit 30. (Of the nine small sherds found in context 71, the fill of a possibly disused post-pit in Partition 4, six probably derive from a single vessel.) No pottery was associated with the 'special deposit' pits (89 and 90) in which so much burnt flint was found. Only a few sherds were found in contexts thought to pre-date the destruction of the structure (all being at the structure's east end), but there is no apparent difference between these and the material found in contexts deemed to post-date the destruction phase. Nor is there any obvious patterning with regard to the distribution of particular shapes or sizes of vessel. The small size and homogeneity of the sherds makes it difficult

to detect instances where parts of the same vessel had ended up in different parts of the site, and such identifications remain tentative, but in most cases the sherds in question come from adjacent or nearby features (*e.g.* rim SF 144 from wall trench 115 and neck SF 254 from post-pit 116/1 (=117), together constituting Pot 17, Fig. 39; other possible links are noted in the full catalogue in archive). Most of the other, longer-distance possible linkages may be due to plough movement, particularly where the material in question (as with SF 136) had been found in the topsoil; but in no instance was the distance thus travelled greater than ten metres (as was the case with sherds from Pot 5, Fig. 37, where one rimsherd (SF 43) was found in post-pit 11 and another (SF 138) came from post-pit 114).

As regards the condition of the pottery and the circumstances of its deposition, the unabraded or lightly abraded condition of virtually all of the sherds suggests that they had probably not lain around for long (or, at least, had not been subject to much wear and tear) before entering the fills of the post-pits and wall trenches in which they were discovered. Furthermore, considering the degree of burning involved in the destruction of the building, remarkably few sherds show any sign of significant heat alteration (*e.g.* oxidation to a pale colour or softening of the fabric), as seen for instance on SF 164 (from 115/1) and SF 210. The latter belongs to Pot 18 and was found in axial pit 30, context 30/2, having apparently arrived with other burnt material – including sherd SF 82 from Pot 11, scorched on one side – shortly after the removal of the post and the burning of the structure. Another sherd from Pot 18, SF 205, which was found in the silt that had subsequently entered pit 30 (30/3), was unburnt. Notwithstanding this paucity of obviously-burnt sherds, a notable feature of the assemblage is the high incidence of spalling, with one third of all the pieces consisting of spalls, or of sherds from which spalls had become detached. While spalling usually occurs during the initial firing of a vessel (Gibson 2002), it can also result from post-depositional burning, as research into the effects of forest fires on buried archaeological material in the United States has confirmed (Winthrop 2004). This work has concluded that spalling takes place when the temperature of the burning exceeds that of the vessel's initial firing (which in the present case may, by analogy with CB pottery from Ireland

(Sheridan 1991), have been around 900°C). As already seen (Murray and Murray, chapter 3.3), the temperature reached by the burning building could, by analogy with experimental results, have reached or exceeded this. Where spalling occurs during firing, the detached spalls are unlikely to remain part of the active ceramic assemblage; but at Warren Field, their frequency suggests that they may well have been produced during the burning of the structure. If they had been protected in some way from the full force of the flames (*e.g.* by fallen roofing material), this might account for their un-oxidised appearance and hardness.

Overall, the presence of small but relatively fresh-looking fragments from numerous vessels, and the position of the pieces within the post-destruction fills of post-pits and wall trenches, suggests the accidental incorporation of material that had been lying in their vicinity inside the building. Plough-truncation of the structure's floor surface will no doubt have led to the destruction of any other pottery, left in the building at the time of its destruction, which may have been associated with the structure's use.

The Crathes Castle Overflow Car Park pottery

The aforementioned two pots from the Crathes Castle Overflow Car Park are as follows:

Pot 1: (CCOC SF 6; not illustrated): represented by a single sherd, probably from the upper belly of a thin-walled, fine-textured carinated bowl with vertical, fairly deeply-indented fingertip fluting on its exterior.

Pot 2: (CCOC SF 1, SF 2, and SF 3; Fig. 44): seven sherds, from the rim, neck and belly of a large, thick-walled shallow bowl, with an estimated rim diameter between 260mm and 290mm, a probable depth of *c.*75mm, and a wall thickness that varies from 16.5mm at the rim, to 13mm at the point of maximum curvature, and 14.5mm at the lower belly. A thin organic encrustation is visible on the interior within this black area, concentrated at the point of the vessel's maximum curvature; again, this represents the last traces of the vessel's former contents (Šoberl and Evershed, chapter 6.2). The sherds' fracture surfaces are generally not markedly abraded so, as with Pot 1, it is unlikely that they had lain around for long before being incorporated within their contexts of discovery. The lithic inclusions of both pots constitute minerals of the same speckly igneous stone as noted in the Warren Field pots.

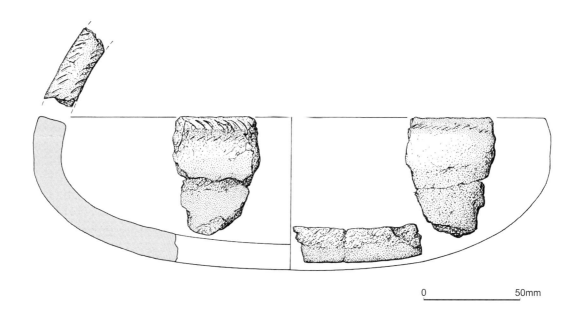

0 _____ 50mm

Figure 44. Crathes Castle Overflow Car Park: reconstruction of Pot 2 (by Marion O'Neil)

The Milton Wood sherd

In 2008, a single sherd (not illustrated) was found in Milton Wood, Crathes Castle Estate (Murray and Murray 2008). It is from a flanged rim, whose upper surface has spalled off; the angle between the rim flange and the neck would have been nearly 90 degrees. The sherd is of the same fine fabric and finish as those from the fine pots from the Warren Field timber hall and from the Crathes Castle Overflow Car Park, and it is very likely to belong to the overall CB tradition. See below on where, in the overall development of the CB tradition, this sherd might belong.

Discussion

The assemblages from the Warren Field and Crathes Castle Overflow Car Park sites are of particular interest because they represent closely-juxtaposed variants of the early Neolithic CB tradition. The Warren Field assemblage constitutes a classic example of the earliest, widespread variant – that is, 'traditional CB', to use the current author's terminology (Sheridan 1985; 1997; 2002; 2007b) – while the Overflow Car Park assemblage, found just c.300 metres away, would appear to represent 'modified CB' pottery of a type mainly seen in northeast Scotland (Henshall's 'northeast style', our 'CBNE': Henshall 1983; 1984). While the latter assemblage remains undated, clues as to its chronological relationship with the Warren Field pottery are provided by another, larger assemblage of CBNE pottery found just across the river at Balbridie, and by a growing body of reliable radiocarbon dates for CBNE pottery elsewhere. This relationship will be explored below. The stylistic attribution and possible dating of the Milton Wood sherd will also be discussed below.

The Warren Field assemblage is typical of traditional CB assemblages in every respect – its vessel shapes (with carinated forms predominating) and sizes, its rim and carination forms, its wall thickness, fabric and surface finish, and its methods of manufacture. These vary little over the large geographical area in which traditional CB pottery has been found (*i.e.* much of Britain and most of Ireland) and this consistency, together with the fact that this pottery has been made by skilled potters, following an established tradition, supports the view that its makers were initially members of immigrant, pioneering farming communities,

rather than acculturated indigenous Mesolithic communities. (See Sheridan 2007b for a detailed discussion of CB pottery, its origins, and its relationship with early farming communities in northern Britain.) That these communities were in contact with each other from a very early stage is demonstrated, at Warren Field, by the presence of imported Arran pitchstone (Warren, chapter 6.3 and *cf.* Sheridan 2007b); it may also be shown in the choice of a speckly igneous stone as the pottery filler, since similar material has been noted in several other traditional CB assemblages in Scotland (*e.g.* at Claish, Stirling (Sheridan 2002) and from Eweford and Pencraig Hill, East Lothian (Sheridan 2007c)). It is also present in the Balbridie CBNE assemblage, although there crushed quartz/ite predominates. This use of the same general kind of stone as a filler in different assemblages need not imply the circulation of the pottery itself, but rather a sharing of knowledge as to what constitutes a good type of stone to protect vessels from thermal shock during firing; diorite and granite, being igneous rocks, are ideal.

The Warren Field assemblage is also typical of those found in comparable early Neolithic timber halls in Scotland – including the newly-discovered example from Lockerbie and also including Balbridie, with its CBNE assemblage – insofar as it is a fairly small assemblage, comprising small amounts of a considerable number of vessels. (By way of comparison, the Warren Field assemblage amounted to *c.*0.55kg of pottery representing 45–52 vessels; at Claish, the figures are *c.*2.7kg and 60–68 vessels; at Balbridie, *c.*2.9kg and 60+ vessels (Cowie, pers. comm); and at Lockerbie *c.*0.8kg and 46+ vessels). This, plus the similarly small lithic assemblages from these buildings, may well relate to the taphonomy of these structures: if each was deliberately decommissioned and burnt down, then some kind of clearing out may have occurred as part of the decommissioning. The size and nature of these ceramic assemblages contrasts with that of some traditional CB assemblages from other kinds of site in Scotland. In terms of the abundance of pottery present, on a square metre by square metre basis the small (*c.*11m × 8m), oval house recently excavated near the mouth of the Dee at Garthdee, Aberdeen (Murray 2005; Murray and Murray 2005b) – and which is associated with reliable radiocarbon dates that are statistically indistinguishable from those relating to Warren Field – has produced a significantly more substantial assemblage than has Warren Field and the other large buildings. Furthermore, several examples could be cited, from other settlement and funerary sites, where much larger body sherds, and/or much greater proportions of individual vessels, are represented (*e.g.* Newbridge, City of Edinburgh; Auchategan, Argyll and Bute; Carzield and Cairnholy, Dumfries and Galloway; and, with CBNE assemblages, Boghead and Easterton of Roseisle, Moray: Sheridan 2007b, Fig. 8; Piggott and Powell 1949; Henshall 1983).

The Warren Field assemblage is one of a growing number of finds of traditional CB pottery in northeast Scotland (Sheridan 2007b, Fig. 1), the next nearest of which comes from a pit at Park Quarry, Durris, less than 7 kilometres to the east along the Dee (Shepherd and Greig 1991). The aforementioned Garthdee find is *c.*20 kilometres to the northeast along the river; and the broader distribution of this type of pottery suggests that its users were attracted to the rich agricultural soils of this part of Scotland. The radiocarbon dates obtained for the Warren Field assemblage – with the results of Bayesian analysis placing its use between *3810–3760 cal BC* (start) and *3780–3700 cal BC* (end) (*68% probability*: see Marshall, chapter 5) – are consistent with the overall picture that has been emerging for traditional CB pottery throughout its area of distribution (Sheridan 2007b). As far as most of Britain and Ireland is concerned, it constitutes the earliest type of pottery to be used.

Just as the number of finds of traditional CB pottery is growing in northeast Scotland, so are the finds of CBNE pottery, as seen for example at the Crathes Castle Overflow Car Park and at Balbridie nearby (see Sheridan 2007b, Fig. 1 for a distribution map). The main characteristics of CBNE pottery were originally defined by Audrey Henshall (1983) and have been reviewed recently by the author in the light of more recent discoveries (Sheridan 2007b). Essentially, this type of pottery represents an early and innovative deviation from the 'traditional CB' canon, while still retaining very close links to its 'parent' tradition. The links are demonstrated, for example, in the continuing use of certain vessel forms, with carinated bowls featuring prominently (as at Balbridie) and being represented in Pot 1 at the Crathes Castle Overflow Car Park; similarly, the tiny pinch-pot 'cup' form noted in the Warren Field assemblage (Fig. 41) is also present at Balbridie (Cowie and Greig forthcoming). The continuing use of fingertip fluting is reflected in the

Balbridie assemblage, and is again represented in Pot 1 in the Overflow Car Park. Where the CBNE style deviates from traditional CB pottery is in a greater variability in vessel form, wall thickness, surface finish and fabric (with a greater incidence of relatively coarse fabrics); a greater incidence of fingertip fluting and of fluted, or 'ripple' burnishing; and also the occasional use of lugs or of impressed or incised decoration, as seen in Pot 2 in the Overflow Car Park (Fig. 44). Indeed, it is this latter pot that has determined the Overflow Car Park assemblage's attribution to the CBNE style since, on its own, the fingertip-fluted sherd representing Pot 1 could equally have belonged to a traditional CB assemblage. The Overflow Car Park Pot 2 finds generalised parallels in other CBNE assemblages: its *comparanda* include the slightly coarse but still nevertheless carinated bowls from Easterton of Roseisle, Moray (Henshall 1983, Fig. 3.21–2) and the four angular bipartite coarseware bowls from Balbridie (Ralston 1982, Fig. 1; Cowie and Greig forthcoming). The latter, along with other angular-profiled decorated vessels from CBNE assemblages (*e.g.* Urquhart, Moray: Henshall 1983, Fig. 5.3.7 and Spurryhillock, Aberdeenshire: Cowie 1997, illus 6, SF 2) have plausibly been proposed as forerunners of the Unstan Bowl, as seen in Orkney and in the Western Isles in contexts dating from *c.*3600 cal BC (Henshall 1983; Cowie 1997).

As regards the chronological relationship between traditional CB pottery and the CBNE style – and, more specifically, between the Warren Field assemblage and those from the Crathes Castle Overflow Car Park and Balbridie – it has been recognised for some time that CBNE pottery represents a very early case of 'style drift', emerging not long after the initial appearance of the tradition as a whole (Sheridan 2002). Marshall's Bayesian analysis of the Balbridie and Warren Field radiocarbon dates (chapter 5) makes it clear, unfortunately, that the currently-available set of dates from Balbridie do not allow us to make a definitive statement about sequence and interval here; the addition of half a dozen new high-quality dates for the Balbridie structure would help resolve the uncertainty. However, looking at the wider picture for well-dated CBNE assemblages (Sheridan 2007b, Fig. 6 and Appendix), it seems likely – even without carrying out Bayesian analysis – that CBNE could have emerged within a few generations of the first appearance of CB pottery. The newly-obtained radiocarbon date of 4995±35

BP (GrA-34772, 3940–3660 cal BC for cremated human bone associated with CBNE pottery at the funerary monument at Midtown of Pitglassie (Shepherd 1996; Sheridan and Bradley 2007) confirms this impression. In this author's opinion, then, the CBNE pottery found at Balbridie and in the Crathes Castle Overflow Car Park postdates the Warren Field pottery, but not necessarily by very long: by one or two generations at the most. Indeed, it could be that the Balbridie structure was built by the immediate descendants of the people who built and burned down the Warren Field structure – or even by those people themselves. The pottery suggests that it is not necessary to posit exact contemporaneity (and intervisibility) between these two large buildings.

A final point relates these observations on ceramics to the dynamics of the hypothetical colonisation process, as elaborated elsewhere by the author (Sheridan 2007b). As Fig. 34 demonstrates, the construction of large structures such as Warren Field occurred over a short period at the beginning of the CB Neolithic. (The subsequent revival of the practice several centuries later, for instance at Littleour, need not concern us here.) One plausible explanation would be to see the construction of Warren Field as a communal house for a group of immigrant farmers from the Continent. The suggested ceremonial initiation of the structure by planting its axial posts, and its subsequent labour-intensive construction, would both express and reinforce the incomers' identity, and stake a claim to the land.

The last pottery to be considered here is the single sherd found in the Milton Wood tree planting pit; and here the fact that it was a single stray find, unassociated with any other sherds, means that one has to approach its 'reading' with caution. While the angularity of the rim flange does not find any close parallels among the CB pottery at Warren Field, or among the CBNE pottery at Balbridie, nevertheless it could, theoretically, belong within either variant of the CB tradition. It could also conceivably belong to a slightly later development of the CB tradition. The earliest kind of CB pottery in Scotland does indeed include some carinated bowls with markedly everted rims (*e.g.* at Carzield, Dumfries and Galloway (pot 1: Sheridan 1993) and Auchategan, Argyll and Bute (Marshall 1978, fig. 13c); and although the Warren Field building assemblage contains no vessels with rims closely comparable to this, an early stage

in the CB tradition cannot be ruled out. Flanged rims are apparently rare in the CBNE repertoire, although one example is known from Midtown of Pitglassie (Shepherd 1996, illus 14.6). They feature prominently in a slightly later variant of CB pottery, found in several parts of Scotland and also in Northern Ireland (*e.g.* at Achnacree and at Balloch Hill, Argyll and Bute: Henshall 1972, 303; Peltenburg 1982, fig. 12, 250).

A radiocarbon date relevant to this variant has recently been obtained from a site at Culduthel, Highland, indicating its use *c.*3600–3500 cal BC (Cook pers. comm.). However, with these slightly later pots, the rims are usually heavier than the Milton Wood example. Whatever its actual date, however, it is likely that this sherd belongs within the first half of the fourth millennium BC.

6.2 Organic residue analysis of pottery from Warren Field timber hall and the Crathes Castle Overflow Car Park site

Lucija Šoberl and Richard Evershed

Introduction

The porous nature of unglazed pottery vessels ensures that, during the processing of food and other organic materials, lipids become absorbed into the vessel wall. These lipids include remnant animal fats, plant oils and plant waxes, which are known to survive in archaeological deposits for several thousand years (Evershed *et al.* 1999). They are recoverable by solvent extraction, and are then quantified and identified by high temperature-gas chromatography (HTGC), GC/mass spectrometry (GC/MS; Evershed *et al.* 1990) and GC-combustion-isotope ratio mass spectrometry (GC-C-IRMS; Evershed *et al.* 1994; Mottram *et al.* 1999).

Identifying from lipid extracts the types of commodity processed in the pottery vessels rests on detailed knowledge of diagnostic compounds and their associated degradation products arising during the use or burial of the pot. For example, triacylglycerols, which are the major constituents of modern animal fats and vegetable oils, are degraded to diacylglycerols, monoacylglycerols and free fatty acids during burial/vessel use. In archaeological pottery, free fatty acids commonly dominate lipid extracts (Evershed 1993), with their origins having been verified through laboratory degradation experiments (*e.g.* Charters *et al.* 1997; Dudd and Evershed 1998; Evershed 2008).

Compound-specific stable carbon isotope determinations, using GC-C-IRMS, allow the carbon stable isotope ($\delta^{13}C$) values of individual compounds (within a mixture) to be determined, providing an important complementary criterion for classifying the origins of lipids. $\delta^{13}C$ values of the principal fatty acids ($C_{16:0}$ and $C_{18:0}$) present in degraded animals fats are effective in distinguishing between different animal fats, *e.g.* ruminant and non-ruminant adipose (body) fats and dairy fats (Evershed *et al.* 1997a; Dudd and Evershed 1998), as well as in the identification of the mixing of commodities (Evershed *et al.* 1999; Copley *et al.* 2001).

Lipid residue analyses were undertaken on eighteen sherds of pottery from Warren Field and two from the Crathes Castle Overflow Car Park site in order to provide insights into vessel use, food processing and animal husbandry at the settlements. The latter is of particular importance in light of the poor survival of animal bone on the sites.

Materials and methods

Lipid analyses were performed using established protocols which are described in detail elsewhere (Evershed *et al.* 1990; Charters *et al.* 1993). HTGC and GC/MS analyses were undertaken to quantify and identify compounds in the lipid extracts, seeking to determine the presence of: (i) an animal fat or plant oil, and/or (ii) plant epicuticular waxes, and/or (iii) beeswax, and/or (iv) mid-chain ketones indicative of vessel heating (Evershed *et al.* 1995, Raven *et al.* 1997). GC-C-IRMS analyses were used to distinguish between ruminant and non-ruminant adipose fats and dairy fats by investigating their $\delta^{13}C_{16:0}$ and $\delta^{13}C_{18:0}$ values.

Results

The results of the initial HTGC screening are summarised in Table 8 on a sample-by-sample basis, giving the total lipid concentration per gram of powdered sherd, and a brief description of the composition of the preserved lipids. Seven of the twenty sherds sampled (35%) yielded significant lipids (> 5 µg g⁻¹). An eighth sherd (CRA18) was considered possibly contaminated.

The presence of degraded animal fat residues was indicated in seven sherds, characterised by a distribution of free fatty acids exhibiting a high abundance of the $C_{18:0}$ fatty acids, together with mono-, di- and triacylglycerols. Other compounds present were mono-unsaturated ($C_{18:1}$), saturated odd carbon chain number ($C_{15:0}$, $C_{17:0}$) and *iso*- and *anteiso*-branched odd carbon number fatty acids ($C_{15:0br}$, $C_{17:0br}$) which suggest a ruminant source of extracted lipids (Evershed *et al.* 1997a; 1997b; 2002; Mottram *et al.* 1999). Triacylglycerols are the major constituent of fresh animal fat but they degrade with time through hydrolysis into di- and monoacylglycerols and free fatty acids. Mono- and diacylglycerols were detected in six of the sampled lipid extracts together with high abundances of $C_{16:0}$ and $C_{18:0}$ free fatty acids. The intact triacylglycerol distributions observed in the extracts from sherds CRA01, 02, 06, 15, 16 and 19 were attributable to ruminant adipose or dairy fat, while narrower distributions typical of porcine fats were not observed. Although laboratory experiments have shown that such distributions become skewed to higher carbon numbers by degradation, sufficient of the lower carbon number triacylglycerols are often preserved to allow dairy fats to remain recognisable; the parent C_{40} to C_{54} triacylglycerol range narrows to C_{44} to C_{54}.

Mid-chain ketones (in the range of C_{31} to C_{35}) were detected in the extracts of four samples (CRA01, CRA02, CRA15 and CRA16). The presence of ketones can be attributed to two possible sources: either the absorption of epicuticular leaf waxes into the pottery fabric during the cooking of leafy vegetables (Evershed *et al.* 1991; Charters *et al.* 1997), or as a consequence of the ketonic decarboxylation reaction which occurs in unglazed ceramic vessels during heating, when the temperature exceeds 300°C, which leads to the condensation of two fatty acids (Evershed *et al.* 1995; Raven *et al.* 1997). The latter compounds provide direct evidence for the heating of animal fats/plant oils to temperatures greater than might be expected in cooking.

The seven samples that yielded appreciable prehistoric lipid concentrations were submitted to further analysis by GC-C-IRMS to determine the $\delta^{13}C$ values for the major fatty acids; these values are plotted in Fig. 45. The $\delta^{13}C$ values obtained for modern reference animal fats from the major domesticated animals exploited in prehistoric Britain and Ireland are grouped within confidence ellipses, onto which the values from the Crathes pottery samples have been plotted. The $\delta^{13}C$ values for the $C_{18:0}$ fatty acid are more depleted in

Table 8. Summary of the results of the organic residue analyses of potsherds. FA = free fatty acids, MAG = monoacylglycerols; DAG = diacylglycerols; TAG = triacylglycerols; OH = long chain alcohols, K = mid chain ketones, OH-FA = hidroxy fatty acids, ND = no decoration, E = exterior (surface), I = interior (surface)

Bristol sherd number	Description	Site context	Lipid concentration (Mg g⁻¹)	Lipids detected	$\delta^{13}C_{16:0} \pm$ 0.3(‰)	$\delta^{13}C_{18:0} \pm$ 0.3(‰)	Predominant commodity type
Crathes Castle Overflow Car Park							
CRA01	body, ND, charred remains inside?	CCOCP Pot 1	839	FA(16<18, 14, 15, 15br, 17, 17br, 18:1, 19, 20, 21, 22), MAG, K, DAG, TAG, OH-FA?	-27.4	-33.3	ruminant dairy fat
CRA02	body, ND	CCOCP Pot 2	1139	FA(16<18, 14, 15, 15br, 17, 17br, 18:1, 19, 20, 21, 22, 23, 24), MAG, K, DAG, TAG, OH-FA?	-31.0	-34.7	ruminant fat
Warren Field timber hall							
CRA06	body, ND, outer surface missing?	post-pit 3	77.9	FA(16<18, 14, 17, 20), MAG, DAG, TAG	-28.6	-33.2	animal fat
CRA15	body, ND, charred remains inside	post-pit 116/117 SF 252	103	FA(16<18;14, 15, 17, 17br, 20), MAG, K, DAG, TAG	-26.1	-33.3	ruminant dairy fat?
CRA16	belly sherd: thin black encrustation on E & I	post-pit 11/5 SF 54	17.3	FA(16<18, 17, 20), MAG, K, DAG, TAG	-28.1	-33.5	degraded animal fat
CRA18	belly sherd	post-pit 7/1 Pot 19	9.0	plant sterols, DAG, TAG	n/a	n/a	possible contamination
CRA19	neck sherd from large pot with extensive encrustation on E	wall trench 153/1 Pot 20	30.9	FA(16<18, 14, 15, 15br, 17, 17br, 20), MAG, DAG, TAG	-27.8	-33.1	ruminant dairy fat?
CRA20	belly sherd from large, coarse textured pot	hall topsoil Pot 22	40.5	FA(16<18: 14, 15, 15br, 17, 17br, 20)	-26.8	-26.3	degraded animal fat

milk fats than in ruminant adipose fats, thereby enabling distinctions to be drawn between milk and adipose fats from ruminant animals (Dudd and Evershed 1998). This is witnessed in the *c.* 2.5‰ shift between centroids of the reference ruminant adipose fat and ruminant dairy fat ellipses. The less depleted $\delta^{13}C$ values seen for the fatty acids in non-ruminant fats compared to equivalent components in ruminant fat are due to differences in diet and in the metabolic and biochemical processes involved in the formation of body fats in ruminant and non-ruminant animals. The $\delta^{13}C$ values from six of the Crathes samples plot within or adjacent to the ruminant dairy

fat reference confidence ellipse, while only one sample (CRA 20) plots in the region of the porcine adipose fat ellipse.

The modern fats used to construct the reference isotope plot were derived from animals reared on strict C_3 diets of forage/fodder and cereals. The slight displacement of $\delta^{13}C$ isotopic values outside the confidence ellipses may be due to the fact that the animals in prehistory were reared on diets which varied in $\delta^{13}C$ values compared to modern diets affected by today's different environmental influences. $\Delta^{13}C$ values ($\delta^{13}C_{16:0}$–$\delta^{13}C_{18:0}$) are also useful indicators of lipid origin when such variations in isotope values occur. Fig. 46 displays

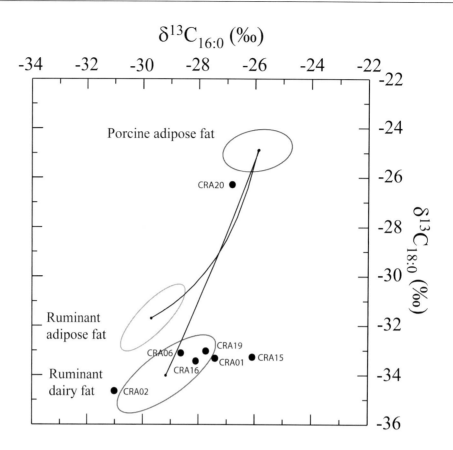

Figure 45. Scatter plot showing the $\delta^{13}C$ values of $C_{16:0}$ and $C_{18:0}$ fatty acids prepared from total lipid extracts of Crathes pottery samples. The values of modern reference fats are represented by confidence ellipses (1 standard deviation). All $\delta^{13}C$ values obtained for modern reference animal fats have been adjusted for the post-Industrial Revolution effects of fossil fuel burning, by the addition of 1.2 ‰. Lines connecting the ellipses represent theoretical $\delta^{13}C$ values obtained through the mixing of these fats

the $\Delta^{13}C$ values plotted against $\delta^{13}C_{16:0}$ values for the Crathes samples. The ranges on the left side of the plot are from the modern reference fats. $\Delta^{13}C$ values obtained for the Crathes samples again strongly confirm the presence of ruminant dairy lipids in six pottery samples and also the presence of porcine adipose fat in sample CRA20.

Discussion

The analyses of the twenty early Neolithic pottery samples from Crathes have shown 35% of the sherds to contain appreciable contemporary lipid residues (>5µg g^{-1} sherd), higher than often observed for British Neolithic pottery (Copley *et al.* 2005b). The high degree of preservation overall was also reflected in the survival of acylglycerol components (monoacylglycerols, diacylglycerols, triacylglycerols) in a significant proportion of lipid extracts. Mid-chain ketones were identified in extracts of four sherds, which confirmed extensive heating of the vessels or sherds from which they derived.

Most of the extracts containing preserved triacylglycerols displayed a wide acyl carbon number distribution, including lower molecular weight species diagnostic of milk fats, which was confirmed by GC-C-IRMS analyses. Although none of the samples contained triacylglycerol distributions typical of porcine fats, the extract of CRA20, which lacked triacylglycerols, contained fatty acids exhibiting $\delta^{13}C$ values consistent with processing pig products.

Recently it has been demonstrated that dairy products were important commodities in prehistoric southern Britain, established through the survival of residues of dairy fats preserved in cooking vessels (Copley *et al.* 2003; 2005). The vast majority

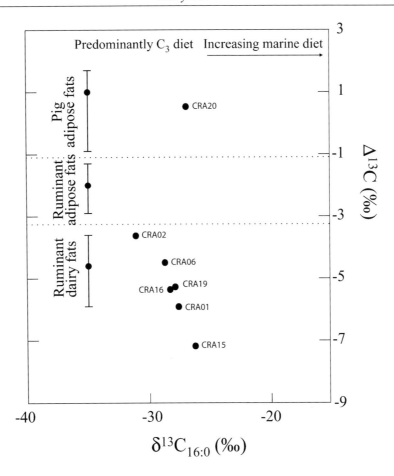

Figure 46. A plot showing the difference between $\Delta^{13}C$ values ($\delta^{13}C_{18:0}$–$\delta^{13}C_{16:0}$) and $\delta^{13}C$ values obtained from the $C_{16:0}$ fatty acids extracted from the Crathes pottery samples. The ranges for the modern reference fats are plotted to the left of the diagram

of southern British prehistoric sites showing dairy fat residues yielded faunal assemblages dominated by cattle. Notable examples of early Neolithic sites yielding high proportions of cattle bones and abundant dairy fats include: Eton Rowing Lake, Windmill Hill and Hambledon Hill (Copley *et al.* 2003; 2005).

In summary, while acidic soil conditions meant that the faunal remains at Crathes were poor, precluding their use in the reconstruction of the settlement subsistence strategies, the lipids preserved in the pottery from both the Warren Field timber hall and the Crathes Castle Overflow Car Park site provide strong evidence for the processing of dairy products (from either cattle or sheep/goat). A single sample from the timber hall suggests some use of pig meat, although this could be from wild or domesticated animals (Mukherjee *et al.* 2007; 2008).

6.3 Stone tools

Graeme Warren

Introduction

This report describes 185 artefacts recovered from excavations at Warren Field and two from the small nearby site at Crathes Castle Overflow Car Park. The detailed presentation of the assemblage is divided into two on spatial grounds – 34 artefacts from the pit alignment (chapter 2) treated separately from the 151 from the timber hall (chapter 3) with an overall concluding discussion. This division facilitates comparisons with other halls. Comments on raw materials and collection standards precede this detail. Finally, a further two flints are discussed from the Crathes Castle Overflow Car Park site, *c.*300m away.

Methodology

Artefacts were classified macroscopically according to standard terminology (Finlayson, Finlay and Mithen 2000). Occasional refits and material links were noted in this process. This classification system describes both primary and secondary technology and the results were stored in an Access database. A full catalogue forms part of the archive. A formal refitting study of all artefacts from the timber hall was carried out by Brian Dolan (2007) and a report is included in the archive.

Collection

Collection of artefacts was predominantly by hand, and screening of all excavated spoil was not carried out. This has undoubtedly impacted on the average size and character of artefacts recovered. A total of 34 artefacts were recovered from samples, of these eleven (40.7%) were chips (*i.e.* <10mm in maximum dimension) and the average size of other artefacts was 15.6±6.0 × 12±4.5mm (n=23). In contrast, of the 151 artefacts recovered by hand only three (2%) were chips and the average size of non-chips was 24.7±10.9 × 18.2±8.3mm (n = 148). The proportion of chips and other small debitage is therefore clearly affected by recovery techniques. This is significant in considering evidence of stone working taking place on site.

Raw materials

The assemblage overall is dominated by flint (n=151, 81.6% of the total) with smaller quantities of pitchstone (n=6, 3.2%), quartz (n=1, 0.5%) and 26 of a poorly understood material (see below). These materials appear in different quantities in different parts of the site and frequencies are given in the detailed discussions below.

The flint is apparently derived from a pebble source. Nearly half (47.7%) of all flint is cortical, with that cortex frequently battered and abraded. The flint is mainly small (average length of complete pieces 24.7±8.9mm), although the presence of some large blades and flakes with lengths of nearly 40mm gives a better indication of the maximum sizes of pebbles available. Many of the flints are affected by burning and do not give an indication of colour, but a range of greys and honeys are present. These characteristics are all in keeping with local beach pebble sources. Beach flint deposits along the eastern coast are mainly derived from sources under the North Sea (Gemmel and Kessel 1979). The Buchan Gravels

contain redeposited flint pebbles, outcropping immediately beneath the modern land surface and in the region tills and other deposits contain high quantities of flint (Bridgeland, Saville and Sinclair 1997). There is no strong evidence at Warren Field for the use of this material.

Six pieces of pitchstone were found in the hall and, importantly, two of these may conjoin (see below for discussion). Four are heavily burnt. Pitchstone is a dark-olive/green-grey volcanic glass with a fine-grained crystalline structure that is found in dykes and sills of the British Tertiary Volcanic Province (*c.*60mya). Archaeological pitchstones in Scotland are ultimately traced to Arran by geochemical analyses (Thorpe and Thorpe 1984) and the presence of small amounts of Arran pitchstone in early Neolithic assemblages in eastern Scotland is relatively common (Warren 2007), even if the reason for this consistent pattern is unclear.

A single possible quartz artefact was recovered from the fill of a large axial pit (30/2). This is a small chunk (? flake) of quartz with the pebble surface forming a flat 'underside': it is possibly a scraper but is not clearly worked (see below). Quartz is common in early Neolithic assemblages in the region generally (Warren 2007).

The most problematic aspect of the assemblage is a group of 26 artefacts (Fig. 47) of a difficult to identify raw material(s), recovered from the upper fills of pit 5 (5/1) of the pit alignment. Geological advice on these pieces has been conflicting, even to the extent of identifying the number of raw materials represented. These pieces were generally in rather poor condition, frequently abraded (18/26; 69.2%) and edge damaged (19/26; 73.1%). The vast majority of pieces (24/26; 92.3%) appear to have been affected by heat, and some, at least, of the fragile character of the artefacts, and the damage they have suffered, can be attributed to weaknesses caused by burning. The cream colour is assumedly due to post-depositional transformation: grey-green siliceous areas can be seen in the centre of modern fracture surfaces and one artefact, SF 501V, is predominantly grey-green with patches of red, and small areas where a cream weathered surface appears to have been removed by flaking. One further artefact (SF 6), recovered from topsoil near the timber hall, is heavily transformed but may be related.

Twenty-four of the artefacts are all clearly manufactured from the same material – a cream-tan coloured, soft, slightly laminate material, with high quality fractures, but a strong tendency to laminar, blocky forms. This material is exceptionally fine grained and has caused considerable difficulty in identification, with advice from both Professor Patrick Shannon (University College Dublin, School of Geological Sciences) and Dr Brian Jackson (National Museums Scotland) acknowledging the complexity of the material and suggesting further thin section and XRF/XRD analysis to establish its character more definitively. This analysis has not been carried out and the following interpretations must be considered as provisional. Dr Jackson suggests that twenty-four of the pieces are best described as an argillite, a sedimentary or slightly metamorphosed material dominated by clay particles. He also argues that two pieces (SF 501 T and V) are a different raw material, possibly a siltstone, but with the possibility that some material has been derived from volcanic ashes. Professor Shannon, based on thin section analysis of material identified by Jackson as an argillite, suggested that it was a very unusual material, possibly some form of tuff. To this author's eye there are not two materials represented, but a continuum of variation, and it may be that clay/silt stones, with some volcanic input, forms the best overarching interpretation of the materials without further analysis. In any case, they are not highly distinctive and, as far as one can tell at present, do not appear to be exotic for the region.

Artefacts from the pit alignment

A total of 34 lithics were recovered from the area of the pit alignment, 26 of clay/silt stone and eight of flint. Five of the flint artefacts were recovered from pit 5 (one each from 5/4, 5/10, 5/12, and two from 5/11), and two from top soil immediately above this pit. One further artefact, a flint flake, was found from topsoil. All 26 of the clay/silt stone artefacts were recovered from context 5/1.

Flint

The flint artefacts from pit 5, contexts 5/10 and 5/11, are in association with Mesolithic radiocarbon dates of between 7180 and 6810 cal BC. They are two abraded, broken regular flakes and an indeterminate burnt flake fragment. All are edge damaged and are best interpreted as residual. One artefact (SF 504) had clearly been struck from a core with a second platform located perpendicularly to the first on the same face, and a second (SF 508) has notable parallelism of dorsal ridges and may, strictly, be a blade fragment. None of the artefacts are strictly diagnostic, but blade and narrow flake industries would be in keeping with Mesolithic stone working in this region. A single blade fragment from 5/12 is later than the dates above and a burnt chunk of flint from 5/4 (SF 502) is presumably also later in date.

Clay/Siltstone

Classification of the artefacts is a little problematic, as many of them do not fit clear morphological categories. Three broad groups could be defined: chunks (6), flakes (13), flakes/chunks with evidence for further removals (7).

Chunks

A total of six 'chunks' were present. These are blocky artefacts with no clear ventral surface, or unconvincing flake morphology. One (SF 501Y) has a small area of high polish or abrasion, and may be an axe fragment, but is not wholly convincing as an axe fragment: indeed it is possible that this surface is a 'natural boss' (Edmonds, Sheridan and Tipping 1992: illus 8). The remaining five have failed or small removals on one face only. SF 501R has opposed removals across a surface only 18mm wide. SF 501Z is a larger fragment (51mm × 26mm × 13mm) with an unusual exterior surface.

Flakes

Thirteen flakes were present, including eight regular, two irregular and three indeterminate examples. Flakes were generally small, characterised by simple, high-angled platforms and feathered terminations. Flakes were generally shallow, but did not exhibit marked curvature. A single flake could be refitted to a chunk/core in four instances (SF 501A/B, SF 501C/D, SF 501E/F, SF 501G/H: Fig. 47).

Worked Flakes/Chunks

A total of seven pieces with further working were identified. These pieces are medium sized, sub-rectangular chunks or flakes with considerable evidence for reworking: in four instances single flakes could be refitted to the chunks or flakes. Removals were found on one or both sides, and were sometimes numerous. In keeping with dorsal evidence on the flakes themselves, removals were made from many different directions. Platforms were frequently simple with high angles, often taking advantage of the natural fracture properties of the material. In some instances however (SF 501U: Fig. 47, SF 501V), bifacial removals and low-angled removals led to the creation of a much lower, more acute edge, akin to a working edge. The generally small size and the limits of the successful refitting should be noted: only one small flake could be refitted to each of four chunks, although, in every instance, the material was not exhausted. In only one of these instances (SF 501G/H) could a 'missing' flake be identified between the refits. The exceptionally limited character of

these working episodes suggests little more than a token attempt at working, and the reasons for the inclusion of these conjoining pieces in the deposits are intriguing. It may be worth speculating that the act of removing flakes was itself of more significance than the products.

Artefacts from the timber hall

A total of 151 artefacts were recovered in association with the timber hall. The assemblage is dominated by flint (94.7%, n=143) with six pitchstone, one quartz, and one unidentified burnt material,

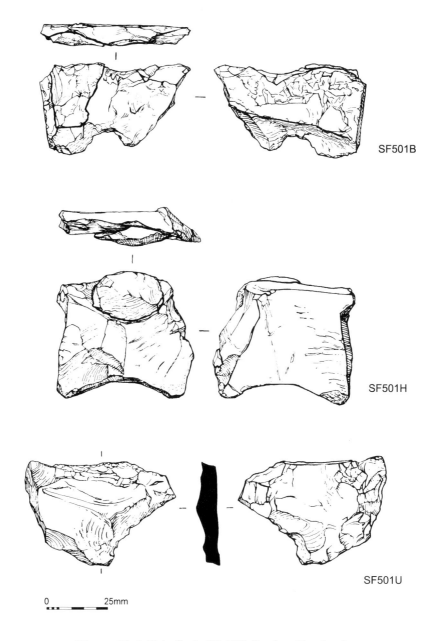

Figure 47. Lithic finds SF 501 (by Jan Dunbar)

possibly related to the clay/silt stones discussed above. The assemblage is broadly homogenous, clearly related to assemblages collected from other timber halls in Scotland, and is generally treated as a unit in this technological discussion. Once the overall character of the assemblage is discussed, the artefacts from pre- and post-destruction contexts are compared.

The condition of the artefacts is affected by the locations in which they were recovered (please note, for consistency of identification, assessments of condition are based on flint artefacts only). For example, 36.4% (n=52) of the assemblage is abraded, but of these 52, 24 were recovered from the topsoil, where 75% of all artefacts are abraded. If topsoil finds are removed, only 24.3% of artefacts are abraded. These are found in low proportions across the site, but are more frequent than average in south wall post-pit 31 (2 of 3) and secondary fills of of an internal pit 89 (7 of 17). There is no consistent difference between pre- and post-destruction contexts in terms of abrasion.

Burning is common across the assemblage, with 59.4% of artefacts clearly burnt. Burning is less frequent in the topsoil assemblage (31.3%) than from features (67.3%). Several individual features show very high levels of burning. In some instances fragmentation caused by burning inflates the 'number' of burnt objects in the assemblage: for example internal pit 90 (90/1) contains 24 individual lithics, all burnt. These include two examples of four fragments which can be reassembled to a single flake and two examples of three fragments.

All refits were within the context. The proportion of burning on artefacts from pre- and post-destruction contexts is discussed below.

Macroscopically identified edge damage is very common, being present on 67.8% of the assemblage as a whole, and is slightly more common in the topsoil assemblage (79.1%) than in that from features (64.5%). Edge damage is also more frequent in the post-destruction assemblage than the pre-destruction assemblage. Edge damage, in many instances then, is likely related to disturbance and other taphonomic processes, rather than use in the past. However, some individual pieces clearly do demonstrate a relationship between edge damage and possible use (*e.g.* SF 24, 256, 276: Fig. 49). Context 71/2 is also notable for having a very low proportion of edge-damaged material. Breakage is also frequent, with 50% of all items broken. Breakages are much more common on blades and flakes than on other artefacts, and are also more likely to affect large artefacts. It is therefore difficult to assess the distribution of broken material.

Primary technology
The primary technology of the assemblage as a whole is dominated by flakes, mainly regular, with a very important aspect of blades (Table 9).

FLINT TECHNOLOGY
As the largest part of the assemblage is flint, it is possible to characterise this in more detail than other aspects. The flint assemblage is strongly

Table 9. Stone artefacts: primary technology

Blank	Flint		Unknown	Pitchstone	Quartz	N
Bipolar core	2	1.4%				2
Blade	24	16.8%		1		25
Chip	13	9.1%		1		14
Chunk	17	11.9%	1			18
Core	1	0.7%		2		3
Flake – indet	15	10.5%		2		17
Flake – irreg	11	7.7%				11
Flake – reg	58	40.6%				58
Indet					1	1
Pebble	1	0.7%				1
Split pebble	1	0.7%				1
	143		1	6	1	151

dominated by flakes, of which regular flakes are very significant. Blades also form a large proportion of the assemblage as a whole. Platform cores are rare in flint, with only one possible example noted (SF 121), a small and possibly fragmentary remnant of an irregular core/bipolar core. The numerical significance of chunks is biased by a large number of burnt fragments included in this total. Taking this into account, the absence of production evidence (chunks, chips, irregular flakes, cores) is notable. Flake and blade production clearly did take place on site; SF 64 (Fig. 48) is a core rejuvenation flake, removing an area of step fracturing on a single platform working face. SF 9 (Fig. 48) is a much more ambiguous piece, with morphology that is difficult to interpret, but is most likely a partial core rejuvenation tablet. Refitting analyses have also demonstrated that core reduction most likely took place on site, with flint raw material groups and some refits possible (Dolan 2007). As noted above, the hand recovery of artefacts has deflated proportions of chips and other small debris but this would not explain the absence of cores and larger production debris. Given the nature of the assemblage it seems likely that production of stone tools did take place on site, but that careful curation of cores and waste was carried out. This is significant in terms of the interpretation of activity on the site.

Platform core techniques: Where platform types could be identified, they were dominated by simple flake or cortical surfaces. A single facetted and a single isolated platform were also present. The presence/absence of 'scrubbing' of the platform edge could only be observed on a small number of pieces, but was more common on blades (40%, n=15) than on regular flakes (9.5%, n=21) suggesting some distinction between these production routines; or at the least, the investment of greater energy in the production of blades. Bulbs were almost exclusively diffuse on platform flakes, and terminations were mainly feathered.

Bipolar techniques: Bipolar techniques were a small but significant component of the assemblage. Two bipolar cores were discovered, both from topsoil, one burnt. A total of eight flakes displayed clear evidence for bipolar techniques, with irregular flakes being much more likely to have derived from a bipolar core (Table 10). Bipolar flakes, cores and a bipolar split pebble were found in low numbers in primary and secondary fills (4 examples) and in disturbed contexts (7 examples). Some bipolar flakes (SF 260 and 268) were in demonstrably pre-destruction contexts and thus provide conclusive evidence that bipolar working is of early Neolithic date in eastern Scotland (see Warren 2007): this is an important contribution to our understanding of stone working in the region. Some spatial evidence suggests that bipolar working was associated with a specific part of the hall; the four stratified examples being from Area C. Bipolar routines are also clearly associated with the production of cortical blanks for convex end scrapers.

PITCHSTONE TECHNOLOGY

The pitchstone assemblage includes small flakes and blades and a possible refit (SF 33: Fig. 48; SF 274 (Refit Group 9?): Fig. 49) (Dolan 2007). Here it must be noted that the refit itself is not certain, and caution is necessary in interpretation. A small pitchstone pebble appears to have been worked using a variety of techniques, including clear evidence of multiple platforms (evidence on SF 33 and opposed removals on SF 274). At some stage in this working, SF 274 was removed from the core using a bipolar technique. SF 274 itself then sees some further removals: possibly irregular retouch, but most likely a very small scale episode of bipolar flaking. The remnant 'core' from which it was removed was also then further worked, using the bipolar technique, leading to the creation of SF 33. Even if the refit is not sound,

Table 10. Bipolar evidence on flint flakes

Blank	Bipolar	% of blank	Not Bipolar	% of blank	Indet	% of blank	Total
Flake – irregular	4	36.4%	3	27.3%	4	36.4%	11
Flake – regular	4	6.9%	34	58.6%	20	34.5%	58

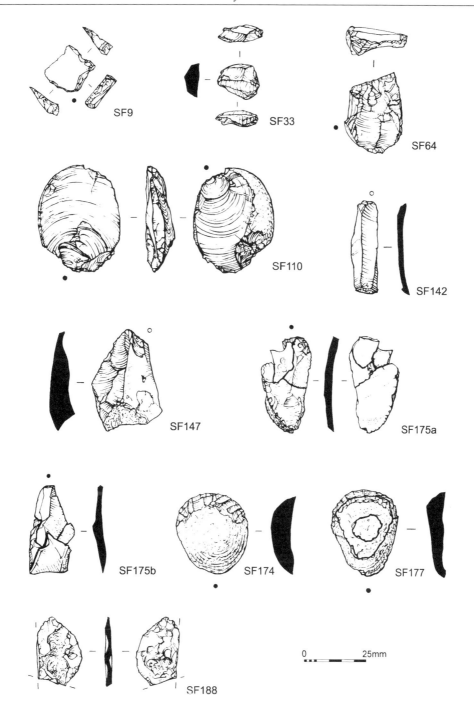

Figure 48. Lithic finds SF 9–188 (by Jan Dunbar)

the variety of reduction techniques used on such a small pitchstone object is impressive.

Secondary technology
Ten artefacts of the assemblage are clearly retouched and two may be. The retouched artefacts comprise three definite scrapers (as well as one possible quartz example and a doubtful rejuvenation flake), four edge-retouched flakes, a projectile point, a serration and a possible truncation.

The scrapers are all manufactured on primary flint flakes and have formal convex scraper edges executed at the distal. They are slightly varied in morphology, but are clearly a related set of

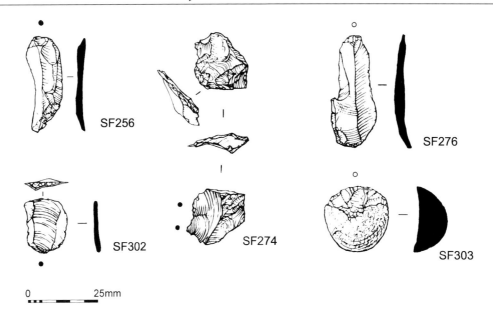

Figure 49. Lithic finds SF 256–303 (by Jan Dunbar)

artefacts (SF 174 and 177: Fig. 48; SF 303: Fig. 49). A small fragment of quartz (SF 211) may also have formed part of a scraper, although the primary flake surface in this instance is on the underside of the tool. Several small flakes appear to have been removed from the edge of the flake (technically these are therefore inverse retouch) forming a slightly irregular possible convex working edge.

The serration (SF 276, Fig. 49) is executed on a formal blade; the serration is slightly irregular, but is accompanied by a very clear gloss. The projectile point (SF 188, Fig. 48) is very heavily burnt and fragmentary but would appear to have been a leaf-shaped arrowhead. The four edge retouched flakes are diverse, and a possible truncation is also present.

Technological discussion
The Warren Field assemblage fits very well into broader contextual understandings of the technology of early Neolithic stone working from timber structures, and also from sites in eastern Scotland more generally (Warren 2007, with references and detail). Comparisons with Balbridie are straightforward (Warren and Sabine forthcoming). Both sites have a flint dominated industry, relying on beach pebble sources. Both assemblages provide clear evidence of both platform and bipolar routines. Cores are rare, but the products of careful platform regimes are

common, suggesting important routines of stone working involving curation of lithic material and careful cleaning and treatment of stone working waste. Retouched objects include a small range of scrapers and edge retouched objects. No pitchstone was present at Balbridie, but it is relatively common in early Neolithic sites in the region; for example, Claish (Barclay, Brophy and MacGregor 2002), Deer's Den (Alexander 2000) and Dubton Farm (Cameron 2002). These patterns are reiterated across the region, where recent reviews (Warren 2007) have highlighted consistent patterns in the relationships between technology and landscape.

Spatial and chronological distribution
The distribution of lithics throughout the timber hall (Fig. 36) allows for some provisional interpretations of relationships between artefacts from pre- and post-destruction contexts and between categories of artefacts and areas of the building and thus allows lithics to make a contribution to the wider interpretation of the site. Caution is necessary here. The lithic assemblage is small. The original floors of the building have been destroyed, and artefacts are only preserved in negative features: some in primary, some in secondary fills. The processes by which material is incorporated into these fills are various: in some instances, lithics clearly form part of structured or

deliberate deposits; in others, they are assumedly residual, in many cases appearing to relate to post-destruction filling of features, with the lithics therefore likely representing material deposited near particular features in the closing stages of the use of the structure. Quantification is further complicated by the dominance of burning and associated fragmentation.

PRE- AND POST-DESTRUCTION

A total of 112 artefacts can be assigned a relative chronology. Of these 52 are clearly associated with pre-destruction contexts and 60 are demonstrably later. Only one of the refits links a pre- and post-destruction context: Refit Group 7 includes two flint flakes from a small platform core. SF 194 came from the remains of a partition (71/2) and SF 67 from the eastern axial pit 30 (30/2) (Dolan 2007).

The general composition of the pre- and post-destruction assemblages is very similar (Table 11), with both dominated by flakes and blades. As noted above, due to the extent of burning and fragmentation of the pre-destruction assemblage, formal statistical comparison of the composition is difficult. The post-destruction assemblage includes more chips, but fewer chunks (a pattern that is not explained by sampling biases) and much more pitchstone (five pieces as opposed to one), but it is not clear what the significance of these patterns is. Four retouched artefacts were found in pre-destruction contexts: these include two scrapers (SF 174, 177), the leaf-shaped arrowhead (SF 188)

and an edge retouched flake. These artefacts are securely dated to before destruction of the structure and thus have a *terminus ante quem* of *3780–3690 cal BC* (Marshall, chapter 5). This is valuable dating evidence for the appearance of these forms in Scotland. Retouched artefacts from post-destruction contexts include edge retouched flakes, a possible serration and a scraper. As noted above, the presence of bipolar flakes in unambiguous pre-destruction contexts is an important contribution to understanding the date of appearance of this stone-working technique in eastern Scotland.

SPATIAL ANALYSIS

Refitting analyses, carried out by Brian Dolan (2007), show refits or material groups extending across the structure as a whole: testimony to complex deposition and/or disturbance. Notwithstanding these problems, a cautious examination of the distribution, taken at face value, does reveal some interesting patterns, although the provisional nature of these discussions must be stressed.

The burnt pitchstone was found in internal pits only (30/3, 50/3, 90/1), albeit distributed across the length of the structure. The two possibly refitting pitchstone fragments also stretch across the structure, linking an internal post of partition 4 (70) with a south wall post-pit (31/1). All of the pitchstone is in post-destruction contexts with the exception of SF 213, from an internal pit (90/1). If we assume that the post-destruction contexts

Table 11. Stone artefacts: composition of pre-destruction and post-destruction assemblages

	Pre-Destruction		Post-Destruction		
Blank	Flint	Pitchstone	Flint	Pitchstone	Quartz
Blade	6	1	12		
Chip	1		11	1	
Chunk	8		2		
Core				2	
Flake – indeterminate	9		5	2	
Flake – irregular	5		2		
Flake – regular	21		22		
Pebble	1				1
	51	1	54	5	1

Table 12. Spatial distribution of flint blanks, controlled for fragmentation. Part = partition (Fig. 36)

Blank	Area A	Area B	Area C	Area D	Part. 1	Part. 2	Part. 3	Part. 4	Disturbed	Total
Bipolar core									1	1
Blade		1	1	2	1				1	6
Chip	1	1	1	6		1		1	1	12
Chunk	2		2	1				2	5	12
Flake – irreg			2					1	2	5
Flake – reg	4		3	2		3			4	16
	7	2	9	11	1	4	0	4	14	52

Table 13. Spatial distribution of bipolar flint, controlled for fragmentation. Part = partition (Fig. 36)

Bipolar Flake	Area A	Area B	Area C	Area D	Part. 1	Part. 2	Part. 3	Part. 4	Disturbed	Total
Indeterminate	4	1	5	8		1		4	8	31
No	3	1	2	3	1	1			5	16
Yes			2			2			1	5

Table 14. Spatial distribution of flint by reduction sequence, controlled for fragmentation. Part = partition (Fig. 36)

	Area A	Area B	Area C	Area D	Part. 1	Part. 2	Part. 3	Part. 4	Disturbed	Total
Primary			1						1	2
Secondary	4		5	3	1	3		2	6	24
Tertiary	2	1	2	2				1	6	14

have been filled from material in their vicinity, this distribution would suggest that the use of pitchstone took place inside the structure.

As noted above, the condition of artefacts varies across the site as a whole, and is clearly impacted on by taphonomic processes. Some patterns still appear, however. Burning, for example, appears to be more common on internal pits or partitions than in wall post-pits or trenches. Some of these are clearly associated with structured deposits of material, including formal retouched objects. Post-destruction fills of the large axial pit 30 contain five burnt artefacts from a total of eight. These are blades and flakes and include a core rejuvenation

flake. Context 71/2, the pre-destruction primary fill of an internal post-pit of partition 4, has seven burnt items out of eight, including small fragments of flakes and a broken and heavily burnt leaf-shaped arrowhead (SF 188). Finally, in pit 140, a post-destruction context contained five burnt objects from a total of eight (once burnt artefacts are reassembled). These again include blades, flakes and a burnt convex end scraper (SF 303). All of these pits suggest associations between burning and retouched artefacts in the context of deliberate depositions of material. That the patterns are identical before and after destruction is notable.

Initial observations of the assemblage suggested

that it was possible to identify areas within the structure that may have been focal points for stone working. Quantifying such an observation, however, is complicated by small sample sizes, burning and associated fragmentation. In the following, no attempt is made to distinguish between pre- and post-destruction contexts. Tables 12–14 show only complete flint artefacts in an attempt to control for these biases.

Assuming that we can interpret the organisation of space from the distribution of stone tools, some evidence suggests that Area C may have been associated with the production of stone tools. This area has a higher proportion of irregular flakes and cortical material than many other areas, and, along with the adjacent partition 2, the only spatially constrained bipolar evidence. This evidence, not as strong as one would desire, not least because the variables are not truly independent, implies that this part of the structure was used for stone tool production, including bipolar production, but that cores etc. were removed from the area – exactly as one would anticipate within a structure. Further work, especially comparison with other sites, is required to consolidate this observation.

Artefacts from Crathes Castle Overflow Car Park

Two flints were recovered on the Crathes Castle Overflow Car Park site. One (CCOC SF 4) was a heavily abraded secondary flake of grey/honey flint with extensive invasive retouch on the left lateral edge, generally forming an acute edge. The other (CCOC SF 5) was a lightly abraded secondary regular flake of honey coloured flint with extensive edge damage. Cortical evidence demonstrates that both flints were ultimately derived from pebble sources. SF 5 is very undiagnostic, whereas SF 4 would be broadly in keeping with the Neolithic date suggested by the pottery (Sheridan, chapter 6.1).

Overall discussion

The stone tool assemblage from the Warren Field sites is of considerable interest. The assemblage includes a small component of Mesolithic stone working. It is important to note that this material is not truly distinct from the rest of the assemblage, and that, without the dates, a typological and/or technological analysis is very unlikely to have identified this phase.

The formal deposition of burnt, flaked material in the pit alignment pit 5, in association with an early Neolithic radiocarbon date, is also important. This material, probably a clay/silt stone, has caused some difficulties in analysis, but indicates, in keeping with sites across Britain and Ireland, an early Neolithic interest in the properties of varied raw materials.

The assemblage from the timber hall itself is very significant and the detailed chronological relationships modelled in the structure add to the importance of the collection. Warren Field provides some of the best dates for the appearance of technical routines and retouched forms in the region. Put simply the assemblage suggests that stone tool production took place on site, possibly within a constrained area of the structure. Hints of use-wear evidence on some pieces would also imply that stone tools were used on site. Careful curation and structuring of stone tools is evidenced in the composition of the assemblage, and is borne out by regional comparisons. The small size of many early Neolithic assemblages is notable. Stone tools also clearly form part of deliberate deposits both before and possibly after the destruction of the building: these include retouched forms and, again, indicate that stone working was embedded in wider values and understandings.

6.4 A possible carbonised wooden vessel

Anne Crone

Several fragments of carbonised wood retrieved from the post-destruction fill (30/2) of axial pit 30 in the Neolithic timber hall were registered as possible vessel fragments (Fig. 36). These were examined (Crone 2007) and five pieces of birch (*Betula* sp.) identified which are all very similar in that the tangential surface on each is larger than the vertical plane, *i.e.* the plane in which the direction of the grain lies. This alone suggests that they are fragments of a deliberately fashioned object because the charcoal is unlikely to have fractured in this way.

The morphology of the largest fragment, SF 68 (Fig. 50), has raised the possibility that the birch fragments are the remains of a wooden vessel. SF 68 is a triangular fragment, 32mm by 18mm and 11mm thick with a slight curvature along the longest axis. The two tangential surfaces are smooth and there are very faint striae running

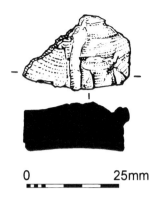

0   25mm

Figure 50. Carbonised wood SF 68 (by Jan Dunbar)

across the grain that could be marks made in manufacture. The outer surface bears what appear to be incised grooves, the clearest of which are two parallel grooves running with the grain of the wood. These could represent carved decoration although the extent is too small to make sense of the marks. Possible chevrons or a representation of an ear of cereal have been suggested.

The other fragments of birch (SF 78, 91, 92 and 94b) vary in thickness from 7 mm to 14 mm but as most of them do not have smooth surfaces on both sides it is likely that these are not original thicknesses. The curvature in the tangential plane is not marked on any of the fragments. The only other fragment which bears possible manufacture marks is SF 78 which has striae similar to those on SF 68 on its only smooth surface.

Discussion

Overall, the general morphology of the birch fragments is suggestive of a relatively thin-walled container of some sort. Wooden containers of Neolithic date are relatively rare so it is difficult to make any useful comparisons, not least because

amongst the limited assemblage there are quite a variety of types. In the British Isles these include carved boxes (Killybeg, Co. Antrim: Coles, Heal and Orme 1978; Sweet Track, Somerset: Coles and Coles 1986), carved bowls (Storrs Moss, Lancashire: Powell, Oldfield and Corcoran 1971; Timoney, Co. Tipperary: Earwood 1993, 38) and boxes made of bark (Lower Horton, Berkshire: Earwood 1993, 42; Runnymede Bridge, Berkshire: Heal 2000, 141). Even within the largest assemblage found to date, a group of four bowls found in a late Neolithic pit in one of the ditch segments of the causewayed enclosure at Etton, Cambridgeshire (Taylor 1998) there is great variation in shape, ranging from a shallow, flat-bottomed dish-like vessel to a deep round-bodied bowl. These were fashioned (by charring and scraping) from alder coppice stools and Taylor suggests that the varying styles of the vessels were mainly dictated by the character of the wood, although at least one of the vessels was an imitation of a contemporary pottery vessel. One example had rim decoration consisting of transverse cuts, similar to that found on Peterborough and Mildenhall pottery. The possible carved decoration on the Warren Field fragments may also be emulating pottery decoration. This group of vessels ranges in wall thickness from 10mm to 18mm; with the exception of one particularly thin fragment, the Warren Field fragments fit within this range.

All of the examples mentioned above have been found in waterlogged conditions; there are no other known examples of carbonised vessels of Neolithic date. This may simply be a question of sampling strategies and recognition; carbonised fragments of turned wooden bowls of Early Historic date have now been found at Hoddom, Dumfriesshire (Crone 2006) and Kintore, Aberdeenshire (Crone 2008). Kintore has also produced carbonised fragments of carved wooden vessels of Roman date.

Epilogue

... there are known knowns: there are things we know we know. We also know there are known unknowns; that is to say we know there are some things we do not know. But there are also unknown unknowns – the ones we don't know we don't know.

Donald Rumsfeld, Former United States Secretary of Defense

The practice of archaeology takes place in a very specific 'real-world' context: while grappling with the traces of past people's lives, archaeologists are embedded within their own, modern world – their own time and place. And this, of course, influences the way they think about the past, no matter how 'objective' they may strive to be. By the time excavations began in the Warren Field, Donald Rumsfeld's remarks at a news conference had become legendary. Left over from a museum exhibition on the enigmatic carved stone balls of northeast Scotland, an interpretation panel bearing

his words sat in the site office, presiding over tea breaks, the steady flow of finds, and discussions about the evidence slowly emerging from the sands and gravels. They were a salutary reminder not to get ahead of ourselves.

When we began, all we actually knew was that in this field lay two monuments – both of rare type, neither very well understood – and a range of other features, which might or might not have been created by people. We knew we did not know how much of them survived below ground, where in time they sat, or whether they were related to

Figure 51. The Warren Field excavations in the wider landscape with Crathes Castle in the background. (Photograph by Moira Greig. © Aberdeenshire Archaeology Service. AAS-05–02–CT34)

each other in time as well as space ... much less what they were for. For this we had a framework of knowledge and a spectrum of logical possibilities within which to work: these were the 'known knowns' and the 'known unknowns' around which we structured our research strategy.

But it was the 'unknown unknowns' which led us places we could never have predicted. That the carbonised remains of early Neolithic birchwood artefacts lay within one of the hall's great axial post-pits – to emerge, (perhaps predictably after all!), on the last day of the first season's excavations. That one monument would bear the traces of human effort stretching across four thousand years. That we would find ourselves puzzling over what hunting and gathering communities could *possibly* have been doing to produce elevated levels of metals in the soil. Or that, at the end, we would find it incredibly difficult to relinquish the sites back to their protective layers of soil and turf, and the Warren Field to the cattle. But then, given that archaeology explores the endless creativity of human endeavour, it will always be the unknown unknowns that are the best of all.

Appendices

Appendix 1. Details of features in the timber hall (Table 15)
Hilary Murray and Charles Murray

No	Wood id	Sectioned	Timber	Dimensions (mm)	Depth (mm)	Detail	Charred
Features of east wall of timber hall							
002	willow/poplar	Yes	round	430diam	200–250		sides+base
003	oak	Yes	round	500–600diam	280		sides+base
004		Yes	round	300–340diam	150		sides+base
006		Yes	round	350diam	180		sides+base
007		Yes	-	140	030	not post?	
008		Yes	round	360–400	180		
009		Yes	round	520	400	secondary	sides+base
010		Yes	split	150–200×440	100		
011	ash	Yes	round	500–540	150	secondary	
012		Yes	split?	420×260	100		
013	oak	Yes	round	600–650	430		sides+base
014		No	round	250–300diam			
032		Yes	round	420–480diam	150		sides+base
033		Yes	round	170–280	100		sides+base
034		Yes	round	300diam	200		sides+base
036		Yes	round	450diam	250	secondary	
037	oak	Yes	round	350–380diam	160	stone packing	sides+base
039		Yes	unclear	180diam	180		
046		No	round	340–400diam			sides
047		Yes	round?	520×330	150		sides+base
048		Yes	post-pit	*c.*400diam	*c.*300		
049		Yes	unclear	200–300	-	rabbit disturbance	
159		Yes	round	240diam	130	secondary	sides+base
160		Yes	pipe only	190diam	240	secondary	

No	Wood id	Sectioned	Timber	Dimensions (mm)	Depth (mm)	Detail	Charred
Features of west wall of timber hall							
051		Yes	round	300diam	300	-	base
053		Yes	n/a	3400×280–480	120–180	wall slot	
055		Yes	n/a	430	320	post-pit	-
056		Yes	round	150diam	130	stone packing	-
057		Yes	round	130diam	160	-	-
058		Yes	unclear	300	150		
059		Yes	n/a	320	80	post-pit	-
075		Yes	split	450×250	80	base tapered	sides+base

Appendix 1. Details of features in the timber hall *continued*

Features of south wall of timber hall

No	Wood id	Sectioned	Timber	Dimensions (mm)	Depth (mm)	Detail	Charred
031	oak	Yes	round	700	320		sides+base
042		Yes	round	450–600diam	400		
044	oak	Yes	round	280	170		sides
045		No	round	380–400diam	-		
076		No	round	580–600diam	-		sides
077	willow/ poplar	Yes	round	600diam	320		sides+base
081		No	unclear	330×350	-		
082		No	split	470×250	-		sides
083		No	round	450diam	-		sides
084		Yes	round	400–430diam	280	section not published	sides+base
085	willow/ poplar	Yes	round	530diam	230		sides+base
086		Yes	split	800×480	290		sides+base
102		No	unclear	330×400	-		
103		No	split	420–600×90–150	-	packing stones to N	
104		No	round	400–420diam	-		sides
108		Yes	round	500diam	240		sides+base
109		No	split	550×320	-		sides
110		Yes	unclear	350–420diam	150		traces sides and base
111	oak/ash	Yes	round	400–420diam	380		sides+base
113		Yes	round?	300–380diam	250		
121		No	round	500–600diam	-		
122		No	round	600–620diam	-		
135		Yes	split	500×150	180		base
141		No	round	350–400diam	-		
142		Yes	round	380–460diam	200		sides +base
146		Yes	split	800×450	210		sides+base
147		No	round	320–340diam	-		
149		No	round	500	-		
150		Yes	unclear	320	210		sides+base

Features of north wall of timber hall

No	Wood id	Sectioned	Timber	Dimensions (mm)	Depth (mm)	Detail	Charred
038		Yes	round	680–700diam	230		sides+base
060		Yes	round	600–620diam	220		sides+base
061		Yes	split?	180×160	100	secondary	
065		No	split?	300diam			
066		Yes	round	320–360diam	150		sides+base

Appendix 1. Details of features in the timber hall *continued*

No	Wood id	Sectioned	Timber	Dimensions (mm)	Depth (mm)	Detail	Charred
Features of north wall of timber hall							
067		No	split	400×350	-		sides
072		Yes	round	270–360diam	160		sides+base
073		No	split	640×300	-		sides
092		No	split	700×360	-		
094		No	split	700×350	-		sides
096		No	unclear	600×400	-		
117		No	split	830×380–400	-		sides
118		Yes	split	600×380	350		sides+base
119		Yes	round	500–650diam	250		sides+base
120		No	split	480×280	-		sides
131		Yes	round	200–250diam	160	secondary	sides+base
155		No	split	520×300	-		sides
161		No	round	550–580diam	-		sides
162		No	round	400–450	-		sides
163		No	round	300diam	-		
164		No	round	350diam	-		sides
165		Yes	split	640×420	300		sides
166		Yes	split	350×270	150		sides+base
167		Yes	split	550×350	350	secondary	sides+base
168		No	round	420×500	-		
169		No	round	400diam	-		
172		No	split	490×220	-		sides
173		Yes	round	260diam	220		sides
174		No	split	560×240	-		sides
175		No	split	1000×250	-		sides

No	Wood id	Sectioned	Timber	Dimensions (mm)	Depth (mm)	Detail	Charred
Internal features of timber hall							
041		Yes	split	300–350×160	270	041A	
041		Yes	split	300–350×120	300	041B	
043	oak	Yes	round	200–250	200	secondary	sides
062		Yes	n/a	290	120	stake hole?	-
068		Yes	split?	150×200	100		
069		Yes	split?	280×390	160	069A secondary	sides+base
069		Yes	split	180×380	110	069B	
070		Yes	unclear	200×230	140		
071		Yes	n/a	900×680	450	post-pit	
078	willow/ poplar	Yes	split	130×180	200	78/2	

Appendix 1. Details of features in the timber hall *continued*

\multicolumn{8}{l}{**Internal features of timber hall**}
No	**Wood id**	**Sectioned**	**Timber**	**Dimensions (mm)**	**Depth (mm)**	**Detail**	**Charred**
---	---	---	---	---	---	---	---
078		Yes	split	120×400	330	78/3	
078		No	split?	120×300	-	78/7	
078		Yes	round	350–400diam	230	78/8	
087		Yes	round	430diam	200		
088		Yes		440×370	80	post-pit	
089		Yes	n/a	350diam	470	deposition pit?	
090		Yes	n/a	420×670	400	pit/post-pit	
099		Yes	split	200×400	300	099A	
099		No	split	280×500	-	099B	
101		Yes	unclear	200×300	160		
107		Yes	split	300×140	100		top of sides only
112		Yes	post-pit	420×580	320	post-pit	
114		Yes	split	280×380	330		
123		Yes	split	530×150	350		
124		Yes	split	150–210×310	160	cuts 123	
125	oak	Yes	split	200x80–150	130	125A	
125	willow/ poplar	Yes	split	170x50–70	180	125B	
126		Yes	split	120–140×350	150		
127		Yes	n/a	400×640	230	post-pit, post removed	
128		Yes	split?	360×200	270	cuts 127	
130		Yes	n/a	500×920	510	post-pit	
138		Yes	unclear	220×100	280	stone packing	
139		Yes	n/a	370×650	250	post-pit	
140		Yes	split	300×80	150	140A	
140		Yes	split	200×120	250	140B	
140		Yes	split	220×100	130	140C	sides
143		Yes	n/a	1800×400	140	wall slot	
144		Yes	round	340diam	250	stone packing	sides+base
145		Yes	n/a	330×420	300	post-pit?	
148		Yes	n/a	380diam	170	post-pit?	
157		Yes	unclear	200×250	140		sides+base

Appendix 2. Thin-section descriptions (Table 16)
Stephen Lancaster

Context No.	Sample No.	Zone No.	Mineral Components	Organic Components	Fabric	Microstructure	Pedofeatures
Pit alignment pits 5 and 16							
5/1	1	1	Very dominant quartz, 'free' grains 5mm–400μm, occasional fragments of metamorphic rock. Coarse mineral fraction unsorted. Grains and fragments sub-angular to rounded. Fine mineral fraction, <400μm, mostly <50μm, similar range of mineral types.	Occasional charcoal fragments (750μm). Frequent fine charcoal (down to 5μm) incorporated into organo-mineral fine material.	Brown to yellow brown fabric, chitonic, locally gefuric, C/F limit 400μm, C/F ratio 1:3.	Intergrain aggregate. Porosity: 40–50%, channels and packing voids.	Dominant bacillo-cylindrical excrements, very rare to rare partially reddened mineral grains.
5/4	1	2	Very dominant quartz, 'free' grains 5mm–400μm, occasional fragments of metamorphic rock. Coarse mineral fraction poorly sorted. Grains and fragments angular to sub-rounded. Fine mineral fraction, <400μm, mostly <50μm, similar range of mineral types.	Occasional charcoal fragments (550μm). Very rare tissue fragments. Frequent to common fine charcoal (down to 5μm) incorporated into organo-mineral fine material, common organic pigment.	Dark brown, fabric, chitonic, locally gefuric, C/F limit 150μm, C/F ratio 1:8.	Intergrain aggregate (few grains). Porosity: 30–40%, channels and packing voids.	Dominant bacillo-cylindrical excrements, occasional pale orange weakly impregnated ferruginous nodules (20–40μm) very rare partially reddened mineral grains. Rare large mamillated/round/ovoid dense yellow brown organo-mineral excrements, up to 3mm in length, frequent comminuted charcoal.
5/3	1	3	Very dominant quartz, 'free' grains 4.3mm–250μm, occasional fragments of metamorphic rock. Coarse mineral fraction moderately to poorly sorted. Grains and fragments sub-angular to rounded. Single fragment of burnt bone. Fine mineral fraction, <250μm, mostly <50μm, similar range of mineral types.	Occasional charcoal fragments (600μm). Very rare tissue fragments. Frequent fine charcoal (down to 5μm) incorporated into organo-mineral fine material.	Brown to dark brown fabric, enaulic to chitonic, C/F limit 150μm, C/F ratio 2:1.	Intergrain aggregate. Porosity: 30–35%, channels and packing voids.	Dominant bacillo-cylindrical excrements, very rare partially reddened mineral grains. Rare mamillated dense brown organo-mineral excrements, up to 500μm in length.

Appendix 2. Thin-section descriptions *continued.*

Context No.	Sample No.	Zone No.	Mineral Components	Organic Components	Fabric	Microstructure	Pedofeatures
Pit alignment pits 5 and 16							
5/3	2	1	Dominant quartz, 'free' grains 4.5mm–200μm, sub-angular to sub-rounded, common fragments of metamorphic rock, 6.5mm–750μm, rounded to sub-angular. Coarse mineral fraction poorly sorted. Fine mineral fraction, <200μm, mostly <50μm, similar range of mineral types. Frequent phytoliths.	Occasional charcoal fragments (600μm). Rare tissue fragments, heavily degraded. Frequent fine charcoal (down to 5μm) incorporated into organo-mineral fine material.	Brown to dark brown fabric, chitonic, C/F limit 200μm, C/F ratio 4:1.	Intergrain aggregate. Porosity: 25%, packing voids and possible channels.	Dominant bacillo-cylindrical excrements, occasional partially reddened mineral grains. Rare mamillated dense brown organo-mineral excrements, up to 500μm in length.
5/18	2	2	Dominant quartz, 'free' grains 5mm–200μm, sub-angular to sub-rounded, common fragments of metamorphic rock, 6.3mm–75μm, rounded to sub-angular. Coarse mineral fraction unsorted. Fine mineral fraction <200μm, mostly <50μm, similar range of mineral types. Occasional phytoliths.	Frequent charcoal fragments (500μm–2.5 mm). Common fine charcoal (down to 5μm) incorporated into organo-mineral fine material, common organic pigment.	Brown fabric, chitonic to enaulic, C/F limit 200μm, C/F ratio 2:1–3:2.	Intergrain aggregate. Porosity: 25%, packing voids and possible channels.	Common to dominant bacillo-cylindrical excrements, occasional pale orange weakly impregnated ferruginous nodules (20–40μm).
16/17	8	1	Abundant quartz and feldspars, frequent fragments of metamorphic rock. Coarse mineral fraction poorly to moderately sorted. Grains and fragments sub-angular to rounded. Fine mineral silt sized, similar range of mineral types.	Rare charcoal fragments. Common comminuted charcoal incorporated into organo-mineral fine fraction.	Pale yellow brown fabric, C/F limit 50μm, C/F ratio 6:1	Intergrain microaggregate to pellicular granular. Porosity 30–40%, mainly channels.	Common to frequent bacillo-cylindrical excrements. Single possible reworked mamillated excrement. Occasional to rare partially reddened mineral grain.
16/10	8	2	Dominant quartz, abundant feldspars, frequent fragments of metamorphic rock. Coarse mineral fraction poorly to moderately sorted. Grains and fragments sub-angular to rounded. Fine mineral silt sized, similar range of mineral types.	Rare charcoal fragments. Abundant comminuted charcoal incorporated into organo-mineral fine fraction.	Yellow brown fabric, C/F limit 50μm, C/F ratio 4:1	Intergrain microaggregate Porosity 40%, mainly channels.	Common to frequent bacillo-cylindrical excrements. Rare to very rare partially reddened mineral grain.

Appendix 2. Thin-section descriptions *continued*

Context No.	Sample No.	Zone No.	Mineral Components	Organic Components	Fabric	Microstructure	Pedofeatures
Timber hall Pit 30							
30/11	3	1	Common to dominant quartz. Common feldspars, frequent fragments of metamorphic rock, including granite. Coarse mineral fraction poorly sorted. Grains and fragments sub-rounded to rounded, rarely sub-angular. Many cracked quartz grains. Mineral suite generally has a 'battered', weathered appearance. Fine mineral silt sized, similar range of mineral types.	Coarse organic absent except single fungal spore. Fine material organo-mineral, with amorphous organic matter and comminuted charcoal.	Light brown fabric, enaulic, C/F limit 50μm, C/F ratio 10:1	Intergrain aggregate, density of aggregates variable. Void space approx. 40%, packing voids.	Frequent bacillo-cylindrical excrements, highly fused. Possible rare reworked mamillated excrements. Rare reddened mineral grain.
30/12	3	2	Common to dominant quartz. Common feldspars, frequent fragments of metamorphic rock, including granite. Coarse mineral fraction moderately to poorly sorted. Grains and fragments sub-rounded to rounded, rarely sub-angular. Some cracked quartz grains. Slightly less weathered appearance to the mineral suite. Fine mineral silt sized, similar range of mineral types.	Frequent sand sized fragments of charcoal. Fine material organo-mineral with amorphous organic matter and comminuted charcoal.	Light buff brown fabric, enaulic to monic, C/F limit 50μm, C/F ratio 20:1	Granular to intergrain microaggregate Porosity: 25%	Occasional to common bacillo-cylindrical excrements, highly fused. Possible rare reworked mamillated excrements. Rare reddened mineral grain.
30/12	4	1	Common to dominant quartz. Common feldspars, frequent fragments of metamorphic rock, including granite. Coarse mineral fraction poorly sorted. Grains and fragments sub-angular to rounded. Few cracked quartz grains. Fine mineral silt sized, similar range of mineral types.	Occasional fragments of amorphous organic matter (125μm), battered sand sized fragments of charcoal. Occasional to common comminuted charcoal incorporated into organo-mineral fine fraction.	Light brown fabric, enaulic to monic, C/F limit 50μm, C/F ratio 15:1	Intergrain microaggregate Porosity: 30%.	Common bacillo-cylindrical excrements, highly fused in places. Possible rare reworked mamillated excrements. Rare partially reddened mineral grain.

Appendix 2. Thin-section descriptions *continued*

Context No.	Sample No.	Zone No.	Mineral Components	Organic Components	Fabric	Microstructure	Pedofeatures
Timber hall Pit 30							
30/2	4	2	Dominant quartz, common feldspars, frequent fragments of metamorphic rock, including granite. Coarse mineral fraction poorly sorted. Grains and fragments sub-rounded to rounded. Some cracked quartz grains. Fine mineral silt sized, similar range of mineral types.	Frequent charcoal fragments (up to 8mm) and frequent fragments of humified material. Fine material more humic and contains more comminuted charcoal than Zone 2.	Dark yellow brown fabric, enaulic, C/F limit 50μm, C/F ratio 10:1	Intergrain microaggregate Porosity: 25%	Frequent bacillo-cylindrical excrements, highly fused/dense in places. Rare partially reddened mineral grain. Single large topsoil fragment.
30/6	5	1	Dominant quartz, occasional feldspars, frequent fragments of metamorphic rock. Coarse mineral fraction poorly sorted. Grains and fragments sub-angular to rounded. Fine mineral silt sized, similar range of mineral types, but feldspars frequent.	Occasional charcoal and lignified plant remains. Frequent comminuted charcoal and humified matter incorporated into organo-mineral fine fraction.	Dark yellow brown fabric, enaulic, C/F limit 50μm, C/F ratio 3:1	Intergrain microaggregate Porosity: 20%	Frequent bacillo-cylindrical excrements, highly fused/dense in places. Rare partially reddened mineral grain.
30/2	5	2	Dominant quartz, occasional feldspars, frequent fragments of metamorphic rock. Coarse mineral fraction poorly sorted. Grains and fragments sub-angular to rounded. Fine mineral silt sized, similar range of mineral types.	Frequent charcoal and lignified plant remains. Frequent to abundant comminuted charcoal and humified matter incorporated into organo-mineral fine fraction.	Dark brown to black fabric, gefuric, C/F limit 50μm, C/F ratio 4:1	Intergrain microaggregate Porosity: 25–30%, including possible biological channels	Frequent bacillo-cylindrical excrements. Rare partially reddened mineral grain.
30/2	5	3	Abundant quartz and feldspars, frequent fragments of metamorphic rock, including granite. Coarse mineral fraction poorly sorted. Grains and fragments sub-angular to rounded. Significant chemical weathering of feldspars. Fine mineral silt sized, similar range of mineral types.	Occasional sand sized battered charcoal. Occasional but ubiquitous comminuted charcoal incorporated into organo-mineral fine fraction.	Pale buff fabric, monic to enaulic, C/F limit 50μm, C/F ratio 10:1	Granular to intergrain microaggregate Porosity: 40%	Occasional to common bacillo-cylindrical excrements. Rare to very rare partially reddened mineral grain.

Appendix 2. Thin-section descriptions *continued*

Context No.	Sample No.	Zone No.	Mineral Components	Organic Components	Fabric	Microstructure	Pedofeatures
Timber hall Pit 30							
30/13	6	1	Abundant quartz and feldspars, frequent fragments of metamorphic rock. Coarse mineral fraction poorly sorted. Grains and fragments sub-rounded to rounded. Some cracked quartz grains. Fine mineral silt sized, similar range of mineral types.	Occasional comminuted charcoal incorporated into organo-mineral fine fraction.	Pale brown fabric, enaulic, C/F limit 50μm, C/F ratio 10:1	Intergrain microaggregate Porosity: 40%	Occasional bacillo-cylindrical excrements.
30/6	6	2	Abundant quartz and feldspars, frequent fragments of metamorphic rock. Coarse mineral fraction poorly sorted. Grains and fragments sub-rounded to rounded. Some cracked quartz grains. Fine mineral silt sized, similar range of mineral types.	Frequent charcoal fragments. Abundant comminuted charcoal incorporated into organo-mineral fine fraction.	Dark yellow brown fabric, chito-gefuric, C/F limit 50μm, C/F ratio 3:1	Dense intergrain microaggregate Porosity: 25–35%	Frequent to abundant bacillo-cylindrical excrements. Rare to partially reddened mineral grain.
30/6, 30/5	7		Abundant quartz and feldspars, frequent fragments of metamorphic rock. Coarse mineral fraction unsorted. Grains and fragments sub-angular to rounded. Fine mineral silt sized, similar range of mineral types.	Occasional to common charcoal fragments, of battered appearance. Abundant comminuted charcoal incorporated into organo-mineral fine fraction.	Pale buff brown fabric, C/F limit 50μm, C/F ratio 3:1	Intergrain microaggregate to channelled granular. Porosity varies across slide: 60% at top, reducing to 30% at base.	Occasional to common bacillo-cylindrical excrements. Rare partially reddened mineral grain. Very rare iron impregnated plant tissue pseudomorphs.

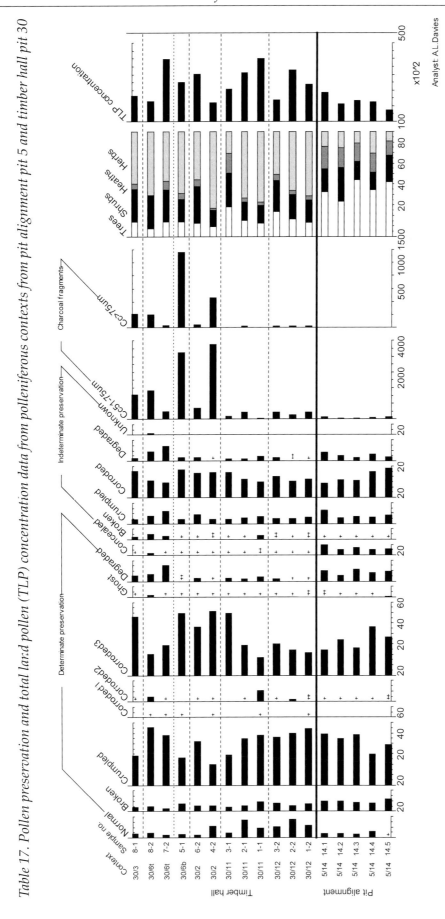

Appendix 3 Pollen data

Althea Davies, Richard Tipping and Robert McCulloch

Table 17. Pollen preservation and total land pollen (TLP) concentration data from polleniferous contexts from pit alignment pit 5 and timber hall pit 30

Table 18. Results of pollen preservation analysis for fully analysed pollen samples from the pit alignment pit 5 and timber hall pit 30. Test numbers 5 and 8 are additional to those proposed by Bunting and Tipping (2000). Failure indicated in bold font

Test (cut-off limit)	1 TLP sum (<300)	2 Total pollen concentration (<3000)	3 No. of main sum taxa (<10)	4 % severely deteriorated grains (degraded) (>35)	5 % severely deteriorated grains (>75% corroded) (>50)	6 % indet. pollen & spores. (%TLP+gp) (>30)	7 % resistant taxa (>6)	8 % resistant taxa (incl. more taxa than test 7) (>15)	9 % Pteropsida (monolete) indet. (%TLP+gp) (>40)	10 Spore:pollen concentration ratio (>0.66)	11 Spore:pollen taxa ratio (>0.66)	No. fails
Sample												
Pit alignment: Pit 5												
5/14/1	334.0	18577.0	19	9.9	24.6	**45.2**	0.60	9.58	18.14	0.25	0.32	1
5/14/2	317.0	11194.6	17	5.7	34.4	**35.3**	0.63	**11.99**	24.77	0.36	0.18	2
5/14/3	325.0	13421.0	14	11.4	26.2	**35.0**	0.62	8.31	16.12	0.22	0.29	1
5/14/4	311.0	12551.7	13	8.4	46.6	**43.5**	2.57	**16.40**	15.87	0.22	0.31	2
5/14/5	**126.0**	7172.5	10	9.5	36.5	**46.6**	0.00	5.56	16.23	0.22	0.20	2
Timber hall: Pit 30: Context 30/3												
P8–1	339.0	12792.2	20	5.3	**56.0**	**35.9**	**13.27**	**18.58**	27.21	**1.29**	0.30	5
Context 30/6 (top)												
P8–2	**141.0**	16278.3	19	7.1	20.6	**40.3**	**7.09**	**17.02**	22.57	0.58	0.26	4
P7–2	351.0	39664.9	24	15.1	29.1	**44.5**	**11.40**	**16.52**	23.01	**0.99**	0.21	4
Context 30/6 (base)												
P5–1	310.0	12082.1	20	1.9	**59.4**	**35.8**	**15.16**	**33.23**	14.03	**1.29**	0.30	5
Context 30/2												
P6–2	330.0	25262.2	24	2.7	46.7	**37.1**	**13.64**	**22.12**	18.43	0.57	0.25	3
P4–2	336.0	30026.3	21	0.9	**61.0**	**31.8**	**33.04**	**41.96**	13.38	0.35	0.29	4
Context 30/11												
P3–1	308.0	13762.1	20	2.9	**59.1**	**33.0**	2.60	5.84	25.12	**0.98**	0.30	3
P2–1	387.0	32799.8	20	2.1	28.7	27.7	**7.24**	**18.86**	11.58	0.29	0.30	2
P1–1	314.0	23697.6	25	4.5	17.2	**31.6**	4.78	**16.56**	14.89	0.34	0.24	2
Context 30/12												
P3–2	338.0	20744.3	21	2.7	30.2	**30.2**	**6.80**	**13.91**	15.38	0.46	0.29	3
P2–2	358.0	31082.0	20	1.1	24.3	24.3	3.91	13.13	9.36	0.31	0.20	0
P1–2	330.0	40046.3	20	0.6	21.8	26.7	5.15	12.12	8.89	0.23	0.25	0

Table 19. Pollen size measurements of large Poaceae (grass) pollen grains >8 μm from timber hall pit 30 and their assignation to cereal type. Identification (1) is based on all measures. Identification (2) is based on annulus diameter (anl-D)

Context	anl-D (um)	M+ (um)	M- (um)	Size (um)	Index	Preservation	Identification (1)	Identification (2)
30.12	10	45	38.75	41.88	1.16	crumpled	Hordeum group	Hordeum group
	8.75	45	31.25	38.13	1.44	crumpled	Hordeum group	Hordeum group
	8.75	28.75	27.5	28.13	1.05	crumpled	undiff.	Hordeum group
	8.75	40	22.5	31.25	1.78	crumpled	undiff.	Hordeum group
	8.75	40	21.25	30.63	1.88	crumpled	undiff.	Hordeum group
	8.75	36.25	32.5	34.38	1.12	crumpled	Hordeum group	Hordeum group
	11.25	36.25	33.75	35.00	1.07	crumpled	Avena/Triticum group	Avena/Triticum group
	10	45	25	35.00	1.80	crumpled	Hordeum group	Hordeum group
	8.75	30	27.5	28.75	1.09	crumpled	undiff.	Hordeum group
	8.75	33.75	26.25	30.00	1.29	crumpled	undiff.	Hordeum group
	8.75	43.75	33.75	38.75	1.30	crumpled	Hordeum group	Hordeum group
	8.125	32.5	26.25	29.38	1.24	crumpled	undiff.	Hordeum group
30.11	10.625	?	27.5	?		broken	undiff.	Avena/Triticum group
	10	37.5	26.25	31.88	1.43	crumpled	undiff.	Hordeum group
	10	31.25	27.5	29.38	1.14	crumpled	undiff.	Hordeum group
	10	28.75	22.5	25.63	1.28	crumpled	undiff.	Hordeum group
	10	27.5	25	26.25	1.10	crumpled	undiff.	Hordeum group
	8.75	40	27.5	33.75	1.45	crumpled	Hordeum group	Hordeum group
	8.75	38.75	30	34.38	1.29	crumpled	Hordeum group	Hordeum group
	8.75	32.5	31.25	31.88	1.04	crumpled	undiff.	Hordeum group
	8.75	28.75	22.5	25.63	1.28	crumpled	undiff.	Hordeum group
	8.125	31.25	25	28.13	1.25	crumpled	undiff.	Hordeum group
	11.25	33.75	27.5	30.63	1.23	crumpled	undiff.	Avena/Triticum group
	8.75	33.75	30	31.88	1.13	crumpled	undiff.	Hordeum group
30.2	8.125	35	30	32.50	1.17	crumpled	Hordeum group	Hordeum group
	11.25	51.25	37.5	44.38	1.37	crumpled	Avena/Triticum group	Avena/Triticum group
	11.25	40	30	35.00	1.33	crumpled	Hordeum group	Avena/Triticum group
	10	32.5	26.25	29.38	1.24	crumpled	undiff.	Hordeum group
	8.75	40	21.25	30.63	1.88	crumpled	undiff.	Hordeum group
	8.75	37.5	30	33.75	1.25	crumpled	Hordeum group	Hordeum group
	8.75	32.5	27.5	30.00	1.18	crumpled	undiff.	Hordeum group
	8.75	31.25	27.5	29.38	1.14	crumpled	undiff.	Hordeum group

Table 19. continued

Context	anl-D (um)	M+ (um)	M- (um)	Size (um)	Index	Preservation	Identification (1)	Identification (2)
30.6	10	35	33.75	34.38	1.04	crumpled	*Hordeum group*	*Hordeum group*
	10	33.75	23.75	28.75	1.42	crumpled	undiff.	*Hordeum group*
	10	26.25	23.75	25.00	1.11	broken	undiff.	*Hordeum group*
	8.75	42.5	18.75	30.63	2.27	crumpled	undiff.	*Hordeum group*
	8.75	40	26.25	33.13	1.52	crumpled	*Hordeum group*	*Hordeum group*
	8.75	38.75	28.75	33.75	1.35	crumpled	*Hordeum group*	*Hordeum group*
	8.75	30	20	25.00	1.50	broken	undiff.	*Hordeum group*
	10	40	27.5	33.75	1.45	crumpled	*Hordeum group*	*Hordeum group*
	10	37.5	31.25	34.38	1.20	crumpled	*Hordeum group*	*Hordeum group*
	8.75	42.5	18.75	30.63	2.27	crumpled	undiff.	*Hordeum group*
	8.75	40	33.75	36.88	1.19	crumpled	*Hordeum group*	*Hordeum group*
	8.75	36.25	20	28.13	1.81	crumpled	undiff.	*Hordeum group*
	8.75	36.25	15	25.63	2.42	ghost	undiff.	*Hordeum group*
	8.75	33.75	32.5	33.13	1.04	crumpled	*Hordeum group*	*Hordeum group*
	8.75	33.75	21.25	27.50	1.59	crumpled	undiff.	*Hordeum group*
	8.75	33.75	17.5	25.63	1.93	crumpled	undiff.	*Hordeum group*
	8.75	33.75	16.25	25.00	2.08	crumpled	undiff.	*Hordeum group*
	8.75	32.5	21.25	26.88	1.53	crumpled	undiff.	*Hordeum group*
	8.75	31.25	30	30.63	1.04	crumpled	undiff.	*Hordeum group*
	8.75	31.25	27.5	29.38	1.14	crumpled	undiff.	*Hordeum group*
	8.75	31.25	26.25	28.75	1.19	crumpled	undiff.	*Hordeum group*
	8.75	31.25	20	25.63	1.56	corroded 3	undiff.	*Hordeum group*
	8.75	30	27.5	28.75	1.09	corroded 3	undiff.	*Hordeum group*
	8.75	30	23.75	26.88	1.26	crumpled	undiff.	*Hordeum group*
	8.75	30	21.25	25.63	1.41	crumpled	undiff.	*Hordeum group*
	8.75	28.75	27.5	28.13	1.05	crumpled	undiff.	*Hordeum group*
	8.75	28.75	27.5	28.13	1.05	crumpled	undiff.	*Hordeum group*
	8.75	28.75	23.75	26.25	1.21	crumpled	undiff.	*Hordeum group*
	8.75	25	18.75	21.88	1.33	crumpled	undiff.	*Hordeum group*
	8.75	23.75	18.75	21.25	1.27	crumpled	undiff.	*Hordeum group*
	8.75	22.5	18.75	20.63	1.20	crumpled	undiff.	*Hordeum group*
	10	37.5	31.25	34.38	1.20	crumpled	*Hordeum group*	*Hordeum group*
	10	37.5	21.25	29.38	1.76	crumpled	undiff.	*Hordeum group*
	8.75	31.25	26.25	28.75	1.19	crumpled	undiff.	*Hordeum group*
	8.75	31.25	26.25	28.75	1.19	crumpled	undiff.	*Hordeum group*
	8.75	30	20	25.00	1.50	crumpled	undiff.	*Hordeum group*
	8.75	27.5	26.25	26.88	1.05	crumpled	undiff.	*Hordeum group*

Table 19. continued

Context	anl-D (um)	M+ (um)	M- (um)	Size (um)	Index	Preservation	Identification (1)	Identification (2)
	8.75	31.25	20	25.63	1.56	corroded 3	undiff.	*Hordeum* group
	8.75	30	27.5	28.75	1.09	corroded 3	undiff.	*Hordeum* group
	8.75	30	23.75	26.88	1.26	crumpled	undiff.	*Hordeum* group
	8.75	30	21.25	25.63	1.41	crumpled	undiff.	*Hordeum* group
	8.75	28.75	27.5	28.13	1.05	crumpled	undiff.	*Hordeum* group
	8.75	28.75	27.5	28.13	1.05	crumpled	undiff.	*Hordeum* group
	8.75	28.75	23.75	26.25	1.21	crumpled	undiff.	*Hordeum* group
	8.75	25	18.75	21.88	1.33	crumpled	undiff.	*Hordeum* group
	8.75	23.75	18.75	21.25	1.27	crumpled	undiff.	*Hordeum* group
	8.75	22.5	18.75	20.63	1.20	crumpled	undiff.	*Hordeum* group
	10	37.5	31.25	34.38	1.20	crumpled	*Hordeum* group	*Hordeum* group
	10	37.5	21.25	29.38	1.76	crumpled	undiff.	*Hordeum* group
	8.75	31.25	26.25	28.75	1.19	crumpled	undiff.	*Hordeum* group
	8.75	31.25	26.25	28.75	1.19	crumpled	undiff.	*Hordeum* group
	8.75	30	20	25.00	1.50	crumpled	undiff.	*Hordeum* group
	8.75	27.5	26.25	26.88	1.05	crumpled	undiff.	*Hordeum* group
	8.125	37.5	26.25	31.88	1.43	crumpled	undiff.	*Hordeum* group
	8.125	33.75	26.25	30.00	1.29	crumpled	undiff.	*Hordeum* group
	8.125	31.25	28.75	30.00	1.09	crumpled	undiff.	*Hordeum* group
	8.125	30	26.25	28.13	1.14	crumpled	undiff.	*Hordeum* group
30.3	11.25	46.25	28.75	37.50	1.61	crumpled	undiff.	*Avena/Triticum* group
	10	35	23.75	29.38	1.47	crumpled	undiff.	*Hordeum* group
	10	35	17.5	26.25	2.00	crumpled	undiff.	*Hordeum* group
	10	31.25	28.75	30.00	1.09	corroded 3	undiff.	*Hordeum* group
	8.75	41.25	30	35.63	1.38	crumpled	*Hordeum* group	*Hordeum* group
	8.75	40	21.25	30.63	1.88	crumpled	undiff.	*Hordeum* group
	8.75	38.75	25	31.88	1.55	crumpled	undiff.	*Hordeum* group
	8.75	38.75	21.25	30.00	1.82	crumpled	undiff.	*Hordeum* group
	8.75	35	27.5	31.25	1.27	corroded 3	undiff.	*Hordeum* group
	8.75	35	26.25	30.63	1.33	crumpled	undiff.	*Hordeum* group
	8.75	33.75	28.75	31.25	1.17	crumpled	undiff.	*Hordeum* group
	8.75	31.25	27.5	29.38	1.14	crumpled	undiff.	*Hordeum* group
	8.75	31.25	21.25	26.25	1.47	crumpled	undiff.	*Hordeum* group
	8.125	42.5	36.25	39.38	1.17	crumpled	*Hordeum* group	*Hordeum* group
	8.125	32.5	31.25	31.88	1.04	broken	undiff.	*Hordeum* group

Bibliography

Alexander, D. 1997. Excavation of pits containing decorated Neolithic pottery and early lithic material of
possible Mesolithic date at Spurryhillock, Stonehaven,
Aberdeenshire. *Proceedings of the Society of Antiquaries of
Scotland* 127, 17–27.

Alexander, D. 2000. Excavation of Neolithic pits, later
prehistoric structures and a Roman temporary camp
along the line of the A96 Kintore and Blackburn Bypass,
Aberdeenshire. *Proceedings of the Society of Antiquaries of
Scotland* 130, 11–75.

Allen, M. J. 1995a. Before Stonehenge. In R. M. J. Cleal, K. E.
Walker and R. Montague, *Stonehenge in its landscape*, 41–56.
London: English Heritage.

Allen, M. J. 1995b. Before Stonehenge: Mesolithic human
activity in a wildwood landscape. In R. M. J. Cleal, K.
E. Walker and R. Montague, *Stonehenge in its landscape*,
470–72. London: English Heritage.

Allen, M. J. and Gardiner, J. 2002. A sense of time: cultural
markers in the Mesolithic of southern England? In B.
David and M. Wilson (eds), *Inscribed Landscapes: marking
and making places*, 139–53. Honolulu: University of Hawai'i
Press.

Armit, I., Murphy, E., Nelis, E. and Simpson, D. 2003. Irish
Neolithic houses. In I. Armit, E. Murphy, E. Nelis and D.
Simpson (eds), *Neolithic settlement in Ireland and western
Britain*, 146–8. Oxford: Oxbow Books.

Ashmore, P. 1999. Radiocarbon dating: avoiding errors by
avoiding mixed samples. *Antiquity* 73, 124–30.

Ashmore, P. 2004. Absolute chronology. In I. A. G. Shepherd
and G. J. Barclay (eds), *Scotland in Ancient Europe: the
Neolithic and Early Bronze Age of Scotland in their European
context*, 125–36. Edinburgh: Society of Antiquaries of
Scotland.

Atkinson, J. A. 2002. Excavation of a Neolithic occupation site
at Chapelfield, Cowie, Stirling. *Proceedings of the Society of
Antiquaries of Scotland* 132, 139–192.

Atkinson, J. A., Donnelly, M., and MacGregor, G. 1997.
Ben Lawers Historic Landscape Project. *Discovery and
Excavation in Scotland* 1997, 63.

Ballin, T. B. 2004. *Chest of Dee, Crathie and Braemar, Aberdeenshire:
the lithic assemblage*. Unpublished report for the National
Trust for Scotland: NTS Sites and Monuments Record.

Bankoff, H. A. and Winter, F. A. 1979. A house burning in
Serbia: what do burned remains tell an archaeologist.
Archaeology 32, 8–14.

Barclay, G. J. 1995. Discussion. In J. Kendrick, Excavation
of a Neolithic enclosure and an Iron Age settlement at
Douglasmuir, Angus, 36–39. *Proceedings of the Society of
Antiquaries of Scotland* 125, 29–67.

Barclay, G. J. 1996. Neolithic buildings in Scotland. In T.
Darvill and J. Thomas (eds), *Neolithic Houses in Northwest
Europe and Beyond*, 61–75. Oxford: Oxbow Books.

Barclay, G. J. 2000. Between Orkney and Wessex: the search
for the regional Neolithics of Britain. In A. Ritchie (ed.),
Neolithic Orkney in its European Context, 275–86. Cambridge:
McDonald Institute for Archaeological Research.

Barclay, G. J. 2001. 'Metropolitan' and 'parochial'/'core' and
'periphery': a historiography of the Neolithic of Scotland.
Proceedings of the Prehistoric Society 67, 1–18.

Barclay, G. J. 2003a. The Neolithic. In K. J. Edwards and I.
B. M. Ralston (eds), *Scotland after the Ice Age: environment,
archaeology and history, 8000 BC–AD 1000*, 127–49. 2nd ed.
Edinburgh: Edinburgh University Press.

Barclay, G. J. 2003b. Neolithic settlement in the lowlands of
Scotland: a preliminary survey. In I. Armit, E. Murphy, E.
Nelis and D. Simpson (eds), *Neolithic Settlement in Ireland
and Western Britain*, 71–83. Oxford: Oxbow Books.

Barclay, G. J. 2004. '... Scotland cannot have been an inviting
country for agricultural settlement': a history of the
Neolithic of Scotland. In I. A. G. Shepherd and G. J.
Barclay (eds), *Scotland in Ancient Europe: the Neolithic and
Early Bronze Age of Scotland in their European context*, 31–44.
Edinburgh: Society of Antiquaries of Scotland.

Barclay, G. J. and Brophy, K. 2004. A rectilinear timber
structure and post-ring at Carsie Mains, Meikleour,
Perthshire. *Tayside and Fife Archaeological Journal* 10, 1–22.

Barclay, G., Brophy, K. and MacGregor, G. 2002. Claish, Stirling:
an early Neolithic structure in its context. *Proceedings of the
Society of Antiquaries of Scotland* 132, 65–137.

Barclay, G. J. and Maxwell, G. S. 1991. Excavation of a
Neolithic long mortuary enclosure within the Roman
legionary fortress at Inchtuthil, Perthshire. *Proceedings of
the Society of Antiquaries of Scotland* 121, 27–44.

Barclay, G. J. and Maxwell, G. S. 1998. *The Cleaven Dyke and
Littleour: monuments in the Neolithic of Tayside*. Edinburgh:
Society of Antiquaries of Scotland.

Barclay G. J. and Russell-White, C. J. (eds) 1993. Excavations in
the ceremonial complex of the fourth to second millennium
BC at Balfarg/Balbirnie, Glenrothes, Fife. *Proceedings of the
Society of Antiquaries of Scotland* 123, 453–210.

Barnatt, J., Bevan, B. and Edmonds, M. 2002. Gardom's Edge:
a landscape through time. *Antiquity* 26, 50–6.

Barrett, J. C. 2005. Material culture, humanity and the
beginnings of the Neolithic. In T. L. Kienlen (ed.), *Die

Dinge als Zeichen: Kulturelles Wissen und Materielle Kultur, 111–24. Bonn: Habelt.

Barrett, J. C. 2006. A perspective on the early architecture of Western Europe. In J. Maran, C. Juwig, H. Schwengel and U. Thaler (eds), *Constructing Power: architecture, ideology and social practice*, 15–30. Hamburg: Lit Verlag.

Bayliss, A., Bronk Ramsey, C., van der Plicht, J. and Whittle, A. 2007. Bradshaw and Bayes: towards a timetable for the Neolithic. *Cambridge Archaeological Journal* 17, 1–28.

Begg, P. and Hewitt, J. 1991. The Warren Field, Crathes Castle. Unpublished report for the National Trust for Scotland: NTS Sites and Monuments Record.

Bennett, K. D. 1989. A provisional map of forest types for the British Isles 5000 years ago. *Journal of Quaternary Science* 4, 141–4.

Birks, H. J. B. 1973. *Past and Present Vegetation of the Isle of Skye: A Palaeoecological Study*. Cambridge: Cambridge University Press.

Birks, H. J. B. 1989. Holocene isochrone maps and patterns of tree-spreading in the British Isles. *Journal of Biogeography* 16, 503–40.

Bloch, M. 1995. People into places: Zafimaniry concepts of clarity. In E. Hirsch and M. O'Hanlon (eds), *The Anthropology of Landscape: perspectives on place and space*, 63–77. Oxford: Clarendon Press.

Bowman, S. 1990. *Radiocarbon Dating*. London: British Museum Publications.

Boyd, W. E. and Kenworthy, J. B. 1992. The use of wood as a natural resource at a Scottish Mesolithic site. *Glasgow Archaeological Journal* 17 (1991–2), 11–23.

Bradley, R. 2003. Neolithic expectations. In I. Armit, E. Murphy, E. Nelis and D. Simpson (eds), *Neolithic settlement in Ireland and Western Britain*, 218–22. Oxford: Oxbow Books.

Bradley, R. 2005. *Ritual and domestic life in prehistoric Europe*. London: Routledge.

Brennand, M. and Taylor, M. 2003. The survey and excavation of a Bronze Age timber circle at Holme-next-the-Sea, Norfolk, 1998–9. *Proceedings of the Prehistoric Society* 69, 1–84.

Bridgeland, D. R., Saville, A. and Sinclair J. M. 1997. New evidence for the origin of the Buchan Ridge Gravel, Aberdeenshire. *Scottish Journal of Geology* 33.1, 43–50.

Britnell, W. J. 1984. The Gwernvale long cairn, Crickhowell, Brecknock. In W. J. Britnell and H. N. Savory, *Gwernvale and Penywyrlod: two Neolithic long cairns in the Black Mountains of Brecknock*, 41–154. Cardiff: Cambrian Archaeological Association.

Bronk Ramsey, C. 1995. Radiocarbon calibration and analysis of stratigraphy: The OxCal program. *Radiocarbon* 37, 425–30.

Bronk Ramsey, C. 1998. Probability and dating. *Radiocarbon* 40, 461–74.

Bronk Ramsey, C. 2001. Development of the radiocarbon program OxCal. *Radiocarbon* 43 (2A), 355–63.

Brophy, K. 2007. From big houses to cult houses: early Neolithic timber halls in Scotland. *Proceedings of the Prehistoric Society* 73, 75–96.

Broström, A., Sugita, S. and Gaillard, M-J. 2004. Pollen productivity estimates for the reconstruction of past vegetation cover in the cultural landscape of southern Sweden. *The Holocene* 14, 368–81.

Broström, A., Sugita, S., Gaillard, M-J. and Pilesjo, P. 2005. Estimating the spatial scale of pollen dispersal in the cultural landscape of southern Sweden. *The Holocene* 15, 252–62.

Brown, I. M. 1992. *Deglaciation of the Dee Valley, N. E. Scotland*. Unpublished PhD thesis, University of Aberdeen.

Brown, I. M. 1993. Pattern of deglaciation of the last (Late Devensian) Scottish ice sheet: evidence from ice-marginal deposits in the Dee valley, northeast Scotland. *Journal of Quaternary Science* 8, 235–50.

Brunskill, R. W. 1999. *Timber Building in Britain*. London: Cassell.

Buck, C. E., Cavanagh, W. G. and Litton, C. D. 1996. *Bayesian Approach to Interpreting Archaeological Data*. Chichester: Wiley.

Bullock, P., Federoff, N., Jongerius, A., Stoops, G. and Tursina, T. 1985. *Handbook for Soil Thin Section Description*. Wolverhampton: Waine Research Publications.

Bunting, M. J. 2002. Detecting woodland remnants in cultural landscapes: modern pollen deposition around small woodlands in northwest Scotland. *The Holocene* 12, 291–301.

Bunting, M. J. and Tipping, R. 2000. Sorting dross from data: possible indicators of post-depositional assemblage biasing in archaeological palynology. In G. Bailey, R. Charles and N. Winder (eds), *Human Ecodynamics*, 63–68. Oxford: Oxbow Books.

Cameron, K. 2002. The Excavation of Neolithic pits and Iron Age souterrains at Dubton Farm, Brechin, Angus. *Tayside and Fife Archaeological Journal* 8, 19–76.

Caseldine, C. J. 1981. Surface pollen studies across Bankhead Moss, Fife, Scotland. *Journal of Biogeography* 8, 7–25.

Charters, S., Evershed, R. P., Goad, L. J., Leyden, A., Blinkhorn, P. W. and Denham V. 1993. Quantification and distribution of lipid in archaeological ceramics: implications for sampling potsherds for organic residue analysis and the classification of vessel use. *Archaeometry* 35, 211–23.

Charters, S., Evershed, R. P., Quye, A., Blinkhorn, P. W. and Reeves, V. 1997. Simulation experiments for determining the use of ancient pottery vessels: the behaviour of epicuticular leaf wax during boiling of a leafy vegetable. *Journal of Archaeological Science* 24, 1–7.

Clarke, A. 2007. Mar Lodge Estate, Aberdeenshire: report on three lithic scatters – Chest of Dee, Caochanan Ruadha, Carn Fiaclach Beag. Unpublished report for the National Trust for Scotland: NTS Sites and Monuments Record.

Clark, S. H. E. 2002. *Holocene environmental change in northeast Scotland: a palaeontomological approach*. Unpublished PhD thesis, University of Sheffield.

Clark, S. H. E. and Edwards, K. J. 2004. Elm bark beetle in Holocene peat deposits and the northwest European elm decline. *Journal of Quaternary Science* 19, 525–8.

Coles, J. 1973. *Archaeology by Experiment*. London: Hutchinson.

Coles, B. and Coles, J. 1986. *Sweet Track to Glastonbury*. London: Thames and Hudson.

Coles, J. M., Heal, S. V. E. and Orme, B. J. 1978. The use and character of wood in prehistoric Britain and Ireland. *Proceedings of the Prehistoric Society* 44, 1–45.

Collins, T. and Coyne, F. 2004. Early Mesolithic features at Hermitage, Castleconnell, Co. Limerick. *Irish Quaternary Association Newsletter* 32 (April 2004), 8–10.

Cooney, G. 1997. Images of settlement in the landscape in the Neolithic. In P. Topping (ed.), *Neolithic Landscapes*, 23–31. Oxford: Oxbow Books.

Cooney, G. 2000. *Landscapes of Neolithic Ireland.* London: Routledge.

Cooney, G. 2003. Rooted or routed? Landscapes of Neolithic settlement in Ireland. In I. Armit, E. Murphy, E. Nelis and D. Simpson (eds), *Neolithic Settlement in Ireland and Western Britain*, 47–55. Oxford: Oxbow Books.

Copley, M. S., Rose, P. J., Clapham, A., Edwards, D. N., Horton, M. C. and Evershed, R. P. 2001. Processing palm fruits in the Nile Valley – biomolecular evidence from Qasr Ibrim. *Antiquity* 75, 538–42.

Copley, M. S., Berstan, R., Dudd, S. N., Docherty, G., Mukherjee, A. J., Straker, V., Payne, S. and Evershed, R. P. 2003. Direct chemical evidence for widespread dairying in prehistoric Britain. *Proceedings of the National Academy of Sciences* 100, 1524–9.

Copley, M. S., Bland, H.A., Rose, P., Horton, M. and Evershed, R. P. 2005a. Gas chromatographic, mass spectrometric and stable carbon isotopic investigations of organic residues of plant oils and animal fats employed as illuminants in archaeological lamps from Egypt. *Analyst* 130, 860–71.

Copley, M. S., Berstan, R., Dudd, S. N., Aillaud, S., Mukherjee, A. J., Straker, V., Payne, S. and Evershed, R. P. 2005b. Processing of milk products in pottery vessels through British prehistory. *Antiquity* 79, 895–908.

Copp, A. and Toop, N. 2005. Nosterfield Quarry, North Yorkshire: Watching Brief. Unpublished interim report. Field Archaeology Specialists Ltd, York.

Cowie, T. G. 1997. The Neolithic pottery sherds. In D. Alexander, Excavation of pits containing decorated Neolithic pottery and early lithic material of possible Mesolithic date at Spurryhillock, Stonehaven, Aberdeenshire, 22–3. *Proceedings of the Society of Antiquaries of Scotland* 127, 17–27.

Cowie, T. G. and Greig. M. Forthcoming. The pottery. In I. B. M. Ralston, *The Neolithic Timber Hall at Balbridie, Aberdeenshire.*

Council for British Archaeology. 1951. Sixth Report of the Scottish Regional Group, Council for British Archaeology.

Crone, A. 2006. Wooden artefacts. In C. Lowe, *Excavations at Hoddom, Dumfriesshire*, 135–7. Edinburgh: Society of Antiquaries of Scotland.

Crone, A. 2007. A possible carbonised wooden vessel from the Warren Field, Crathes Castle Estate, Aberdeenshire. Unpublished full report in site archive (archived in the National Monuments Record of Scotland, Edinburgh).

Crone, A. 2008. Carbonised wooden artefacts. In M. Cook and L. Dunbar, *Rituals, Roundhouses and Romans: Excavations at Kintore 2000–2005. Volume 1: Forest Rd*, 238–42. Edinburgh: Scottish Trust for Archaeological Research.

Cross, S. 2003. Irish Neolithic settlement architecture – a reappraisal. In I. Armit, E. Murphy, E. Nelis and D. Simpson (eds), *Neolithic settlement in Ireland and Western Britain*, 195–202. Oxford: Oxbow Books.

Cummings, V. 2000. Myth, memory and metaphor: the significance of place, space and the landscape in Mesolithic Pembrokeshire. In R. Young (ed.), *Mesolithic Lifeways: Current Research from Britain and Ireland*, 87–95. Leicester: University of Leicester.

Darvill, T. 1996. Neolithic buildings in England, Wales and the Isle of Man, 77–111. In T. Darvill and J. Thomas (eds), *Neolithic Houses in Northwest Europe and Beyond.* Oxford: Oxbow Books.

Davies, A. L., Tipping, R. and McCulloch, R. 2007. Crathes Warren Field: Assessment, analysis and interpretation of pollen contents from Pits 5, 16 and 30. Unpublished report in site archive (archived in the National Monuments Record of Scotland, Edinburgh).

Didden, W. A. M. 1993. Ecology of Terrestrial Enchytraeidae. *Pedobiologia* 37, 2–29.

Dolan, B. 2007. Warren Field. Stone tools: Refitting. Unpublished report in site archive (archived in the National Monuments Record of Scotland, Edinburgh).

Dudd, S. N. and Evershed, R. P. 1998. Direct demonstration of milk as an element of archaeological economies. *Science* 282, 1478–81.

Earwood, C. 1993. *Domestic wooden artefacts in Britain and Ireland from Neolithic to Viking times.* Exeter: Exeter University Press.

Edmonds, M. 1999. *Ancestral geographies of the Neolithic.* London: Routledge.

Edmonds, M., Sheridan, A. and Tipping, R. 1992. Survey and excavation at Creag na Caillich, Killin, Perthshire. *Proceedings of the Society Antiquaries of Scotland* 122, 77–112.

Edwards, K. J. 1989. The cereal pollen record and early agriculture. In A. Milles, D. Williams and N. Gardner (eds), 113–35. *The beginnings of agriculture.* Oxford: British Archaeological Reports.

Evershed, R. P. 1993. Biomolecular archaeology and lipids. *World Archaeology* 25, 74–93.

Evershed, R. P. 2008. Experimental approaches to the interpretation of absorbed organic residues in archaeological ceramics. *World Archaeology* 40, 26–47.

Evershed, R. P., Heron, C. and Goad, L. J. 1990. Analysis of organic residues of archaeological origin by high-temperature gas-chromatography and gas-chromatography mass-spectrometry. *Analyst* 115, 1339–42.

Evershed, R. P., Heron, C. and Goad, L. J. 1991. Epicuticular wax components preserved in potsherds as chemical indicators of leafy vegetables in ancient diets. *Antiquity* 65, 540–4.

Evershed, R. P., Arnot, K. I., Collister, J., Eglinton, G. and Charters, S. 1994. Application of isotope ratio monitoring gas-chromatography mass-spectrometry to the analysis of organic residues of archaeological origin. *Analyst* 119, 909–14.

Evershed, R. P., Stott, A. W., Raven, A., Dudd, S. N., Charters, S. and Leyden, A. 1995. Formation of long-chain ketones in ancient pottery vessels by pyrolysis of acyl lipids. *Tetrahedron Letters* 36, 8875–8.

Evershed, R. P., Mottram, H. R., Dudd, S. N., Charters, S., Stott, A. W., Lawrence, G. J., Gibson, A. M., Conner, A., Blinkhorn, P. W. and Reeves, V. 1997a. New criteria for the identification of animal fats preserved in archaeological pottery. *Naturwissenschaften* 84, 402–6.

Evershed, R. P., Vaughan, S. J., Dudd, S. N. and Soles, J. S. 1997b. Fuel for thought? Beeswax in lamps and conical cups from the late Minoan Crete. *Antiquity* 71, 979–85.

Evershed, R. P., Dudd, S. N., Charters, S., Mottram, H., Stott, A. W., Raven, A., van Bergen, P. F. and Bland, H. A. 1999. Lipids as carriers of anthropogenic signals from prehistory. *Philosophical Transactions of the Royal Society of London Series B-Biological Sciences* 354, 19–31.

Fairbairn, A. S. 2000. On the spread of crops across Neolithic Britain. In A. S. Fairbairn (ed.), *Plants in Neolithic Britain and Beyond*, 67–121. Oxford: Oxbow Books.

Fairweather, A. D. and Ralston, I. B. M. 1993. The Neolithic timber hall at Balbridie, Grampian Region, Scotland: the building, the date and the plant macrofossils. *Antiquity* 67, 313–23.

Finlay, N. 2000. Microliths in the making. In R. Young (ed.), *Mesolithic Lifeways: Current Research from Britain and Ireland*, 23–31. Leicester: University of Leicester.

Finlayson, B., Finlay, N. and Mithen, S. 2000. The cataloguing and analysis of the lithic assemblages. In S. J. Mithen (ed.), *Hunter-Gatherer Landscape Archaeology: The Southern Hebrides Mesolithic Project 1988–98.* Vol. 1, 61–72. Cambridge: McDonald Insitute.

Fraser, S. M. 2003. Chest of Dee: prehistoric lithic scatter. *Discovery and Excavation in Scotland* 4 (new series), 16.

Fraser, S. M. 2005. Caochanan Ruadha, Mar Lodge Estate: lithic scatter. *Discovery and Excavation in Scotland* 6 (new series), 14.

Gelfand, A. E. and Smith, A. F. M. 1990. Sampling approaches to calculating marginal densities. *Journal of American Statistical Association* 85, 398–409.

Gemmell, A. M. D. and Kesel, R. H. 1979. Developments in the study of the Buchan flint deposits. *Scottish Archaeological Forum* 9, 66–77.

Gibson, A. M. 2002. *Prehistoric Pottery in Britain and Ireland.* Stroud: Tempus.

Gilks, W. R., Richardson, S. and Spiegelhalter, D. J. 1996. *Markov Chain Monte Carlo in Practice.* London: Chapman and Hall.

Gooder, J. and Hatherly, C. 2003. North-East Quarry, Dunbar. *Discovery and Excavation in Scotland* 4 (new series), 56.

Grieve, M. 1931. *A Modern Herbal.* London: Jonathan Cape.

Grogan, E. 1996. Neolithic houses in Ireland. In T. Darvill and J. Thomas (eds), *Neolithic Houses in Northwest Europe and beyond*, 41–60. Oxford: Oxbow Books.

Halinen, P. 2005. Prehistoric hunters of northernmost Lapland: settlement patterns and subsistence strategies. *Iskos* (Suomen Muinaismuistoyhdistys) 14.

Hall, V. A. 1989. A study of the modern pollen rain from a reconstructed 19th century farm. *Irish Naturalists Journal* 23, 82–92.

Hardy, K. 2009.Worked bone from Sand. In K. Hardy and C. R. Wickham-Jones (eds), *Mesolithic and Later Sites around the Inner Sound, Scotland: the work of the Scotland's First Settlers Project 1998–2004*, Scottish Archaeological Internet Reports.

Hastie, M. 2004. Assessment of samples from Crathes, Warren Field. Unpublished report in site archive (archived in the National Monuments Record of Scotland, Edinburgh).

Hayden, C. 2006. *The Prehistoric Landscape at White Horse Stone, Aylesford, Kent.* Oxford: Channel tunnel rail link: Oxfordshire Wessex Archaeology Joint Venture.

Heal, V. 2000. The technology of the worked wood and bark. In S. Needham, *The Passage of the Thames: Holocene Environment and Settlement at Runnymede*, 140–7. London: British Museum.

Hemp, W. J. 1930. The chambered cairn of Bryn Celli Ddu. *Archaeologia* 80, 179–214.

Henshall, A. S. 1972. *The Chambered Cairns of Scotland.* Volume 2. Edinburgh: Edinburgh University Press.

Henshall, A. S. 1983. The Neolithic pottery from Easterton of Roseisle, Moray. In A. O'Connor and D. V. Clarke (eds), *From the Stone Age to the 'Forty-Five*, 19–44. Edinburgh: John Donald.

Henshall, A. S. 1984. The pottery. In H. A. W. Burl, Report on the excavation of a Neolithic mound at Boghead, Speymouth Forest, Fochabers, Moray, 1972 and 1974, 59–66. *Proceedings of the Society of Antiquaries of Scotland* 114, 35–73.

Holden, T. 1998. *The Archaeology of Scottish Thatch.* Edinburgh: Historic Scotland.

Hope-Taylor, B. 1980. Balbridie ... and Doon Hill. *Current Archaeology* 72, 18–19.

Hugh-Jones, C. 1979. *From the Milk River: Spatial and Temporal Processes in Northwest Amazonia.* Cambridge: Cambridge University Press.

Hugh-Jones, C. 1996. Houses in the Neolithic imagination: an Amazonian example. In T. Darvill and J. Thomas (eds), *Neolithic Houses in Northwest Europe and Beyond*, 185–93. Oxford: Oxbow Books.

Humphrey, C. 1995. Chiefly and Shamanist landscapes in Mongolia. In E. Hirsch and M. O'Hanlon (eds), *The Anthropology of Landscape: Perspectives on Place and Space*, 135–62. Oxford: Clarendon Press.

Isbister, A. 2009. Pigment resources report: excavations at Sand. In K. Hardy and C. R. Wickham-Jones (eds) *Mesolithic and Later Sites around the Inner Sound, Scotland: the Work of the Scotland's First Settlers Project 1998–2004.* Scottish Archaeological Internet Reports.

Johnston, D. A. 1997. Biggar Common, 1987–93: an early prehistoric funerary and domestic landscape in Clydesdale, South Lanarkshire. *Proceedings of the Society of Antiquaries of Scotland* 127, 185–253.

Jones, R. E. 2000. Geophysical surveys on the Crathes Castle Estate, Kincardineshire. Unpublished report for the National Trust for Scotland: NTS Sites and Monuments Record.

Kendrick, J. 1995. Excavation of a Neolithic enclosure and an Iron Age settlement at Douglasmuir, Angus. *Proceedings of the Society of Antiquaries of Scotland* 125, 29–67.

Kenworthy, J. B. 1981. Nethermills Farm, Crathes: excavations 1978–1980. Unpublished interim report.

Kenworthy, J. B. 1982. The flint. In J. C. Murray (ed.), *Excavations in the Medieval Burgh of Aberdeen*, 200–15. Edinburgh: Society of Antiquaries of Scotland.

Kidd, R. S. 2004. Resistivity Survey Report. Unpublished report in site archive (archived in the National Monuments Record of Scotland, Edinburgh).

Kinnes, I. 1985. Circumstance not context: the Neolithic of Britain as seen from the outside. *Proceedings of the Society of Antiquaries of Scotland* 115, 15–57.

Kinnes, I. 2004. Context not circumstance: a distant view of Scottish monuments in Europe. In I. A. G. Shepherd and G. J. Barclay (eds), *Scotland in Ancient Europe: the Neolithic and Early Bronze Age of Scotland in their European context*, 139–42. Edinburgh: Society of Antiquaries of Scotland.

Kirby, M. 2006. Smarter schools PPP Project. Lockerbie Academy, Lockerbie, Dumfriesshire: Archaeological evaluation and excavations. Unpublished Data Structure Report 1182, CFA Archaeology Ltd, Edinburgh.

Lancaster, S. 2007a. Analysis of soil thin sections from Warren Field, Crathes, Aberdeenshire. Unpublished report in site archive (archived in the National Monuments Record of Scotland, Edinburgh).

Lancaster, S. 2007b. Analysis of soil thin sections from Pit 5, Warren Field, Crathes, Aberdeenshire. Unpublished report in site archive (archived in the National Monuments Record of Scotland, Edinburgh).

Lewis, J. and Brown, F. 2006. Hunter-gatherers and first farmers: the Mesolithic wildwood to the end of the monumental landscape of the Neolithic (10,000 BC–1700 BC). In J. Lewis *et al.*, *Landscape Evolution in the Middle Thames Valley: Heathrow Terminal 5 Excavations*, Volume 1: *Perry Oaks*, 27–94. Oxford and Salisbury: Framework Archaeology.

Mann, L. M. 1903. Report on the excavation of prehistoric pile structures in pits in Wigtownshire. *Proceedings of the Society of Antiquaries of Scotland* 37 (1902–3), 370–415.

Marshall, D. N. 1978. Excavations at Auchategan, Glendaruel, Argyll. *Proceedings of the Society of Antiquaries of Scotland* 109 (1977–8), 36–74.

Marshall, P. D., Kenney, J., Grootes, P. M., Hogg, A. and Prior, C. 2007. Radiocarbon dating. In J. Kenney, Parc Bryn Cegin, Llandygai. Unpublished report, Gwynedd Archaeological Trust.

Marshall, P. D. 2007. Radiocarbon dating. Unpublished full report in site archive (archived in the National Monuments Record of Scotland, Edinburgh).

McCullagh, R. 1989. Excavation at Newton, Islay. *Glasgow Archaeological Journal* 15, 23–51.

McLaren, F. S. 2000. Revising the wheat crops of Neolithic Britain. In A. S. Fairbairn (ed.), *Plants in Neolithic Britain and Beyond*, 91–100. Oxford: Oxbow Books.

Meharg A. and Deacon C. 2007. Notes on the chemical analysis of soils from the pit alignment, Warren Field, Crathes. Unpublished report in site archive (archived in the National Monuments Record of Scotland, Edinburgh).

Mellars, P. 1999. Revising the Mesolithic at Star Carr. *British Archaeology* 48, 8–11.

Mercer, R. 2004. Enclosure and monumentality, and the Mesolithic – Neolithic continuum. In R. Cleal and J. Pollard (eds), *Monuments and Material Culture: Papers in Honour of an Avebury Archaeologist: Isobel Smith*, 39–46. Salisbury: Hobnob Press.

Milner, N. 2009. Mesolithic middens and marine molluscs: procurement and consumption of shellfish at the site of Sand. In K. Hardy and C. R. Wickham-Jones (eds), *Mesolithic and Later Sites around the Inner Sound, Scotland:*

the Work of the Scotland's First Settlers Project 1998–2004, Scottish Archaeological Internet Reports.

Mook, W. G. 1986. Business meeting: recommendations/ resolutions adopted by the Twelfth International Radiocarbon Conference. *Radiocarbon* 28, 799.

Mottram, H. R., Dudd, S. N., Lawrence, G. J., Stott, A.W. and Evershed, R. P. 1999. New chromatographic, mass spectrometric and stable isotope approaches to the classification of degraded animal fats preserved in archaeological pottery. *Journal of Chromatography A* 833, 209–21.

Mukherjee, A. J., Berstan, R., Copley, M. S., Gibson, A. M. and Evershed, R. P. 2007. Compound-specific stable carbon isotope detection of pork consumption applied to the British Late Neolithic. *Antiquity* 81, 743–54.

Mukherjee, A. J., Gibson, A. M. and Evershed, R. P. 2008. Trends in pig product processing at British Neolithic Grooved Ware sites traced through organic residues in potsherds. *Journal of Archaeological Science* 35, 2059–73.

Murray, H. K. 2005. David Lloyd Leisure Centre, Garthdee Road, Aberdeen. *Discovery and Excavation in Scotland* 6 (new series), 8–9.

Murray, H. K. and Murray, J. C. 2004. Warren Field, Crathes, Aberdeenshire. *Discovery and Excavation in Scotland* 5 (new series), 11.

Murray, H. K. and Murray, J. C. 2005a. Warren Field, Crathes, Aberdeenshire. *Discovery and Excavation in Scotland* 6 (new series), 12–13.

Murray, J. C. and Murray, H. K. 2005b. Garthdee Road, Aberdeen. *Discovery and Excavation in Scotland* 6 (new series), 165.

Murray, H. K. and Murray, J. C. 2006. Warren Field, Crathes, Aberdeenshire. *Discovery and Excavation in Scotland* 7 (new series), 15.

Murray, H. K. and Murray, J. C. 2008. Forestry Compartment 23, Milton Wood, Crathes Castle Estate, Aberdeenshire. Unpublished report for the National Trust for Scotland: NTS Sites and Monuments Record.

Nielsen, S. 1966. Eksperiment. *Skalk* 3.

Noble, G. 2006. *Neolithic Scotland: Timber, Stone, Earth and Fire*. Edinburgh: Edinburgh University Press.

Peltenburg, E. J. 1982. Excavations at Balloch Hill, Argyll. *Proceedings of the Society of Antiquaries of Scotland* 112, 142–214.

Piggott, S. and Powell, T. G. E. 1949. The excavation of three Neolithic chambered tombs in Galloway, 1949. *Proceedings of the Society of Antiquaries of Scotland* 83 (1948–9), 103–61.

Pitts, M. 2006. Sensational new discoveries at Bryn Celli Ddu. *British Archaeology* 89 (July–August 2006), 6.

Pitts, M. 2007. Oldest cremation burials. *British Archaeology* 93 (March–April 2007), 9.

Pollard, J. 2000. Neolithic occupation practices and social ecologies from Rinyo to Clacton. In A. Ritchie (ed.), *Neolithic Orkney in its European Context*, 363–9. Cambridge: McDonald Institute for Archaeological Research.

Pollard, T. 1997. Excavation of a Neolithic settlement and ritual complex at Beckton Farm, Lockerbie, Dumfries and Galloway. *Proceedings of the Society of Antiquaries of Scotland* 127, 69–121.

Powell, T. G. E., Oldfield, F. and Corcoran, J. X. W. P. 1971. Excavation in Zone VII peat at Storrs Moss, Lancashire, England 1965–67. *Proceedings of the Prehistoric Society* 37, 112–37.

Price, T. D. 1989. The reconstruction of Mesolithic diets. In C. Bonsall (ed.), *The Mesolithic in Europe*, 48–59. Edinburgh: John Donald.

Proudfoot, E. 2001. Fordhouse Barrow. *Discovery and Excavation in Scotland* 2 (new series), 122.

Ralston, I. B. M. 1982. A timber hall at Balbridie Farm. *Aberdeen University Review* 168, 238–49.

Ralston, I. B. M. 1984. Notes on the archaeology of Kincardine and Deeside District. *The Deeside Field* 18, 73–83.

Ralston, I. B. M. and Reynolds, N. 1981. Balbridie: Excavations 1977–80. Unpublished interim report.

Rasmussen, M. (ed.) 2007. *Iron Age Houses in Flames: Testing House Reconstructions at Lejre*. Lejre: Historical-Archaeological Experimental Centre.

Raven, A. M., Van Bergen, P. F., Stott, A. W., Dudd, S. N. and Evershed, R. P., 1997. Formation of long chain ketones in archaeological pottery by pyrolysis of acyl lipids. *Journal of Analytical and Applied Pyrolysis* 40/41, 267–85.

Ray, K. and Thomas, J. 2003. In the kinship of cows: the social centrality of cattle in the earlier Neolithic of southern Britain. In M. Parker Pearson (ed.), *Food, Culture and Identity in the Neolithic and Early Bronze Age*, 37–44. Oxford: British Archaeological Reports.

Reimer, P. J., Baillie, M. G. L., Bard, E., Bayliss, A., Beck, J. W., Bertrand, C. J. H., Blackwell, P. G., Buck, C. E., Burr, G. S., Cutler, K. B., Damon, P. E., Edwards, R. L., Fairbanks, R. G., Friedrich, M., Guilderson, T. P., Hogg, A. G., Hughen, K. A., Kromer, B., McCormac, G., Manning, S., Ramsey, C. B., Reimer, R. W., Remmele, S., Southon, J. R., Stuiver, M., Talamo, S., Taylor, F. W., van der Plicht, J. and Weyhenmeyer, C. E. 2004. IntCal04 Terrestrial radiocarbon age calibration, 0–26 Cal Kyr BP. *Radiocarbon* 46, 1029–58.

Rennie, E. B. 1984. Excavations at Ardnadam, Cowal, 1964–82. *Glasgow Archaeological Journal* 11, 13–39.

Rennie, E. B. 1985. Dunloskin: charcoal-burning platform, hut foundations. *Discovery and Excavation in Scotland* 1985, 37.

Reynolds, P. 1995. The life and death of a post-hole. *Interpreting Stratigraphy* 5, 21–5.

Rideout, J. S. 1997. Excavation of Neolithic enclosures at Cowie Road, Bannockburn, Stirling, 1984–5. *Proceedings of the Society of Antiquaries of Scotland* 127, 29–68.

Rowley-Conwy, P. 2004. How the West was lost: a reconsideration of agricultural origins in Britain, Ireland and Southern Scandinavia. *Current Anthropology* 45 (Supplement), 83–112.

Russell-White, C. J. 1995. The excavation of a Neolithic and Iron Age settlement at Wardend of Durris, Aberdeenshire. *Proceedings of the Society of Antiquaries of Scotland* 125, 9–27.

Scientific American. 1885. Report of the Committee of the American Society of Civil Engineers on the preservation of timber, presented and accepted at the annual convention, June 25, 1885. *Scientific American Supplement*, 514.

Scott, E. M. 2003. The third international radiocarbon intercomparison (TIRI) and the fourth international radiocarbon intercomparison (FIRI) 1990–2002: results, analyses, and conclusions. *Radiocarbon* 45, 135–408.

Selkirk, A. 1980. Balbridie. *Current Archaeology* 70, 326–8.

Semenov, S. A. 1968. *Razvitie tehniki v kamenom veke*. Institut Arkheologii: Academia Nauk SSSR.

Shepherd, A. 1996. A Neolithic ring-mound at Midtown of Pitglassie, Auchterless, Aberdeenshire. *Proceedings of the Society of Antiquaries of Scotland* 126, 17–51.

Shepherd, I. A. G. and Barclay, G. J. (eds) 2004. *Scotland in Ancient Europe: the Neolithic and Early Bronze Age of Scotland in their European context*. Edinburgh: Society of Antiquaries of Scotland.

Shepherd, I. A. G. and Greig, M. 1991. Park Quarry (Durris parish): Neolithic pit. *Discovery and Excavation in Scotland* 1991, 35.

Sheridan, J. A. 1985. *The Role of Exchange Studies in 'Social Archaeology', with Special Reference to the Prehistory of Ireland from the Fourth to the Early Second Millennium BC*. Unpublished PhD thesis, University of Cambridge.

Sheridan, J. A. 1991. Pottery production in Neolithic and Early Bronze Age Ireland: a petrological and chemical study. In A. Middleton and I. Freestone (eds), *Recent Developments in Ceramic Petrology*, 305–35. London: British Museum

Sheridan, J. A. 1993. Pottery. In D. Maynard, Neolithic pit at Carzield, Kirkton, Dumfriesshire, 28–30. *Transactions of the Dumfriesshire and Galloway Natural History and Antiquarian Society* 68, 25–31.

Sheridan, J. A. 1997. Pottery. In D. A. Johnston, Biggar Common, 1987–93: an early prehistoric funerary and domestic landscape in Clydesdale, South Lanarkshire, 202–23. *Proceedings of the Society of Antiquaries of Scotland* 127, 185–253.

Sheridan, J. A. 2000. Achnacreebeag and its French connections: vive the 'Auld Alliance'. In J. C. Henderson (ed.), *The Prehistory and Early History of Atlantic Europe*, 1–15. Oxford: British Archaeological Reports.

Sheridan, J. A. 2002. Pottery and other ceramic finds. In G. J. Barclay, K. Brophy and G. MacGregor, (eds), Claish, Stirling: an early Neolithic structure in its context, 79–88. *Proceedings of the Society of Antiquaries of Scotland* 132, 65–137.

Sheridan, J. A. 2003. French connections I: spreading the *marmites* thinly. In I. Armit, E. Murphy, E. Nelis and D. Simpson (eds), *Neolithic Settlement in Ireland and Western Britain*, 3–17. Oxford: Oxbow Books.

Sheridan, J. A. 2005. Pitfalls and other traps … why it is worth looking at museum artefacts again. *The Archaeologist* 58, 20–1.

Sheridan, J. A. 2007a. The pottery. Unpublished full archive report in site archive (archived in the National Monuments Record of Scotland, Edinburgh).

Sheridan, J. A. 2007b. From Picardie to Pickering and Pencraig Hill? New information on the 'Carinated Bowl Neolithic' in northern Britain. In A. W. R. Whittle and V. Cummings (eds), *Going Over: The Mesolithic-Neolithic Transition in North-West Europe*, 441–492. London: British Academy.

Sheridan, J. A. 2007c. Traditional Carinated Bowl pottery from the Area 5 Early Neolithic funerary monument, Eweford West; and Pottery from Pencraig Hill (both East

Lothian). Archive report associated with O. Lelong and G. MacGregor 2007, *The Lands of Ancient Lothian: Interpreting the Archaeology of the A1*. Edinburgh: Society of Antiquaries of Scotland.

Sheridan, J. A. and Bradley, R. J. 2007. Radiocarbon dates arranged thorugh National Museums Scotland during 2006/7, *Discovery and Excavation in Scotland* 8 (new series), 220–1.

Slota, P. J. Jr., Jull, A. J. T., Linick, T. W. and Toolin, L. J. 1987. Preparation of small samples for ^{14}C accelerator targets by catalytic reduction of CO. *Radiocarbon* 29, 303–6.

Smith, A. G. K. and Higginbottom, G. 2008. Investigating the possibility of astronomical connections at the Crathes Warren Field site. Unpublished report in site archive (archived in the National Monuments Record of Scotland, Edinburgh).

Smith, C. 2007. The mammal bone from Warren Field, Crathes, Aberdeenshire. Unpublished report in site archive (archived in the National Monuments Record of Scotland, Edinburgh).

Šoberl, L. and Evershed, R. P. 2008. Organic residue analysis of pottery from Crathes (Overflow Car Park and Warren Field samples), Scotland. Unpublished report in site archive (archived in the National Monuments Record of Scotland, Edinburgh).

Spikins, P. 2000. Ethno-facts or ethno-fiction? Searching for the structure of settlement patterns. In R. Young (ed.), *Mesolithic Lifeways: Current Research from Britain and Ireland*, 105–18. Leicester: University of Leicester.

Stevanovic, M. 1997. The age of clay: the social dynamics of house destruction. *Journal of Anthropological Archaeology* 16, 334–95.

Stevanovic, M. 2002. Burned houses in the Neolithic of southeast Europe. In D. Gheorghiu (ed.), *Fire in Archaeology*, 55–62. Oxford: British Archaeological Reports.

Stuiver, M. and Kra, R. S. 1986. Editorial comment. *Radiocarbon* 28 (2B), ii.

Stuiver, M. and Polach, H. A. 1977. Reporting of ^{14}C data. *Radiocarbon* 19, 355–63.

Stuiver, M. and Reimer, P. J. 1986. A computer program for radiocarbon age calculation. *Radiocarbon* 28, 1022–30.

Stuiver, M. and Reimer, P. J. 1993. Extended ^{14}C data base and revised CALIB 3.0 ^{14}C age calibration program. *Radiocarbon* 35, 215–30.

Sugita, S., Gaillard, M.-J. and Broström, A. 1999. Landscape openness and pollen records: a simulation approach. *The Holocene* 9, 409–21.

Tallantire, P. A. 1992. The alder [*Alnus glutinosa* (L.) Gaertn.] problem in the British Isles: a third approach to its palaeohistory. *New Phytologist* 122, 717–31.

Taylor, M. 1998. Wood and bark from the enclosure ditch. In F. Pryor, *Etton: Excavations at a Neolithic Causewayed Enclosure near Maxey, Cambridgeshire, 1982–7*, 115–59. London: English Heritage.

Thomas, J. 1991. *Rethinking the Neolithic*. Cambridge: Cambridge University Press.

Thomas, J. 1996. Neolithic houses in mainland Britain and Ireland – a sceptical view. In T. Darvill and J. Thomas (eds), *Neolithic Houses in Northwest Europe and Beyond*, 1–12. Oxford: Oxbow Books.

Thomas, J. 1999. *Understanding the Neolithic*. London: Routledge.

Thomas, J. 2001. Dunragit Excavations Project 1999–2002. Excavations at Dunragit: 2001. http://orgs.man.ac.uk/research/dunragit/dunragit_2001.htm.

Thomas, J. 2006. On the origins and development of cursus monuments in Britain. *Proceedings of the Prehistoric Society* 72, 229–41.

Thorpe, O. W. and Thorpe, R. S. 1984. The distribution and sources of archaeological pitchstone in Britain. *Journal of Archaeological Science* 11, 1–34.

Timpany, S. 2006a. Analysis of samples from Crathes Warren Field. Unpublished report in site archive (archived in the National Monuments Record of Scotland, Edinburgh).

Timpany, S. 2006b. Palaeoenvironmental analysis of samples from Pits 01, 05 and 06, Crathes Warren Field. Unpublished report in site archive (archived in the National Monuments Record of Scotland, Edinburgh).

Tipping, R. 2000. Pollen preservation analysis as a necessity in Holocene palynology. In J. P. Huntley and S. Stallibrass (eds), *Taphonomy and Interpretation*, 23–33. Oxford: Oxbow Books.

Tipping, R. 2007. Crathes Warren Field: Geomorphic setting. Unpublished report in site archive (archived in the National Monuments Record of Scotland, Edinburgh).

Tipping, R., Carter, S. and Johnston, D. 1994. Soil pollen and soil micromorphological analyses of old ground surfaces on Biggar Common, Borders Region, Scotland. *Journal of Archaeological Science* 21, 387–401.

Tipping, R., Bunting, M. J., Davies, A. L., Murray, H., Fraser, S. and McCulloch, R. 2009. Modelling land use around an early Neolithic timber 'hall' in north east Scotland from high spatial resolution pollen analysis. *Journal of Archaeological Science* 36, 140–9.

Topping, P. 1996. Structure and ritual in the Neolithic house: some examples from Britain and Ireland. In T. Darvill and J. Thomas (eds), *Neolithic Houses in Northwest Europe and Beyond*, 157–70. Oxford: Oxbow Books.

Tringham, R. 2005. Weaving house life and death into places: a blueprint for a hypermedia narrative. In D. Bailey, A. Whittle and V. Cummings (eds), *(Un)settling the Neolithic*, 98–111. Oxford: Oxbow Books.

Vasari, Y. and Vasari, A. 1968. Late- and post-glacial macrophytic vegetation in the lochs of northern Scotland. *Acta Botanica Fennica* 80, 1–120.

Vuorela, I. 1973. Relative pollen rain around cultivated fields. *Acta Botanica Fennica* 102, 1–27.

Ward, G. K. and Wilson, S. R. 1978. Procedures for comparing and combining radiocarbon age determinations: a critique. *Archaeometry* 20, 19–31.

Ware, T. and Hattis, D. 2000. *Residential rehabilitation inspection guide*. Appendix A: *The effects of fire on structural systems*. Washington: National Institute of Building Sciences (for U.S. Department of Housing and Urban Development).

Warren, G. 2005. *Mesolithic lives in Scotland*. Stroud: Tempus.

Warren, G. M. 2007. Chipped stone tool industries of the earlier Neolithic in Eastern Scotland. *Scottish Archaeological Journal* 28, 27–47.

Warren, G. M. and Sabine, K. Forthcoming. Chipped Stone.

In I. B. M. Ralston, *The Neolithic Timber Hall at Balbridie, Aberdeenshire*.

Whittle, A. 1996. *Europe in the Neolithic: the Creation of New Worlds*. Cambridge: Cambridge University Press.

Whittle, A. 1999. The Neolithic Period, *c.*4000–2500/2200 BC. In Hunter, J. and Ralston, I. B. M. (eds), *The Archaeology of Britain: an Introduction from the Upper Palaeolithic to the Industrial Revolution*, 58–76. London: Routledge.

Whittle, A. 2003. *The Archaeology of People: Dimensions of Neolithic life*. London: Routledge.

Wickham-Jones, C. R. 1990. *Rhum: Mesolithic and Later Sites at Kinloch, Excavations 1984–86*. Edinburgh: Society of Antiquaries of Scotland.

Winterbottom, S. and Tipping, R. 2007. Crathes Warren Field: Intervisibility analyses. Unpublished archive report in site archive (archived in the National Monuments Record of Scotland, Edinburgh).

Winthrop, K. 2004. *A Bare Bones Guide to Fire Effects on Cultural Resources*. US Bureau of Land Management: http://www. blm.gov/wo/st/en/prog/more/CRM/fire_and_heritage/ fire_resources.html.

Xu, S., Anderson R., Bryant C., Cook G. T., Dougans A., Freeman S., Naysmith P., Schnabel C. and Scott ,E. M. 2004. Capabilities of the new SUERC 5MV AMS facility for ^{14}C dating. *Radiocarbon* 46, 59–64.